JUL -- 2021

D0090643

ESTES VALLEY
LIBRARY
WITHDRAWN

BY CARROT QUINN

Thru-Hiking Will Break Your Heart

The Sunset Route

THE SUNSET ROUTE

THE SUNSET ROUTE

*FREIGHT TRAINS, FORGIVENESS, AND FREEDOM ON
THE RAILS IN THE AMERICAN WEST*

CARROT QUINN

THE DIAL PRESS NEW YORK

Copyright © 2021 by Carrot Quinn

All rights reserved.

Published in the United States by The Dial Press, an imprint of Random House, a division of Penguin Random House LLC, New York.

THE DIAL PRESS is a registered trademark and the colophon is a trademark of Penguin Random House LLC.

LIBRARY OF CONGRESS CATALOGING-IN-PUBLICATION DATA
Names: Quinn, Carrot, author.
Title: The sunset route : a memoir / by Carrot Quinn.
Description: New York : The Dial Press, [2021]
Identifiers: LCCN 2020044466 (print) | LCCN 2020044467 (ebook)
| ISBN 9780593133286 (hardcover) | ISBN 9780593133293 (ebook)
Subjects: LCSH: Quinn, Carrot. | Street children—Alaska—Biography.
| Alternative lifestyles—United States.
Classification: LCC HV883.A4 Q56 2021 (print) | LCC HV883.A4 (ebook)
| DDC 305.48/442 [B] —dc23
LC record available at https://lccn.loc.gov/2020044466
LC ebook record available at https://lccn.loc.gov/2020044467

Printed in Canada on acid-free paper

randomhousebooks.com

9 8 7 6 5 4 3 2 1

First Edition

Book design by Jo Anne Metsch

For John, who was there.
And for Tara, who understands.

Here is the world.
Beautiful and terrible things will happen.
Don't be afraid.

—FREDERICK BUECHNER,
Beyond Words

Author's Note

The stories in this book are crafted from my journals, from conversations I've had with others, and from my own memory. While all of the events in this memoir are real and true and did happen, some dialogue has been reconstructed, some exact dates and timelines have been estimated, and the names and some identifying characteristics of several people mentioned in the book have been changed.

THE SUNSET ROUTE

crouch in the dark railcar, gripping a plastic tarp around me. The cold wind beats at my face. Beyond the metal lip of the car is the black fir forest of Oregon's Cascade Mountains, the trees silhouettes against the bright, moonlit snow. These trees bear witness to my train rushing past, train cars rocking and groaning as we hurtle along the track at sixty miles an hour. I press my numb fingers into my palm, counting off the hours until dawn. One, two, three, four. I pull the water bottle from my pack and shake it—empty. When did I drink the last of it? I can't remember. All night I've been drifting in and out of a dim, strange place without time, too cold to really sleep. I remember the moment, earlier today, when I lost my sleeping bag to the train. I'd just woken from a nap. The thundering of the train was ceaseless, the slice of sky visible above the lip of our railcar empty of trees. I looked over at my friend Sami, curled in her sleeping bag on the other side of the car, and I figured I'd cross the railcar to talk to her, since there was too much noise for us to shout. For stability, I gripped the underside of the semi-truck trailer that sat in the railcar as I worked my way along the narrow ledge between the two large holes in the floor of the car, over to Sami's side. I sat next to her on her sleeping pad and we shouted about our wonder and shared a bag of dried mango. The train slowed and then lurched, picking up speed again. This turned the four-foot-wide hole in the floor into a vacuum of strong, sucking wind, and my zero-degree sleeping bag, which I'd just shoplifted the day before for this trip, rose from the foam pad onto which I'd unstuffed it, tumbled a bit, and was slurped into the hole as if into a hell-mouth, gone forever.

I started laughing, dried mango stuck to my teeth, too shocked to do anything else. Sami stared at the hole, horrified. It was February, and the low farmlands of the Willamette Valley were dark with gray clouds that never left, resulting in a persistent cold drizzle that stung your cheeks. I might be okay without a sleeping bag here. But in a matter of hours our train would climb into the Cascades, and we weren't entirely sure, but we figured it would be colder up there. Maybe there would even be snow.

"Fuck fuck fuck!" I yelled, into the wind.

"I have a tarp you can use," Sami shouted at me. She pulled a folded blue bundle from the top of her pack. I took it gratefully. It would be dark soon, and there wouldn't be anything to do but bed down in the rumble and the wind and wait for dawn. I crossed back to my side of the car and sat on my foam pad, taking stock of my things. I had a wool sweater, a flannel shirt, a hat, a pair of gloves, a rain jacket. I was wearing heavy, double-knee Carhartts and leather hiking boots, both of which I'd shoplifted.

I'd be warm enough tonight with these things, wouldn't I? How cold did it get in the Cascade Mountains in February, anyway? I had a few days' worth of nuts, dried fruit, and canned beans, and one liter of water. We'd arrived at the trainyard with two liters each, and I'd drunk one of mine while waiting for our train. I was pretty sure my remaining liter wasn't enough to get me the rest of the way to Los Angeles—why hadn't I brought more? Well, there was nothing to be done now.

Now, in this late hour, I know the answer to my earlier question: it is very cold in the Cascade Mountains in February, especially when you are hurtling along at breakneck speed and you have no real protection from the wind. I pull the blue tarp tighter around me, strain to see shapes in the glittering dark. How long until we cross from Oregon into California, and then drop down into the warm desert? And how long until we reach L.A., our destination? One more day? Three? The fir forest blurs past, its hollows piled with snow. The trees observe without judgment, as they have for my entire life.

I think back to two days ago when Sami and I were sitting on the lip of this railcar, having just climbed onto the train.

"It's okay," she said. "This car is safe."

The railcar was shaped like a shoebox with no top, and we were looking down inside it. The car didn't look rideable. It looked dangerous. Instead of a solid metal floor, there were two large holes, each four feet across, through which we could see the train tracks. On either side of each of these holes was just a scrap of floor, about twelve inches wide. This ledge was where we would sleep, eat, and hang out until our train reached L.A. To complicate things further, the back half of a semi-truck was sitting in this railcar. We would have to crawl between the huge truck tires to get to the little ledges where we could rest, each of us on one side of one of the large holes. Our view would be the hoses and grimy pipes of the underside of the truck. The truck's mud flaps would be our only protection from the wind.

"See," said Sami as she jumped down into the car. "Perfectly safe." She pulled off her large canvas military backpack and pushed it in front of her, under the axle of the truck. She reached a ledge and clipped the straps of her pack around a metal pipe that ran the length of the railcar. "You attach your pack to the car so it doesn't fall in the hole when the train is moving. Then you just make sure that *you* don't fall in the hole."

I followed on my hands and knees, gripping the edge of the railcar. A hiss, like a bike tire deflating, ran the length of the train, from one car to the next—the brakes releasing. I had been told to listen for this sound. The train lurched, there was a scream of twisting metal, and the tracks below us began to move. The train was moving. I had climbed onto a freight train and now it was moving!

"Shit!" said Sami. "Get under here, quick! We don't want the bull to see us!"

"Bull," I had recently learned, was what the rail cop was called. We were in Portland, Oregon, on the southern edge of the city, where the tidy grid of houses turned to suburbs and sprawl. We'd caught the train where our friend Andrew, who had ridden so many trains his Carhartt pants shone like waxed canvas on account of all the diesel grease, had told us to catch it—he'd told us which city bus to take south, which stop to get off at, to look for the Burger King and the underpass and the blackberry brambles, to arrive in the morning and wait under a tree out of the rain, that eventually our train would come. He told us what to look for—not grainers with no place to ride, not boxcars like in the movies, not oil tankers. Intermodal trains, that's what you wanted. Double stacks. Two colorful freight containers in a car like an open shoebox. He'd said that most of the double stacks on the train, which might be up to two miles long, would not be rideable. But one or two of them would be. We'd know by the numbers on the side of the car, and whether or not they were ridged or smooth. The train to L.A., when it arrived (it came every day but Sunday, Andrew had said), would stop for fifteen minutes, max. That's all the time that we would have.

Our train had come, it had slowed, it had stilled. We'd run along it on the slanted ballast, lungs burning, tripping over the railroad ties. Our packs jostled against our backs and the resting cars ticked, ticked, as though alive. The units—that's what the engines are called and there were four of them on this train, enough to pull it up and over the Cascades—were far ahead, so far we couldn't see them, nor could we be seen by the engineers that manned them. We'd found this car that was, according to Sami, perfectly safe, we'd climbed inside it, and now the train had begun to move again, toward a road crossing where the bull, Andrew had said, would be parked in an unmarked white SUV. The bull would watch the train go by and look for signs that there were riders. If he saw us, he would stop the train, pull us off, and we'd get a ticket for criminal trespassing. It would be a fine, maybe some community service. Our trip would be over. If we could just make it past that road crossing, though, we'd be safe, free.

As I scrambled into the car, I could already hear the dinging of the metal arms that blocked traffic at the crossing—the sound was growing louder, closer. Blood rushed to my face. If I could just get to the small metal ledge, I could lie down, and the lip of the railcar would hide me. But as I wiggled under the axle of the semi-truck, I was exposed, alarmingly so. What if I was caught by the bull, and arrested? What if he'd already seen us?

I got myself under the truck and turned around, yanking my pack after me. It wouldn't budge. *Oh shit! Oh shit, oh shit!* A stronger pull and the fabric made an awful tearing sound as, at last, I freed it. I scurried onto the ledge, unrolled my foam sleeping pad, and flattened myself onto it, barely breathing, just as we pulled slowly through the road crossing. I clenched my eyes shut, wishing for invisibility. The dinging of the metal arms was all around me now—the sound felt as though it was coming from inside my skull. Why were we moving so slowly through this crossing? Was the train stopping? Were we about to get busted? Finally, the clanging receded and then, after a time, it was gone. I lifted my face and looked at Sami, whose mouth was slack with relief.

"Holy shit," she said. The sound of her words was lost to the rumble of the train, which had picked up speed, but I could see her lips move. I laughed, and my laughter was carried away on the wind.

We were safe. I lay back on my foam sleeping pad on my small metal ledge and watched in wonder as trees and telephone poles passed through the slice of sky between the lip of the car and the underside of the tractor trailer. Rooflines, brick chimneys, traffic lights. Conifers and the bare winter limbs of deciduous trees. The southern outskirts of the city, in cross section. My heart was still racing from our sprint down the stopped train, our narrow miss with the bull, the fact that I was on a freight train at all. I couldn't believe it. I was stowed away on a railcar a mile from the front of the train. I was hidden. I had food and water. I could feel the damp winter air on my face, smell wet forests and woodfires and bakeries. Our train was rocking through traffic crossings, heading toward the open land of rural Oregon. The train would soar over the Cascade Mountains! I'd be carried away into the warm, gentle land of California!

Although I had been told that the train would be loud, it was so much louder than I expected. The sound was like plates of steel being wrenched in half—a sort of screaming that lasted for minutes, tapered away, then began again. And underneath this metallic screaming was the rhythmic rocking of our heavy car on the tracks. And the vibration—every part of the car vibrated, including, and especially, the floor. It was a vibration I could feel in my entire body, even in my teeth. It felt as though I was in the throat of a great, ponderous beast, and I suppose, in a way, I was. How fast were we going? We'd trundled slowly through the intersections in Portland, but now we were positively thundering along. Sixty miles per hour? I closed my eyes, letting the sounds and vibrations of the train hypnotize me.

Once in L.A., the plan was to catch another train to Texas. Instructions from Andrew on where and how to catch this train were written in pencil on a piece of scrap paper that was folded carefully into my journal. Sami had ridden a freight train twice before, and I, before this trip, had never ridden one at all; between her limited knowledge and Andrew's mostly legible instructions, we were hoping that it would all, in the end, work out.

This cold. I don't know what to do about this cold. I lie down on my sleeping pad and wrap myself in the tarp, but I cannot rest.

If only I hadn't lost my sleeping bag! Each time I succeed in gathering the tarp around me, the wind tears it away again, pulling it open with a thousand icy fingers and beating it against the frozen steel of the car. The gaping hole taunts me from beyond my ledge, sucking at the corners of my sleeping pad. I start to panic but remind myself that this sort of thing must happen to my friends who ride trains all the time. *And they're okay, aren't they? I want to be tough like them, don't I?* If Andrew were here, I think—remembering the way he nonchalantly described this route to us, as though riding the train from Portland to L.A. in February was the easiest thing in the world—he'd squat over the hole in the floor and sharpen his knife on the tracks.

When I open my eyes again, it's still nighttime. The trees beyond the train have begun to slow—I can see them more distinctly now. Their boughs, tufted in white, sparkle in the cold, clear air. Is the train stopping? Somewhere up ahead are the units, although I cannot see or hear them—ticking, rumbling engines, four of them, yellow light spilling from their windows. There are engineers in the first unit, but the three rear units will be unmanned. Each unit, I have been told, has a small, heated cockpit, with captain's chairs, a cramped bathroom, and, incredibly, a mini fridge full of bottled water. If the train stops, I can climb out of this car, run down the tracks in the dark, and try to reach those units. Maybe I can ride in one through the night, and be warm. At the very least, I could get some water. How far from my car are the units, though? A mile? More? I feel mumbly with cold, and my thoughts are tangled. Across the car from me, Sami is burrowed in her sleeping bag, the hood cinched around her face so only her nose is visible. As the train pulls to a stop, she does not stir. Now's my chance! I wriggle out from under the truck, lower myself down the three-rung ladder on the outside of the car, and land, with a crunch, in the snow.

When, where, and for how long a train will stop is a riddle that each aspiring train rider must learn to solve, and on which the success of their trip depends. This is what I have learned so far, from my friends: A freight train stops at least every eight hours, to change crews. These crew-change stops are made at specific railyards around the country. Since the train always stops for at least fifteen minutes when it changes crews, this makes a convenient window in which to get on or off a train. We got on in Portland at the specific yard where our train was changing crews, and as our train rumbles south it will stop in a handful of towns, every eight hours or so. Aside from crew-change points, a train might stop on a length of double track to "side" while it allows another train to pass—a train carrying higher-priority freight, maybe, like mail or automobiles—or it might stop in a railyard to refuel or "work," a mysterious affair during which beeping trucks drive up and down the train as it sits motionless under massive floodlights. Or sometimes, like now, on this dark, snowy mountain, the train might stop for no discernible reason at all.

I stumble forward in the snow, willing my numb legs to waken. The train, so full of shrieks and groans just a moment before, is now so silent it's as if it never moved at all, as if it will never move again. The moon casts everything in silver, and the air is fresh and sharp. This is a quiet, wintry land, dazzling and enchanted. I pause for a moment, full of wonder, and then I run, the sound of my boots cracking the stillness like glass shattering on cement. I've gone ten cars toward the front of the train when there's the telltale *hissss* of the brakes releasing. *Fuck! Fuck*

fuck! I spin around and jog as fast as I can back toward my car, slipping a bit on the steep embankment next to the tracks. The train begins to creep forward, so slow at first, not making any noise at all. Then a shudder moves down the string as the slack is pulled out of the couplers between each set of cars. I have to make it back to the car we were riding in—it was yellow, wasn't it? Or was it red?—before the train picks up speed, or I'm fucked. If the train leaves me behind, I'll be stranded here, in the cold forest, in the middle of the mountains. How far to a road? A town? I have no idea.

Unlike what we see in old movies, it's not a good idea to get on or off a moving train. That's called "catching on the fly," and it's dangerous as hell. Train riders in the twenties did it so that they could catch the train once it was past the yard—back then, the rail cops carried batons and would beat you if they found you, so the yards were scary places to get on a train. Getting on and off on the fly is dangerous because the momentum of the train pulls you down toward the tracks, so if you slip and fall, that's where you'll end up. Nowadays, the worst that can happen if you get caught in a trainyard is a trespassing ticket or a night in jail, which is not worth losing your legs to avoid, so the safe thing to do is wait for the train to stop before you get on or off, which you can do without much difficulty as long as you know the crew-change stops. Some people still catch on the fly, of course, but they do it for the thrill, and because they're idiots.

I am terrified of catching on the fly. I've been told that if I absolutely must, as in this situation, where I'm in danger of being left behind, I should pay attention to the three lug nuts on the wheels of the train—if I can make out each individual nut, the train is still going slowly enough for me to get on safely. I glance at the lug nuts as I jog down the string—still in the safe zone.

Then I see our car—yellow, like I thought—and I grab the ladder and pull myself up, struggling against gravity. The cold metal of the ladder rung bites into my hands and I heave myself into the car like a fish flopping into a boat. The inside of the car is in shadow, and through the huge holes in the floor I can see moonlight glinting on the tracks. I wriggle back under the truck and sit on the gritty steel, clutching my pack, heart hammering against my ribs. At least I'm warm now, from the physical exertion and the adrenaline. At least there is that. I feel the trees overhead, all around; I watch them drag slowly past in the moonlight, and my breathing begins to calm. The clean air smells of sharp pinesap. I remember the stillness and quiet of the stopped train sitting in the forest, a quiet so thick it made a rushing in my ears. The train picks up speed, and the wind pulls the heat from me. I wrap the tarp around my body again. I am cold and awake in a magical world, struggling for my survival. I am cold and awake and filled with awe. I feel so alive this strange long night. In the city, I often carry fear and shame like a lead weight; I curl up inside myself like a sprout inside a seed. Out here, I am huge. Expansive. Pieces of me unfurl in all directions, into the open wilderness, up toward the sky. The stillness holds me.

But the cold also reminds me of another time. I haven't been cold like this since I was a child, in Alaska. Being out here, exposed and scared, a little thirsty and a little hungry, takes me back to those days.

I clutch the tarp around me and sit on the vibrating floor of the car, watching the stars. The steady thrumming of the tracks becomes a song that melds with the rhythm of my heart.

1988

I am six years old and the phone is ringing. "Don't pick it up," says Barbara, my mother. She takes a long drag on her Pall Mall cigarette and hisses the words a second time. We are in Anchorage, Alaska, in our small, dim apartment. The blinds are drawn against the outside world and I am sitting on the carpet, picking cheese from an empty pizza box. "Don't you ever pick up the phone," my mother says again.

"I know," I say. "I know."

When I was a baby, we lived in the Chugach Mountains outside of town, in a half-built house. My father worked for the Alaska Railroad and my mother stayed home, singing Dolly Parton songs off-key as she painted the empty rooms. *Your beauty is beyond compare, with flaming locks of auburn hair, with ivory skin and eyes of emerald green.* My brother screamed in the other room with colic but, Barbara later told me, I was always quiet in my bassinet.

"You just watched me," she says to me in the dark apartment. "With your big eyes. You watched everything I did." She lifts her cigarette from the pickle-jar-lid ashtray and inhales again. Her hand is shaking. Barbara is beautiful, a trembling willow tree with shining black hair. She met my father, Bill, in Grand Junction, the dusty town in western Colorado where she was raised. She was nineteen then, living with her parents and five siblings in a brick house that sat on several acres of alfalfa and hay. Her father was a mechanic; her brothers would be mechanics too. Before that, the men in her family had been cowboys, going back five generations in the high desert. Bill wore thick aviator glasses and had a wild, unkempt beard. He told her that he was studying the Bible so that he could live to be three hundred years old, the way that Moses had. He wanted to go to Alaska "before the Russians came." They were married at the courthouse, and she was pregnant soon after.

The house in the Chugach Mountains didn't have siding when I was born, and there were empty holes where the windows should've been. When my parents had first arrived in Alaska, they'd bought a piece of land in a bog that you had to cross a frozen river to reach. A few years later, they were on the mountainside. They moved in fall, the soft early edge of winter, and the poplar trees were flame yellow. The nights began to freeze, and the heat from the woodstove escaped from the empty window frames. Eventually, there wasn't much wood left on the woodpile, and the only food in the house was a box of saltines that Barbara had been using to feed the squirrels.

"That's when the Virgin Mary first spoke to me," says Barbara, returning her cigarette to the pickle jar lid. The cherry of the cigarette flares, and a tendril of smoke reaches up toward the ceiling and dissolves into the haze there. The blinds in our apartment are yellow from smoke. My clothes reek of it. All winter I cough, spitting green phlegm into the bathroom sinks at school.

"I always felt close to the Virgin Mary, but that was the first time I heard her voice," Barbara says, rubbing her palms together. They make a sound like paper rustling. I pick the last of the cheese from the pizza box and lick the grease from my fingers. "I'd stopped sleeping," she continues. "My dreams bled into my waking hours, my waking hours blurring into one long, endless day, a day that grew darker and more brittle by the minute. The Virgin Mary, though, really helped me through that difficult time. I began to hear her voice as clearly as I heard my own. Sometimes I would see her, standing in the shadows of the room. She gave me instructions. Special instructions. Secret information I would have no way of knowing otherwise. I just had to listen and try to obey."

Barbara shakes another cigarette from the pack of Pall Malls and lights it off the dying ember of the last. "We never did finish that house," she says.

The divorce, when it came, was drawn out and terrible. I have few memories of it. I do remember the foster home where I lived for two years, where it was warm and clean, and there were regular meals. Although I have no memory of the separation, I learned later that my brother, Jordan, was in a different foster home. Barbara was eventually awarded custody of us— our father, Bill, had occasional supervised visits, and then he faded completely, leaving only photographs, and then Barbara tore up the photographs and those were gone too. I don't know why Bill left, or where he went. Eventually it became as though he had never existed at all.

I close the pizza box and open it again, trying to make more pizza appear. I am wearing the same clothes I've worn for a week, and I didn't go to school today. I'm not sure where our next meal will come from.

The phone rings again. Is it social services calling? Barbara paces the room, her cigarette twitching in her fingers. Barbara spends most of each day pacing. I can hear her at night, the creak of the floor in her room as she crosses the small space again and again. My teacher has been asking questions: Why are Jordan and I so dirty? Why don't we have any food for lunch? Why are we always falling asleep at our desks? And so Barbara has started keeping us home. She'll keep us home until she finds another school to enroll us in, one where no one knows us. The new school will be a farther walk in the dark winter morning, probably, but we'll manage it—we walk to school alone already, we can do it somewhere else. I like the school where we've been for the past six months, though. I like the black and white tile of the big, open hallway and the carpeted floor of my classroom. I've been stealing food from the other kids' lunches—I can smell the lunch boxes on their metal cart in the coat closet, the turkey sandwiches and Ho Hos wrapped in foil. I've been sneaking into the coat closet and eating the other kids' food when no one is watching. Maybe the teacher found out, and that's why she was asking questions.

Jordan emerges from our room and I follow him around the apartment, parroting his movements as he opens and closes the cupboards. Jordan is eight, and he's clever and resourceful— good at finding food. Before the pizza came a few days ago, I was hungry—my stomach burning and clawing. In the back of one of the cupboards, we found a bag of sugar and a raw potato. We sat on the kitchen floor and ate the potato, as well as spoonfuls of the sugar. Now, Jordan is looking in the cupboards again, but they are even emptier than they were a few days ago. I peek at Barbara in the living room, talking quietly to herself as she paces. Sometimes she is a bright whirlwind, scrubbing the filth from the kitchen counters and entering the apartment in a gust of cold air with paper sacks full of groceries. She'll pick up housekeeping gigs for cash and talk rapidly about how we are going to dig ourselves out of the hole we're in, about how everything is going to change. She is lovely during these periods—her eyes flash, she showers and brushes her long black hair until it shines. She'll put on a clean blouse and some mascara. The apartment sparkles with her laughter. She doesn't eat—she doesn't need to, and there is *too much to do besides!* Jordan and I are buoyed during these times, transported like two small boats on the river of her joy. After a few weeks, though, her ideas begin to take on a ragged edge. Her thoughts become darker and more fantastical, until they unravel and even we can't make sense of them, no matter how hard we try. And then, one morning, Barbara will be on the couch, face pressed into the cushions, unmoving. If you look carefully, you can see the blanket rising and falling just a little with her breaths. She'll stay on the couch this way for weeks, until her long hair is full of mats that will have to be cut out with the orange pair of sewing scissors that lives in the kitchen drawer.

Welfare pays the rent in our low-income apartment complex in Anchorage on a quiet street next to the forest, at the base of the mountains, and food stamps should help buy our food—but Barbara is always forgetting to keep up with the paperwork for the food stamps and I can't remember the last time we had them.

I sit on the floor and poke at the detritus there, the things that have been ground into the carpet since we moved into this apartment. Barbara shakes her pack of cigarettes. Empty. The windows are shut tight against the winter air. The muscles in my legs are cramping, and I cry.

"Shut up!" yells Barbara. In four large strides she is across the living room. She slaps me and *whap!* my head hits the wall. I am wailing now, my world exploding in pain.

"Let's go to our room," says Jordan, pulling my hand. "Come on." Up a flight of stairs, a bare mattress rests on the floor. The carpet is littered with plastic McDonald's toys, headless Barbies, and Taco Bell wrappers. I curl on the mattress and Jordan pushes a stained comforter over me. I cry into the mattress until I am all worn out and the leg cramps are far away. Jordan sits on the edge of the mattress and uses a screwdriver to work apart the pieces of a remote-control car that he found in the dumpster of our apartment building. The baseboard heaters tick-tick-tick. Condensation runs down the window glass, and outside, snow is falling. I walk to the window and press my face to it. The drifting snowflakes are heavy and white in the light from the streetlamp. They heap themselves onto the boughs of the spruce trees. I hear the door across the hall close as Barbara shuts herself in her room. She'll be in there for a long time. Maybe forever.

1989

Barbara wrenches open the heavy wooden door of the church and we duck inside, out of the biting wind. I stamp snow from my boots and pull the gloves from my numb hands. Outside is gunmetal gray with bitter cold, but here is warmth and beams of light from the stained glass in the high stone walls. Outside is the howling storm, but here is such peace that the air barely moves, and dust motes dance languidly in the light. The church smells of frankincense and rose petals and the sulfur of matches and this innocent, unmolested dust. Barbara mutters to herself and twists her hands together. Her long black hair is loose in the light from the stained glass and her eyes are glazed and her body is gaunt beneath her long winter coat. She walks toward the front of the church and looks up at Jesus, hanging gory on the cross, and then ducks into a small room off to the side of the pulpit. I climb the steps to the stage below Jesus. I lift the cloth on the small square table there, searching for something secret, candy or maybe a quarter that somebody dropped. I look at the saints in the stained glass, surrounded by animals and birds and colored light.

In the small room, I find Barbara kneeling on the carpet in front of a metal rack of candles in red glass. She is speaking in tongues while rocking back and forth. *"Shagga-habba-shagga-badda."* It is a language only God can understand.

I find an unlit candle and strike a match. You're supposed to put money in a metal box before you light a candle, but I don't have any money. My lit candle is pretty in its red glass, and I watch the little yellow flame dance for a while. I wonder if, after she is finished here, Barbara will take me to the church gift shop across the street and buy me a new rosary. A wooden one or one made of turquoise plastic. Of course I know she probably won't buy me one, but at least, if we go there, I can look as much as I want. My favorite rosary in the shop is the one made of silver with red crystal beads—it's far too much money for me to ever own. I feel faint, so I leave the small room and sit in one of the pews. I haven't eaten yet today.

I pretend to be praying. I dig through the pamphlets and songbooks. When the dizzy spell passes, I walk around the church in a circle, trying all of the locked doors. Barbara emerges from the small room with the candles and buttons the toggles on her long pink coat. She pulls me out the door, back into the storm. She walks fast, and I struggle to keep from slipping on the ice. At the station where we can catch the city bus back to our apartment, there is a little shop that sells hot dogs and souvenirs, and I fill my pockets with ketchup packets. I surreptitiously squeeze these into my mouth on the bus as we bump along the icy streets. Barbara's face is still shining, her eyes fixed on something far away. I look out the window at the dirty piles of slush—it is the end of winter, and everything is tired.

Barbara has begun to tell Jordan and me that she doesn't just speak to the Virgin Mary, she *is* the Virgin Mary, reincarnated. The Virgin Mary has been reincarnated into a woman who chain-smokes and drinks Mountain Dew from plastic gas station cups. I believe Barbara because this world with my mother is the only one I know. What is the Virgin Mary? What is God? The incense, the wooden pews, the speaking in tongues. My mother's visions. She is strong beyond belief—she can open pickle jars and carry gallons of milk and buy us Jolly Ranchers from the corner store. She is stronger than the sun. And she is so *sure*. Why would she lie?

I look at Barbara's face, her eyes resting on something beyond this world. I imagine the Virgin Mary with her pale blue eyes and sandaled feet. The complicated drapery of her clothing and her plump, open palms. I wonder if Barbara is the Virgin Mary right now. If she is floating on a cloud of God's grace high above the city, where no pain can touch her.

n the morning my tongue is swollen in my mouth. *Fuck, seriously, why didn't I bring more water?* Sami is thirsty as well,
and together we watch the sun rise over the pine forest on the
dry side of the Cascade Mountains from our narrow metal ledges
on the train, feel the sun's light on our ruddy cheeks. I uncurl my
stiff body, try to stretch a little, wipe the salt from my eyes. I may
have slept a bit after all, or I simply forgot whole hours of the
night. I never did reach the units at the front of the train, although I tried two more times after the first attempt, each time
turning around and racing back to our car when I heard the hiss
of the brakes releasing. As the morning lengthens, the wind becomes warm and dry, but each time the train stops and we hop
out to pee or stretch our legs, we are still in the mountains, still
in the forest, still far from the desert. I pick my nose as I watch
the gold sky fade to blue. My boogers are black—being on a

train means breathing diesel exhaust, so much heavy diesel exhaust. Is that why I feel loopy this morning? Or is it the nonstop thundering and rhythmic shaking of the train, which lulls me into a sort of hypnosis? I'm hungry, but I'm more thirsty than hungry, and the thought of putting food into my dry, sandy mouth makes me nauseated. The jar of peanut butter I pull from my pack is unappealing, and I put it away again. I've never been thirsty like this, and I feel alarmed. But also high, and delirious from the long night waiting for morning to come. My heart soars on the horizon with the sun.

All there is to do today is nap and watch the world go by, wait for the day to pass and for night to come again. But surely, we think, by the time it's dark, we will be safe in the warm California desert! And yet night arrives, with its stars and bitter cold and whipping wind, and we are still in the dark mountains of Northern California, stopping in the eerie black forest and then hurtling forward at a speed that feels like it will shake the fillings from our mouths. So there is another night of misery, of trembling in the cold wind; of wishing I had twenty times as many tarps, a sleeping bag fifteen feet thick, an entire gallon of spring water.

Dawn comes again and we emerge from our bedrolls into a delicate world of pink and gold light, a warmth that softens our stiff bodies, a wind turned gentle and kind. The California desert! We've reached the desert! We sit on the metal porch at the front of our car, chewing dried mango, watching the land go by. Finally our layers come off; finally the balmy air caresses our skin. At last our train breaches the dusty outskirts of early-morning Los Angeles. The train slows a great deal, from a shaking rumble to a gentle creep, and stops and starts often as it moves through industrial neighborhoods and road crossings, where commuters are backed up behind the dinging metal crossing arm, watching our train, oblivious to the two riders on sleeping pads, just hidden by the lip of the car.

We'd like to get off before our train reaches the huge labyrinthine trainyard, if possible, with its endless expanse of glimmering, parallel tracks and tangles of strings of cars bound for nowhere, and so when the train stops again we stuff our things into our packs and hop over the side, eardrums vibrating as we stand on the ballast, gathering our bearings.

We are hungry and dehydrated, and we have no idea where we are. My tongue feels like a balled-up sock in my mouth. We walk a few blocks along a wide, empty boulevard, past teenagers selling heart-shaped balloons and baskets of candy. It's Valentine's Day, we realize. We round a corner, and in front of us is a faded strip mall with a taqueria, shimmering like a mirage.

In the taqueria I suck down a huge Styrofoam cup of ice water and feel my cells expanding like a million tiny sponges. I eat a massive burrito, and in the bathroom I scrub the grime from my hands and face with paper towels. Sami and I slump, bleary and contented, in the red plastic booth, nibbling on paper cups of pickled carrots, the wreckage of our meal before us. The proprietors watch us from the back of the restaurant, twisting dishcloths in their hands. At last it's time to ship out and we heave our packs up, newfound energy pumping through our bodies. Outside, we stand in the sunlight, unsure of our next move. We've got to catch the train to Texas, but I also need to acquire a sleeping bag somehow.

"Maybe I'll call my dad?" says Sami. We both laugh. Neither of us grew up knowing our fathers, and we're not sure what a father even is, or what they're supposed to do. The whole concept is absurd to us. But Sami reconnected with her father for the first time a year ago—they even met in person—and they've been talking on the phone once a month, albeit awkwardly, ever since. He lives a thirty-minute drive away.

The bus drops us in Burbank and we walk a few blocks to Sami's dad's house—white, with a tidy lawn and a palm tree, and a red sports car parked in the drive. His wife, who is a costume maker in Hollywood, opens the door and frowns at us. We are filthy with diesel grime and smell of unwashed clothes.

"Leave your packs on the porch," she says. We step inside, to thick beige carpet and glass-fronted china cabinets.

"Can you take us to Trader Joe's?" Sami asks her dad, after we've both showered, leaving gray streaks in the tub and muddying a pile of white towels, which we've left crumpled on the bathroom floor. "We need to dumpster some food for the rest of our trip."

"This is crazy," Sami whispers to me as we pull up behind Trader Joe's in her dad's shiny red sports car. We root around in the dumpster in the warm afternoon sun, the wealthy patrons in the parking lot too oblivious to really understand what we're doing. We load up the trunk of the car with expired sushi, flour tortillas, baby greens, bags of tangerines. I lift a bright bunch of cut flowers in the air, twirl it around in the blue sky, and then toss it behind me, back into the dumpster. I think about my own father—my whole life I've made up stories about how he's dead, or in prison, and that's why he never was there for us when Jordan and I were kids, why he never appeared like a magical Santa Claus when we were starving or had no place to go. I wonder for the millionth time if I should try to find him, now that I'm an adult. Maybe he and I could be friends, the way Sami and her dad are friends now. *What would it be like to have a father?* I drop the thought in the dumpster with the flowers, and keep digging.

Sami and I climb back into her dad's car, the tread of our shoes caked in coffee grounds and mashed plums, and he ferries us to a large chain outdoor store, where I return my rain gear, which I shoplifted in Portland for this trip but figure I will no longer need, and use the store credit to buy the warmest sleeping bag on the shelf. The salesperson tries to talk me out of selecting such a warm sleeping bag.

"Where are you going camping?" he keeps asking me. "The Arctic? You don't need that." I wave him away. I've decided that I'm never going to be cold again.

That evening, Sami's dad and stepmom take us out for Thai food. As we inhale our noodles, Sami's stepmom tells us about her job working in Hollywood, the long days and the way the work consumes her life.

"Are you happy?" I ask.

She fiddles with the snow peas on her plate.

"No," she says. "Not really. I wish, at this point, that I could do something else."

"Oh, I'm sorry," I mumble, suddenly awkward. Who are Sami and I to be free like this, I think, doing whatever we want?

Sami's dad pays the bill and we walk out into the faded night, warm air rising off the concrete. I know I won't be able to ride trains and live off dumpstered bread forever. But what else is there? I'm not sure.

At a railroad junction outside of L.A., we wait for two days for the train that will take us to Texas. The Union Pacific route that heads east from L.A. through Arizona, New Mexico, and Texas and then continues on through Louisiana, Mississippi, and Alabama before terminating in Georgia is called the Sunset Route, and I've heard stories about it from others—it hurtles across the open desert of the Southwest, changes crews in El Paso, the highest-security railyard in the country, and it's the only long train route in North America that won't freeze you in the wintertime. The junction where we wait for our train is open yellow grass and a warm blue sky and we build a three-sided shelter out of tumbleweeds in which to hide. At night, we lie in our tumbleweed house and watch the stars, drifting in and out of sleep as trains that aren't ours blow past. During the day, birds wheel overhead and I finish a February issue of *The New Yorker*, open it at the beginning and start again. Time pools into a great sea with waves lapping all around us and we forget where we are, or how we ever got to this place.

The second morning, I walk across the tracks into the tall weeds to take a shit and, after relieving myself, I glance down and see that my poop is writhing with small white worms. I stand there for a moment, wordless, and then I shriek.

"We need the internet," says Sami, when I give her my report. She's stuffing away her sleeping bag. "The internet will tell us what to do."

We hike along the sun-washed roadsides, asking strangers for directions until we find a small, squat public library, where Google tells me that I have pinworms. I look up holistic remedies. Eat raw garlic every day, says the internet. And not any sugar. In two weeks they'll be gone. I buy a half dozen heads of garlic at a small tienda, peel a clove, and chop it with my pocket knife, using the double knee of my Carhartts as a cutting board. I sprinkle this onto a cold corn tortilla spread with almond butter. It tastes pretty good. I call the Wych Elm, the punk house in Portland where Sami and I live, on a payphone outside the tienda. Does anyone there have pinworms? Children, I have learned, are the ones most likely to get them, and they are spread by poor hygiene—adults in the U.S. usually bathe too much for it to really be a thing. I think of the narrow bathroom at the Wych Elm house. A pungent yellow toilet bowl, a single filthy towel. As far as I know, that bathroom has never been cleaned. And in spite of the cramped nature of the house, the shower is never occupied . . . because no one wants to shower. People boast about how they don't bathe except for the occasional swim in a natural body of water, or how they never wash their clothes. White clothes age with sweat and dirt and black clothes fade from the sun, until everything is the same transcendent shade of brown. People smell strong, but not in a bad way. Not like my mother's stress sweat, from weeks of cowering in her room, chain-smoking in terror while she hallucinated. This is the smell of fresh air and warm bodies and good, clean sweat that's been baked by the sun. It's like how horses have a smell.

"I'll be right back," says Ryan. I hear a knock as the phone's receiver is set on the kitchen table. There is laughter, and a rustling as he picks up the phone again. "Yeah, I have pinworms," he says. "I just had Lisa look at my asshole. I got 'em."

"Oh my God," I say. I think of the time I was dumpstering with Ryan in the rain. We were in the dumpster behind a grocery store, up to our knees in wilted produce. At the bottom was four inches of standing trash-water. Ryan picked a floating carrot out of this water and ate it.

That night, after I eat all that garlic, the itching in my butthole goes away—an itching that I had noticed and been annoyed by, but hadn't known was from the worms. Sami and I sit up playing cards by the light of the nearby streetlamp, and grow antsy with each passing train that still, somehow, does not stop for us. At last, around midnight, I take Andrew's directions from my journal and smooth them, and we reexamine the cryptic words and drawings, wondering if we could've misinterpreted them somehow.

"Wait wait wait," I say, tracing my finger over the scrawls on the paper. "Maybe instead of taking the number five bus to *Fourth* Street, that four is actually a nine, and we were supposed to get off at *Ninth* Street? And that's why we never saw the abandoned Pizza Hut, and the hole in the fence wasn't where it was supposed to be?"

"My God," says Sami.

An hour later we're at a stretch of double track in another part of this brightly lit industrial neighborhood, and by dawn, we're in our sleeping bags headed east, on a train to Texas.

W e are driving. I have no idea what time it is. Outside the windows of our little blue Ford, the world is dark, save for the bare snow illuminated in the streetlamps. We are circling Anchorage in great, aimless loops as Barbara burns one cigarette after another and switches the radio dial, never settling on a song. The volume on the radio is turned up as far as it can go, and the thundering of oldies, then country, then pop music, rattles my skull. The cigarette smoke is thick enough to choke on, and my eyes itch and burn. I am carsick and I have to pee.

I know that Barbara drives for hours like this because it calms her. And I know that she likes the radio up this loud because it helps drown out the voices in her head. At home, the TV stays on 24/7, although the volume is lower so as not to bother the neighbors. At home, the effect is subtler—a dull background noise, inane chatter. Cheery bright commercials and the dumb banter of sitcoms follow me around the apartment as I search for food, wash my hair with dish detergent, or dig through the pile of dirty laundry in the hallway, looking for a shirt or pair of socks that don't reek of mildew.

I press my face against the cold window of the car and soften my gaze, letting the yellow streetlights hypnotize me as they pass. I scratch shapes into the frost with my fingernails. It's so cold out there, so clean. The city this late at night is empty, and the fresh snow is unbroken. I search the dark shapes of the forest beyond the streetlights, let my eyes travel into the hollows there. I am no longer in the car—I am in the woods, I am rising up into the sky. I am in the stars.

We pull into the parking lot of a 7-Eleven and Barbara shuts the engine off. The noise of the radio dies and the silence is deafening, a loudness that flutters in my ears.

"Here," says Barbara. She twists in the seat and hands us each a one-dollar food stamp bill. The slug of dead ashes from the end of her cigarette lands on the leg of my sweatpants. "Buy a piece of candy. Nothing more than twenty-five cents, okay?"

The neat racks of candies sorted by color and shape at the front of a convenience store are incredibly pleasing to me. They are low to the ground, where I can reach them, and I touch a candy in each bin, lifting it and turning it in the light, considering. Do I want the watermelon Jolly Rancher, or the Bit-O-Honey that sticks to my molars? The Tootsie Roll isn't as good as the others, but you get the most candy for your money. Jordan is already paying for his Reese's Peanut Butter Cup, and I pick a couple of Jolly Ranchers and stand behind him in line. The clerk hands Jordan three quarters in change, and then she hands the same to me. The weight of the quarters in my palm is its own sort of food, and I savor it as I exit the warm store and step into the bitter cold.

"Give me that," says Barbara. She scrapes the coins out of our palms with her fingernails. She wrenches the car into reverse and we resume our looping drive of the city. Now I have the bright taste of a watermelon Jolly Rancher in my mouth, though, to cut through the sensations of noise and smoke. A few minutes later we park at another convenience store and she hands us each another food stamp dollar.

This time I buy the Tootsie Roll. I'm hungry, and that candy will fill me up better. I'm nodding off in the car, the thundering radio part of my dreams, when we stop at the third convenience store. After our mission inside is complete, Barbara counts the quarters, her fingers shaking, and then she leaves us in the car and returns a moment later with a fresh pack of Pall Malls. She slaps the pack against her palm and pulls off the cellophane, then drops the trash to the floor of the car, where it mingles with the Taco Bell wrappers and empty drink cups. I fish out the cellophane and play with it as we drive, my heart skipping from the sugar. Jordan is asleep, curled against the door of the car.

A few days later Jordan and I come home from school and the car is gone.

"The brakes went out on a hill on the ice," says Barbara. "Some boys helped me push it off the road, and I gave the car to them. The boys were angels, and God told me to give them the car."

"You gave our car away?" shouts Jordan. "Because *God* told you to?" He slams the door of his room and it bounces off the doorframe, rattling bits of plaster from the wall. I follow him into his room and sit on the carpet, in front of the television he found on the side of the road. The TV is tuned to a station called "The Box," where you can call a 1-800 number and pay four dollars to have them broadcast the music video of your choice. Right now no one is calling and the screen is static. Jordan and I often watch The Box for hours after school, waiting for a music video. Jordan's favorite is the Green Jellÿ video for "Three Little Pigs."

"She probably doesn't even have a license," Jordan is saying. "We're better off without the car. She shouldn't even be driving. Crazy bitch!" He's removing his schoolwork from his backpack and filling the backpack with comic books. He lifts the mattress and pulls out his stash of *Hustler* magazines and puts those in the backpack as well.

"Where are you going?" I ask, nervous.

"I'll be back," he says to me. "Don't worry about me. Find something to eat, okay? The hot bar at the grocery store is good to steal from. You can fill a container with food and just walk out with it. Everyone will think you've paid."

"Don't leave!" I'm crying now, my face thick with snot.

"Shh," says Jordan, a finger to his lips. He lifts his bedroom window open and cold fresh air rushes in. The broken blinds snag on his backpack as he climbs out. I hear the crunch of his boots as he lands in the snow. He turns and pulls the window almost, but not quite, shut.

The hallway is dark and silent save for the low mumbling of the radio in Barbara's room. I likely won't see her again for a few days. It's just me, now, in this world. Just me—hardly strong enough to carry a gallon of milk on my own, not yet strong enough to open a jar of pickles. Short enough that I still have to climb onto the kitchen counter to reach the top cabinets. At night I stay up as late as I want reading library books, and I sleep with all the lights on. I walk to school myself, in the dark under the cold stars, the strong Chinook winds pushing me across the ice that's like a skating rink. No one tells me to wash behind my ears. Brushing my teeth is tedious, so I don't do it.

I pull on my snow pants and step into my snow boots. Behind our apartment is a forested hill and I work my way up it, plunging to my hips in the snow with each step. The snow is fresh, replenished each day by the generous gods of winter. Snow is a free and limitless sculpture medium and building material, and having this much of it makes me feel rich. I like to make caves and tunnels, to burrow into it like an animal. I throw snow into the air and at the other neighborhood children, knock it off tree branches, stamp it down, jump off the back porch railing into it. I let it gather on my eyelashes. I sled downhill on a flattened cardboard box. I eat fistfuls of it, and it tastes like the sky.

There is a spruce tree on this hill whose lowest boughs make a small cave, and now I crawl into this hole and lie on my back, breathing in the crisp air and the clean smell of the spruce tree. The cave is warm and I watch the snow fall, flakes pirouetting from the heavy, leaden sky. I will stay as long as I can, until my eyelashes freeze together and my toes go numb. I can feel the tree's quiet sentience, the way that it holds me. Home is chaos, but this tree is solid. There is no love for me at home but here is the love of nature in its entirety, channeled via this one still, snowy tree.

You're safe, the tree whispers. *You're safe.*

1992

When Barbara was a teenager, she was pretty and popular, and she was determined not just to be good, but to be the very best at everything she did. She played basketball and could do flips in the air on the trampoline and she brushed her black hair a hundred times with her wooden paddle brush and rationed her cottage cheese so that her waist was at least an inch narrower than her three sisters', who were also very thin. Her knees were knobby and there was too much gum when she smiled, but there was nothing to be done about that.

When Barbara was given the challenge of sewing a dress for her high school Home Economics class, she became determined to sew the best dress that had ever been made in her school. She spent weeks obsessing over it, sewing and then tearing out the seams in frustration, then sewing again. Her sewing machine was in a corner of the living room, and while her five siblings played freely in the sun outside, she remained bent over the table, focused. She wanted the pleats just so and the poufs on the sleeves were difficult, and then there was the issue of the bust. Dinner came and went, and still Barbara sat. In the end, the dress was perfect. Her Home Ec teacher, who had never paid her any mind at all, absolutely beamed at Barbara, and then used the dress as an example in class. Barbara was elated for the rest of the week. There was nothing she liked better than being the best at something.

"I hated math, though," she says. We're in the living room of our apartment and I am listening, rapt, as she tells me about her life in high school, about the person she was before I was born. She is showing me how to assemble bits of fabric and then run them through the sewing machine to make a simple doll. I take the small cloth leg she just finished and work it with my fingers, turning it inside out so that the seams are hidden. Barbara hands me a bit of fiberfill from a cellophane bag, and I push this stuffing inside the leg. She pinches together the white fabric for the other leg and feeds it through the machine. *Whrrrr* goes the small metal foot. Black thread flies from the spindle. The thread snarls and Barbara stills the metal foot and pulls the thread loose, and then works it through the spindle again. Her Pall Mall smolders and she pauses to lift it with her long fingers and take a drag.

"I was never good at math," she says again, as she clips the thread with a pair of shears and passes the second finished leg to me. "I tried so hard, but I still did poorly. I even had a tutor. The teacher told me I was stupid."

"I'm good at math," I say.

"I know you are," says Barbara. She hands me a rectangle of synthetic black fur. "Cut a square of this, for the hair." I do as I am told, and Barbara pipes glue from the hot glue gun onto the doll's head, which we've already sewn and stuffed. I love the hot glue gun. I love the way it smells, and the way the glue changes form, from solid to liquid and back again.

Recently I've been spending the evenings after school at the public library down the road, curled in a wooden booth in my stained winter coat, reading. It's quiet there and smells comfortingly of musty books and bleach. I can get lost in what I'm reading for hours, and there is toilet paper in the bathroom. Often I stay until the library closes. Last week, in the nonfiction section, I found a book—a huge tome covered in crinkling plastic—titled *Schizophrenia*. I hid the book under the magazines in my arm and rushed back to my wooden booth, coat rustling. Lately I had started to understand that Barbara's world was not real. That there was something going on with her brain. That she was ill. As I read the book, my loyalty to Barbara, to her burning convictions, did battle in my heart with this nascent understanding of mental illness. I flipped through the chapters in the heavy book, reading bulleted lists of signs, symptoms, treatments. Waves of terror and embarrassment washed over me. Was there anything more awful than schizophrenia? It seemed worse than all the other mental illnesses combined. Why did Barbara have to be like this? Why couldn't she get it together? Why couldn't she *snap out of it*? "SNAP OUT OF IT!" I often screamed at her, when I was hungry, when I was afraid. Was she even *trying* to not be sick? There was a chapter of case studies in the book, and I read these carefully. Other people who were like Barbara. Whose brains created monsters from the things they feared most and sent these monsters to torment them endlessly, day and night, for the rest of their lives. People who were sent plummeting down a dark well into a parallel reality of endless suffering, and even though their loved ones could see them, they couldn't reach them to comfort them. Nobody could. It was like some sort of medieval torture situation you wouldn't wish on your worst enemy, or even on the worst person who had ever lived.

I started to cry in my wooden booth, in the quiet corner of the library, under the soft fluorescent lights. My tears spread onto the pages of the book, onto the stories of the other people like Barbara. I closed the book and wrapped my arms around it and rested my head on its cover. I felt as though my guts were turning inside out. As though my tears would become an ocean, and that ocean would drown me. Then I remembered that I was in the library and wiped at the snot coming out of my nose with the sleeve of my coat. I wept quietly on the book until I felt empty and then I returned it to its shelf, pushing it into the spot where I had found it, tidying the books around it. I left the library and reentered the cold winter, the dark of evening. My kid boots crunched on the frozen crust of the snow. Streetlights cast circles of yellow light on the black road. I was alone except for my hunger. My hunger was my constant companion. The wind moaned, knocking itself against the boughs of the trees, wailing against every solid object. Unlike me, I realized, the wind was *free*. It could cut loose its sorrow against the wide, empty night.

I press the square of black fur onto the doll's cloth scalp while Barbara threads a sewing needle with green embroidery thread. The doll will have green eyes and black hair, like Barbara. Barbara's fingers are nimble, and the tiny sewing needle darts in and out of the white cloth. She shows me how to space the stitches closely and precisely, so that no single stitch stands out but instead joins with the others to make a filled-in shape. Like painting with thread. Soon the doll has long black embroidered eyelashes and a red embroidered mouth. Barbara shows me how to whipstitch the legs and arms to the torso, and the head to the neck. I hold the naked doll in my hands, ecstatic at what we have created.

Barbara's hands are beginning to shake. She lights a new cigarette.

"We'll make her clothes another day," she says. She stands up from the table, with its detritus of fabric scraps, and rubs her hands over her face. The apartment is clean—Barbara has been up and about all week. She's scrubbed the crusted food off the stove and counters, washed all the dishes, cleaned the windows, and wiped down the bathroom until everything smells of Windex and Bon Ami. She wrote a bad check at the grocery store and brought home a gallon of milk, two loaves of bread, a jumbo carton of eggs, and a sack of potatoes. She's kept us home from school this week to help her fold laundry, clean our rooms, and make pans of burnt scrambled eggs. At night her bedroom light spills, liquid yellow, into the hallway. I don't know when she last slept.

That night I boil potatoes and Jordan and I eat them with the last of the margarine while watching TV. We've finished the eggs, and the milk and the bread are gone. I leave our dirty dishes in the sink and stand in front of Barbara's bedroom door, the naked doll clutched in my arms. Maybe Barbara can write another bad check and buy us more food. Maybe she will show me how to make clothes for my doll. Maybe I can sleep in her bed tonight with a fistful of her black hair clutched in my hand, the way she sometimes let me when I was small. I knock on the bedroom door but there is no answer, although I can hear the low muttering of the radio. I open the door and thick cigarette smoke spills out, stinging my eyes. Barbara is kneeling on the carpet, in front of the radio, and she is speaking to it.

"Mom," I say. "Mom!" She rocks back and forth while she talks to the radio. "Mom!" I shout, louder. "Mom!" Soon I am screaming her name as loud as I can. Suddenly she leaps to her feet, eyes aflame, and lunges at me. I lurch away but she grabs my arm and drags me into her room. She is hitting me across the back, again and again, as hard as she can. Her eyes have gone dark and blank. She is somewhere else. She is gone. I curl into a protective ball, but she keeps hitting me. She shoves me out the doorway and slams her bedroom door. I curl against the cool wall, making myself as small as possible. The world is a monster, poised to attack. I have to make myself invisible. I cry until I am blank. No feelings. The hallway is silent, the apartment is silent.

Eventually, I make the doll a dress from an old sock so that it won't be naked anymore.

2003

We hurtle east out of L.A., the wind warm on our restless bodies, the desert opening before us like a great sea. It's a thrill, to be this free. This time, we're in a train car that has a floor, and we unroll our bedrolls without fear of falling onto the tracks to our deaths. This train hadn't been hard to catch—it had stopped, the units with their watchful eyes far ahead and us way in back near the rear of the train, hiding in a culvert full of weeds. We had run along the string as it sat silent in the warm dark, recognized this rideable car, and climbed inside, our boots ringing out against the steel.

We make it as far as Yuma, Arizona, before we are pulled off in the dead of night. There's a tower above the tracks where the rail cop hangs out, and from there he can see straight down into our car, where we're sprawled out, asleep. The rail cop is a large, friendly man.

"You don't see too many people riding trains these days," he says to us, grinning. We're standing on the ballast with our packs, half asleep, while our hard-won ride to Texas pulls slowly away until all we can see is the blinking red light on the end of the final car, and then nothing. The rail cop takes a yellow pad from his pocket. "I'm gonna write y'all a citation. You're going to have to come back and appear in court. I want to tell you, though, that once I give this to you, I'm going to go back in that tower, and if you should happen to get another train out of here, I didn't see it."

"Thank you," I say, rubbing my eyes. "Are you so bored up in that tower?"

"You betcha," he says. I have a feeling that we are a welcome interruption in the monotony of his shift. I stuff the ticket absentmindedly into my pack, where I plan on losing it completely. Stay in Arizona long enough for a court date? Yeah, right.

We hide in the desert at the west end of the yard, where the sprawl of industry fades into a lonely stretch of double track, because this is where the back end of our train will be when the front end pulls up to the station. This, says Sami, is the way it usually is in small-town trainyards. You find the wee train station and then walk backward along the tracks for about a mile. There will usually be signs, here, that this is the place to wait—flattened cardboard, a clearing in the trees. Beer cans. The yards in small towns are much simpler than the jungles of big-city railyards, and easier to puzzle out.

An hour later we are lying on our foam pads under the warmth of the glowing stars when there are lights in the distance, a deep rumbling, and then the units of another eastbound intermodal pound past our hiding place, flooding the world with light, followed by the rattling cars. Our hearts are racing—is the train slowing? It is! We stuff our things away with trembling hands and crunch along the ballast until we find our ride, five cars from the back.

We rattle our way through Arizona, our train vibrating with speed, earplugs stuffed into our ears to protect us from the noise. We sit on the grated metal porch of our car and watch the desert go by as our hair tangles in the wind. The Mexico border is just south of us and it's mostly open country here, not a soul in sight. When we do pass through a town, we sit down in our car, where we're hidden by the four-foot walls, and wait there until the dinging of the last road crossing recedes. Cold cans of beans become meals, and games of cards and Hot Dice pass the time. We pee in a gallon jug with the top chopped off and empty it over the side—when we have to shit, we climb into the car behind ours and do it on a piece of cardboard, fling that over the side into the empty desert.

In New Mexico the train really picks up speed and the cinderblock shacks and wild horses blur past, as if there isn't anything worth stopping for in this part of the world. I nap and wake, nap and wake, the blue sky and then the stars whirling above me. I raise my hand in the air and trace the cup of the Big Dipper to the shining North Star. My earplugs fall out while I'm sleeping and the screaming and rocking of the train becomes the soundtrack of my dreams.

Sami and I came up with the idea to go to Texas just two weeks before we caught the train out of Portland. We were curled on the couch in the kitchen of the Wych Elm house, a wool blanket over our laps, drinking dandelion root tea while outside the world was drenched in cold rain. Two friends who'd just come back from Austin were sitting on the kitchen floor, sorting a box of dumpstered flowers from Trader Joe's. Their eyes sparkled and their arms were tanned from the sun. They plucked the good flowers from the wilted bouquets and rearranged them in mason jars.

"There's this punk house in Austin that's so amazing," they said. "It's called Entropy. There are like fifteen people living there. You should go visit, and get out of the rain."

I had never been to Texas. I had hardly been anywhere. South-central Alaska, with its glaciated mountains next to the ocean; the desert mesas of western Colorado; Portland. That was it. What would it be like to ride my first freight train? To go where it was warm in the winter?

Sami had ridden a train twice, from Portland to Eugene, but I had no experience at all. That afternoon, when Andrew gusted in the back door, carrying his banjo case and dripping from the rain, we cornered him.

"We want to ride a train to Texas," we said to him. "How do we do that?"

We cross, at last, into Texas. In the morning the train stops and I sit blinking in the sun on the porch of our car, my ears ringing in the silence. At the front of the train, where the units are, there must be a tiny town, people, movement. But our car sits pinging on a yellow plain, nothing to mark space but a length of wooden fence on the horizon, partly fallen over. I unfold my rail map and compare it with our surroundings. I have no idea where we are. Our gallons of water are lined up at the end of the car. One gallon is still full. I should've gotten up in the night every time we blew through some small road crossing in the middle of nowhere and looked for street signs that could orient us. But I was lazy, hypnotized by the movement, and I slept. The lines on our rail map are like a spider's web—we were hoping to get to Austin but our train, at any point, could've turned north, at which point we should've gotten off at the soonest crew change and caught another train, if possible.

"Where are we?" asks Sami. She's sitting up in her sleeping bag, rubbing the crust from her eyes. Her hands, black from diesel grime, leave streaks across her face. Our train lurches and begins to move again.

"I don't know," I say. I knife open a can of refried beans and sit on the metal floor of the car, eating the beans with a spoon. I can hear the dinging of the road crossing now, in the distance. Then the train slows again and settles to a stop.

There is a sound that no train rider ever wants to hear—the crunch of boots on gravel and the static hiss of a CB radio. My spoon freezes en route to the bean can, and I lock eyes with Sami.

Pong. Pong. Pong. The sound of someone mounting the three rungs of the ladder on the outside of our car. And then he's standing above us, casting us in the shadow of his ten-gallon Stetson hat.

"Y'all need to get off this train," he says. He's wearing cowboy boots and has a mustache. His belt buckle winks in the sunlight. Why is this yard worker pulling us off the train? Couldn't he have just looked the other way, as they often do, as long as they won't get in trouble for it? Now we'll have to get another train, and we're not even sure where we are. I sigh audibly, and root around in my pack for my sleeping bag stuff sack.

"Y'all better hurry it up," says the man. "Y'all are under arrest."

"Oh shit!" says Sami. "You're a rail cop?"

"I saw you, up on the hill." He points to his unmarked SUV parked near an overpass, where he can look down at passing trains and see any riders in the cars.

"Fuck!" says Sami.

"You're in Sweetwater, Texas," says the warden at the jail, which looks, from the outside, like a small-town post office. The warden has big blond Dolly Parton hair and she frowns at me as she presses my fingers into the ink pad to take my fingerprints. "Why do y'all smell so bad?"

"There aren't any showers on the train," I say.

The warden shakes her head. "You're a little gamey."

"You stink," says another warden, who is rifling through our packs, looking for exciting things like drugs. It's been just over a year since 9/11, and when we first arrived at the jail, the Dolly Parton warden gripped the laminate counter and hissed at us:

"You know who rides these freight trains? Terrorists! Terrorists ride these freight trains!"

The second warden is looking in our wallets. She pulls out a stack of traveler's checks.

"What is this?" she says, flapping the paper notes at us. "Canada money?"

I'm trying not to laugh. Sami shoots me a withering look.

It's Sunday, so we'll have to stay overnight, and the judge will see us in the morning. We trade our filthy Carhartts for clean black-and-white-striped uniforms, shower in a cold steel room, and are taken to our cell, which has three bunks and a TV bolted into the corner of the wall. Our cellmate, Leanne, tells us that she's in for check fraud.

"You were riding a freight train?" she says. "Wow, that's cool! Here, lemme show you a card trick." She shuffles a deck, spreads it facedown on the little table in our cell, and when she picks it back up the cards are in order. Dinner is chicken-fried steak and microwaved corn. The movie *Save the Last Dance* comes on the TV and I watch it curled on the top bunk. Then, after the lights go out, I cry. We've traded the wide-open desert and good moving air for this stale cell with no natural light—it might as well be underground. And we can't leave until they say so. Claustrophobia comes and sits on my chest. I feel as though I've been entombed.

Breakfast is gelatinous oatmeal and a small carton of milk, and then we are handed back our clothes, neatly folded and warm from the dryer. The judge meets us in the hallway—he is a huge, friendly man wearing jeans and a button-down shirt.

"I know y'all think this is Bill and Ted's big adventure," he says, "and you're waitin' to see George Carlin in a phone booth." He tells us we've served our time, a night in jail, and now we're free to go.

Outside, the air is fresh and warm and wild, and we laugh with delight as we wander through the tiny town of Sweetwater, Texas, which looks like the set of an old western film, toward the outskirts in hopes of hitching a ride. Our packs are heavy on our backs but our clothes are clean and we're drunk with joy. Cars slow as they pass us, the drivers' expressions flickering with curiosity, or maybe it's disgust. We don't care, though. We're free. Free!

In Austin we follow our crumpled, handwritten directions to the Entropy house. The house is a huge, old Victorian-style structure with a sinking roof and creaking wooden floors. Narrow stairways lead to oddly shaped rooms where residents have built dens of salvaged furniture, lace, and old velvet. The yard is a jungle of overgrown medicinal herbs and sculptures made from welded bike parts. A young man shows us the kitchen pantry, with hundreds of kinds of tea and trash bags of bagels on the floor. "Stay as long as you like," he says. We gather our strength in the yard among the plants, reading Assata Shakur's autobiography aloud and watching the many visitors come and go. I continue to eat peanut butter for most of my meals. After a week, Sami and I put down our books and look at each other.

"Where to next?" we say.

1993

unhinge the stapler and press it into the wooden top of my desk. *Pop.* A little folded staple appears; my first link of chain. *Pop.* There is the second link. I make a few more of these and connect them; now I have a length of miniature chain. My gray elephant eraser wanders over, curious, and next thing he knows the chain is around his leg. Now the elephant is trapped forever, attached to the edge of my desk. I pick up my horse eraser and sniff it. The horse will be next.

"Jennifer," the teacher is saying.

"What?" I look up. The other kids in my row are staring at me.

"We're passing forward our homework. Do you have your homework?"

I open my backpack and shuffle through the papers there. What homework? I don't remember any homework. History?

Math? I can't remember what we've been studying. I pull out my Trapper Keeper with the Lisa Frank neon kitten on the cover, open it, and pick a few papers at random. I pass these papers forward. There are words on the blackboard but the spots in the corners of my vision are bad today, and I can't read what's written there. The teacher is talking about long division. Math! We're studying math. I sniff my horse eraser again. *Pop.* Another link for my chain.

School lunch. A corn dog, some canned green beans, a wet square of cobbler. Carton of milk. Bright yellow mustard. The first things I've eaten all day. I finish my meal and eye the other kids' lunches. I'm still hungry. The other kids have bologna sandwiches and foil packets of fruit snacks. Those kids don't even notice if they have food or not, they're so well-fed.

I like playing four square, but the spots in my vision just won't quit today, so at recess I sit under the wooden playground equipment and play by myself. I have two sticks. One of them is for digging in the dirt, making neat straight lines and then cross-hatching these lines. The other stick walks in the dug dirt after the first, leaving perfect little tracks. I am counting the lines as I make them. When I finish a square of dirt, I erase it, move a foot to the right, and start again. My stomach rumbles and I drop the sticks and walk away from the playground, into the big open field that edges the woods. It's spring, and the field is soft and wet. A girl bumps into me as the four-square ball bounces past.

"Hey," she says, after she fetches the ball. "Don't you want to play?"

"Nah," I say.

"Why do you smell like an ashtray?" she asks. "You smoke? You got cigarettes?"

"I don't smoke." The girl stares at me and then runs away, her arms around the ball. A flash of white in the grass. I drop to my knees. It's an Oreo, gone soggy from the rain. Likely dropped by someone rich, someone who walks around with dollars falling from their pockets. Someone who owns every packaged product in the world, every expensive kind of boxed cereal, every forty-nine-cent fruit pie. I carefully pick the Oreo from the field and eat it.

The explosion comes in the still of the afternoon. I'm in the living room, watching TV. I find Jordan in his bedroom, kneeling on the floor next to a length of PVC pipe. He's gripping one hand in the other, and blood is running down his arm.

"I followed the instructions," he says. "The potato gun was supposed to work." He is crying, freckled cheeks wet, his lips pulled back in rage.

"No, no, no," says Barbara. She kneels next to Jordan and yanks his hands apart. He screams in pain. I can smell her, like a dumpster on a hot day.

"I need to go to the hospital!" cries Jordan.

"No," snaps Barbara. She lifts his arm, dragging him to his feet. "They ask too many questions at the hospital. We can't trust the hospital!" She pulls him, struggling, to the bathroom, and sits him on the edge of the tub while she fills an enamel turkey pan with tap water and a few glugs of hydrogen peroxide.

"Soak your hand in this," she says to Jordan, and pushes his hand into the pot. He is still crying, snot running into his mouth. "Shut up!" she screams at him. I stand in the hall, keeping myself small. Barbara returns to her room and quietly shuts the door. I find some Scotch tape and pull handfuls of toilet paper from the single precious roll in the bathroom. As I fold the toilet paper, I think about how rare it is to have something unsullied, like a fresh roll of toilet paper. That's what wealth is—clean toilet paper. Unused notebook paper. Clothing that doesn't stink. As much as you want, to dirty up however you like. After this roll of toilet paper is gone, I'm not sure where we'll get more. Usually, all we have to wipe with is newspaper. The newspaper is terrible to use dry. But if you hold it under the faucet and get it a little wet, it works okay. Jordan lifts his fist from the water and uncurls his fingers—the skin on his palm is blown wide open.

"I think I need stitches," he says. He pats his hand with his shirt, trying to dry it. He's shaking and breathing through his teeth.

"I know," I say. "But Mom won't go to the hospital."

"I fucking hate her," he says. "I wish she'd die. Then they'd come and take us away."

I hand him the toilet paper and the Scotch tape and he clumsily bandages his hand, wincing when he touches his palm. "The potato gun was supposed to work," he repeats. "It wasn't supposed to blow up like that."

In the kitchen I drop a brick of ramen into a plastic bowl of warm tap water. Our single saucepan is in the sink, crusted with old macaroni and cheese, along with most of our other dishes. We haven't had dish soap in weeks. There isn't a sponge, either, just an old washcloth that hangs stiff over the faucet. I dig a plastic tumbler from the pile in the sink and look inside it. The bottom is a sludge of wet cigarette ashes. I rinse the ashes out and drink some tap water. The water tastes like cigarettes. The ramen in the bowl is beginning to soften and I try to hurry the process along with a spoon, poking the layers of noodles until they separate and an oily film rises to the surface of the water. The noodles never come out quite right, soaking them this way. Sometimes I eat the ramen dry, broken up like chips. I dip each hunk in the flavor packet to season it.

I pick up the flavor packet. It's shiny foil, neat, with CHICKEN CHICKEN CHICKEN printed diagonally across it. Sometimes a whole flavor packet is too much salt, and half a packet is just right. The noodles are good without the flavor packet too. When there is not a single thing in the apartment to eat, somehow I can always still find these flavor packets, littered across the bottom of every kitchen drawer. Flavor packets and rubber bands and the plastic ties from bread bags.

Ramen is twenty-five cents, fifty cents, a dollar, depending on how much I can buy at once. It's a pyramid, and the more money I have to spend, the less the ramen costs. The whole world is set up like this and I am at the bottom. If I am poor enough, ramen will always cost too much. If I am poor enough, I'll feel like a trespasser even going through the automatic sliding doors of the grocery store. I don't have any money and my hunger pulls negative ions from the food and even that feels like stealing. I walk through the doors anyway and take free heat and free light and free non-violence and non-shouting and it is freeing to be around people who aren't hallucinating, at least for a little while.

Ramen is a good friend when I have a quarter, but it doesn't fill me up. My hunger is deeper than the salt mines in an ancient seabed. My insides are catacombs. My muscles are steel cables and my bones are Swiss cheese. My head is a bird's nest made from spiderwebs and my own saliva. I can't think.

I knock on Jordan's door. There is no answer, and I push it open. The room smells of WD-40 and dirty socks. His bed is empty, his window open, the blinds askew. I feel my pulse quicken. This isn't the first time Jordan has run away. Although he's only two years older than me, he seems to grow wilder each year, while I stay the same. He runs away in summer and lives for days in forts that he and his friend build in the woods from plywood stolen from construction sites, while I stay in my room with a book, hiding from the other kids. He eats dumpstered candy bars, their chocolate gone waxy, and sleeps on the forest floor. He runs away in winter, in the snow, without any shoes. Back when we had a car, he would run away when we were stopped at stoplights, hurling open the car door and darting out into oncoming traffic. Now, seeing his open window and his empty room, I sit on his bed and start to cry. I often feel as though I am as alone as it is possible for a person to be, and then something like this will happen. I am learning that there is no bottom to how alone a person can feel. The comforter on the bed smells like Jordan, and I pull his pillow to me. I feel myself rising from the bed and drifting, untethered, up through the clouds and into the blackness of space, where I slowly spin like an astronaut come loose from the space station. Here in space I am connected to nothing and no one. Here in space it is always dark and always cold, and not a single soul knows that I exist. This is the safest place to be. It is also the worst.

I walk west along the busy road that runs in front of our apartment complex, past the forest to the strip mall where there is a bakery thrift store. There's a good blustery wind and I can smell the earth, raw and wet, free from the heavy hush of winter. In a few months the sun won't set anymore and I'll stay outside until eleven at night, collecting leaves and sticks, stringing sunshine dandelions into necklaces and making small dens in the mossy riot of the forest. When summer comes, I'll live on light alone. But for now, I have to eat.

Heaving myself up, I bend at the waist and dip into the dumpster behind the bakery thrift store. Just like the girls on the parallel bars on the school playground, with their jackets draped over the metal bar, going round and round. There are boxes of donuts inside the dumpster and I feel my heart race as I paw through them. White powder donuts, waxy chocolate donuts. Dropping back onto the ground, I cradle these treasures in my arms. I tear one package open as I walk and quickly eat a donut. I eat another as I make my way through the forest, on the narrow dirt paths that lead to the flat, tea-colored lake. I can smell the lake today, the earthy water, the salty ducks. I eat a third donut, biting carefully into its shiny chocolate exterior. The inside is dry yellow cake. It backs up in my esophagus, coats my mouth in chalk. By the time I get home, my head is thumping and I feel dizzy. My thoughts are going in quick circles, knocking into each other, manic and frightening like a Donald Duck cartoon. I lie on my bed, still, and will my stomach to digest the donuts. I drink a cup of lukewarm tap water. The water tastes like metal.

In the summer there won't be free school lunches, but it won't matter. There will be sunshine and warm dirt and bare skin and green, good-smelling plants along the burbling forest streams and wolves howling in the mountains. I'll make necklaces out of chips of wood and small treasures from leaves and grass and bits of spruce pitch. I'll lie belly-down in the moss and stare for hours at the millipedes and the iridescent beetles. I'll climb every single tree within a quarter mile of my house, give them names and stories and remember their smells—sweet and green or sharp and dusty—and peel off thin whorls of their bark to wear on my wrists. I'll avoid going home as much as possible, and at night I'll sleep with all the windows open and the bad air will go out, and drift away into the wind, and dissipate into a million tiny particles and be eaten up by the good light and the green growing things.

As I lie in my bed and wait for my heart to stop racing, I think, as I sometimes do, about my father. *What does he look like? Where is he?* I remember a photograph of him where he has a beard and wears thick, square glasses. But that could be anyone, any living man. *Doesn't he care about us?* I imagine him in prison or long dead. He's definitely in prison, I decide, but he'll be out soon, and then he'll come for Jordan and me. He'll drive us to Taco Bell and buy us bean burritos and we'll wade in the creek. The salmon will be running. He'll look at our dirty clothes and shake his head. He'll buy us new clothes that smell like the store. When we talk to him, he'll understand the words that come out of our mouths and respond in complete sentences. No more word salad. Our life will finally take shape, become regular, with edges and borders that contain it. The dark world of Barbara's demons will stop leaking in, ruining everything. We'll be safe. We'll finally be safe.

"You came home," I say. Jordan is on the couch in the living room, watching *The Simpsons*.

"Yeah," he says, not looking up from the television. "There's nowhere else to go."

2003

The air smells like roses, and the sidewalks are wet from last night's rain. Bigleaf maples cast the street in warm, dappled shadow. I'm headed to the public library on Killingsworth Street, to use the internet. It's been a few months since my train trip to Texas with Sami, and I've been back in Portland working part-time gigs—nannying, house painting, dog walking. Last night, lying awake on my futon at the Wych Elm house, I decided that I would try to find my father. I'm twenty years old, an adult. I've lived long enough with the fantasy of who and where he might be. I want to know for real.

On the library's computer I pull up a people-finder website and enter my father's full name. A wheel spins on the screen as the website dredges its archives for information. My father has a unique name, and suddenly it's there—an exact match. I pull out my debit card and enter my payment information; it costs just three American dollars for the secret this oracle holds. I am rewarded with an address. No phone number or other information. Just an address. I look around at the other patrons in the library, wondering if they realize what an epic moment this is. They don't. I focus again at the screen. The address is in Anchorage. My father lives in Anchorage. He is neither dead nor in prison. He exists on the very same plane of existence that I do.

Google Maps tells me that his residence is only a mile from the low-income apartment complex where we lived for several years. Has he been in this spot for a long time? Was he there, just down the street, when we were starving? When we subsisted on one free school lunch a day and occasionally I'd find five dollars and brave the winter winds to walk to the Burger King on the corner for a sack of things off the dollar menu? When we didn't even have money for soap? I know he gave up his parental rights before he disappeared, but how could he live so close by and never reach out or find some other way to help us?

I feel strange for the rest of the day, like I'm in a fog. I boil quinoa on the stove and eat it with olive oil and salt, sitting on a wooden chair in the sun next to the herb garden in the backyard. Others come and go—there's an old-time music jam on the roof of the warehouse that makes up one wall of the yard. Patrick comes over from the Greasy Spoon, another punk house, looking for canning jars. Some folks arrive with a bunch of green potatoes they've dumpstered, and there's a loud debate in the kitchen over whether or not green potatoes will make you sick. I let my gaze go soft on the rosemary and culinary sage and wait for the fog to leave my body. My father has been in *Anchorage*? Possibly this whole time?

I sketch a father-shaped fantasy in my mind. This fantasy fits neatly into the parent-shaped hole in my heart. I tell myself that my father will be excited to know I'm alive. He'll want to be friends. He'll ask me questions about my life. My father will think I'm *interesting*. He'll say things like *I wish I'd found you sooner* and *Here's a thing or two I've learned in my long life* and *If you're ever in an emergency and need some cash, give me a call.* My father will smile warmly at me. His entire being will radiate nonjudgmental, unconditional love. He'll have a great excuse for his absence. *I was in prison for a while and I'm embarrassed about that. I figured you'd find me when you were ready.*

The wooden gate to the yard creaks and my boyfriend, Joe, pushes his cruiser inside. Joe is a kind dude, with long blond hair and a septum ring, intellectual blackwork tattoos on his forearms. He's into seventies soul records, tofu, and anarchist theory. He's got a huge cock. I don't love Joe, but I feel safe with him, and that counts for a lot.

Joe sits down next to me and offers up a greasy paper bag.

"Vegan banana bread?" he says. "I made it this morning."

"Hitchhike to Alaska with me," I say.

Joe breaks off a piece of banana bread and chews it thoughtfully. "Well," he says, after a moment, "that sounds terrible. Isn't Alaska really far?"

"It'll be okay," I say. "Just come with me. Please?"

I haven't been back to Alaska since I left at fourteen. What if, as soon as I step foot on the trash-strewn streets of Anchorage, my childhood rises up like a sleeping dragon and swallows me? What if I am transported from this new reality in which I am free back into the horror movie of that first place, the original place? Joe is planted squarely in this world. He doesn't even know that the other world exists. If Joe comes with me, he can keep me tethered to this earth.

Realistically, flying to Alaska would be the most efficient way to get there, but Joe and I don't have any money. I've been working just enough to get by. Mostly I've been making zines, screenprinting patches, riding my bike late at night to the tea dumpster, and volunteering with Food Not Bombs. I have a lot of interests, but making money is not one of them. So, as a result, the only way I can get to Alaska is to hitchhike.

I have a scrap of paper with my father's address. I do not know what he looks like. I'm not even entirely sure if the man at this address is him—what if there are two men of the same age with the same unique name living in Anchorage? But I mean to hitchhike to Alaska, knock on his door, and find out.

It's summertime, and the roadsides of the Pacific Northwest are hot and a little humid, not an awesome place to stand for hours on end with a cardboard sign that says, simply, ALASKA. It takes us half the day, bent under the weight of our backpacks, just to reach the outskirts of Portland, that golden bit of countryside between cities that bakes in the strong July sun. And then we are north of Seattle, and then we're across the U.S.-Canadian border, and then we're in British Columbia. Canada! Vancouver overwhelms us with its skyscrapers and fast trains and so many different languages, and then we are north of the city, among the white-capped mountains and cool forested valleys and small towns forgotten by time. Suddenly there's the long light of the Great North, and something wakes inside me. This long light is an old song I haven't heard in years. It brings tears to my eyes. Joe and I catch rides from weathered men in pickup trucks who grip the wheel with one hand and hold a fifth of vodka in the other. Their hearts are broken from solitude and they swerve on the empty two-lane highway and drop us off in front of road-houses built from old boards where dusty bags of potato chips are the only sustenance we can find. We eat our potato chips and look at the taxidermy on the walls, spin the racks of postcards. The proprietors stare at our tattoos.

And then the mountains recede and we reach the boreal forest. The boreal forest rings the top of the planet in a great band. It is a circumpolar forest. Thousands of miles of flat, boggy land, clogged with tilted, spindly spruce trees and glinting with millions of little lakes. This monotonous forest, also known as the taiga, stretches across Alaska, Canada, Iceland, Siberia, northern Kazakhstan, northern Mongolia, and northern Japan. The taiga is hot in the summers, and the mosquitoes rise up in great suffocating clouds. The forest floor is a trampoline of damp moss; the light that filters through the trees is feathery and soft. As soon as we reach the boreal forest and I see that sharp skyline against a pale blue sky, I am overwhelmed with a feeling of home.

We are far enough north on the Alaska Highway, now, that traffic has slowed to a trickle. This trickle consists of one RV every forty-five minutes, mostly, and it soon becomes very difficult to get a ride at all. We're sunburned and covered in mosquito bites and a tad malnourished and our feet ache from standing on the paved shoulder of the highway. The RVs don't even slow for us—they blow past, spitting up gravel, and I take to throwing rocks at them, which Joe doesn't like. I start bickering with Joe because I'm bored and because I can't stand myself any longer.

Since it's summertime in the North, the sun doesn't set, or it sets so late and for such a short period of time that one is never really aware of the darkness. At first we take this as an opportunity to hitch at night, but soon discover that after eight P.M., every driver that stops for us is intoxicated to the point of incoherence and we will be swerving back and forth across the long empty highway while beer cans rattle around our feet. Out of sheer terror, we are forced to ask a number of rides to drop us off again. So we resign ourselves to an eight P.M. cutoff time, after which we will camp. "Camp" is anywhere in the unpopulated forest that stretches on forever on both sides of the highway. We push our way through the trees wherever our last ride for the night leaves us, battling with the undergrowth and the wet, convoluted ground until we find a clearing large enough for our two-person tent, which we pitch on the soft moss. Joe reads me Rumi while the mosquitoes fling themselves against the mesh of our tent and I listen for bears. Now and then a bear passes close by. They always rush past and disappear quickly, but my heart flings itself into my throat anyway. Eventually we fall asleep.

"If you're on your period," says one of our rides, just sober enough to stay on the right side of the road, as we hurtle down the highway in the morning, "I wouldn't camp in these woods. The bears, they can smell it. Last summer, two women were camped out here—"

"Stop!" I say. "Please stop!"

I run out of reading material and buy a book of bear-attack stories at one of the small markets along the highway. This is, and will continue to be, one of the worst decisions I have ever made in my life. After I read this book, my nighttime tent-terror gets so bad that each night I lie in my sleeping bag panicking for hours as Joe snores softly next to me. In the morning I can never remember actually falling asleep. It will take me almost a decade to let go of the unreasonable fear this book instills in me, and to come to understand that bears are predictable creatures whose habits one can come to know and who, like most members of the animal kingdom, are not actively looking for a fight.

We arrive in Anchorage nine days after setting out from Portland. Anchorage is exactly as I remember it—wide, traffic-filled streets, shuttered strip malls, and ragged apartment buildings, trash in the gutters. A dour blanket of clouds hangs low.

There is beauty in the sprawl, though. The greenbelts are still there, the wild stretches of forest that wend their way through the city. In these forests are lakes, and secret sunlit clearings, and creeks where the salmon spawn, and moose and black bears and grizzlies. Beyond the city rise the Chugach Mountains, where my parents had their little house, never finished, when they were together during the first few years of my life. And on the other edge of the city is the sea. The sea is what hits me harder than anything, the smell and sound of it like a heavy warm weight on my chest. The damp salt air, the cries of the seagulls, the feeling that one has reached the end of the world.

The end of the world. Joe and I stand on the mudflats and look out at the inlet. Across the steely gray water is a string of white volcanoes. And beyond that? The roiling Pacific with all its secrets. We're sharing a takeout container of french fries, and my blood is pounding. It has been pounding for days. I wonder if it will ever stop. I'm in Anchorage, and I'm not a child anymore. The city is no longer a thing to which I lack all magic tickets—although poor, I'm now poor in a different way. I can work, I can get magic tickets if I want them. I am in control of my own destiny. I am an adult.

We walk the greenbelts past the cold lakes I used to swim in, to the apartment complex where I lived before Jordan went to juvie. The dingy buildings seem unchanged. Who lives in our apartment now? Are they happy? Are the walls freshly painted and white? Are the cupboards filled with food? Are there ghosts?

I do not cry. We leave the bike path for the woods and pitch our tent in a clearing in the trees. Joe reads me Rumi, and although there are bears here, I am not afraid of them. This is the place that I know.

Tomorrow, we find my father.

The house is one in a row of condos that are all exactly the same, on a cul-de-sac off Northern Lights Boulevard. An American flag swings on a flagpole above the garage, and there are some potted pansies on the windowsills. I knock on the door and wait. Joe is standing behind me. I've instructed him not to speak. "Don't say anything!" I said to him this morning. *"Not one thing!"*

The door opens. A man is standing there, my height, rounded, with a soft head of hair. He looks like no one. Like any man. Or every man, maybe?

"Hi," I say. "I think I'm your daughter?" I watch him looking at me and am suddenly aware of my tattoos, my half-shaved hair tucked under my trucker cap, my camo-printed cargo shorts and unshaven legs.

"I figured you'd show up eventually," he says, fixing me with an odd smile. "Why don't you come inside?"

A football game plays on a big-screen TV. The man picks up a remote and mutes the game, but does not turn it off. We sit in front of the TV on a long leather sofa. A woman stands in the kitchen with her hands folded. The man tells us that she is his wife. She offers us orange juice, but she does not smile.

"No, thank you," I say. She offers a few more times. Joe takes some juice.

"So," says the man. "Where do you live?" I begin to monologue, my words tumbling over each other. The man grips his glass of juice. The odd smile is unwavering, as though his lips are pinned in place.

There's a rushing between my ears and the room fades out, and then back again. The man is staring at me. Did he just ask me another question?

"I don't know," I say. A few beats pass with the four of us looking at each other, silent. I expected to recognize myself in this man's face, but there's nothing there. Football players run down the field on the huge television.

"What do you do for a living?" I ask the man.

"I have a computer business," he says. Another few beats of silence. I turn and look at the television. I've never understood the appeal of football.

"You never paid child support," I say. "You were living just down the street this whole time."

"I gave up my parental rights," he says. His smile is still there, but his eyes are flat, as though made of glass. The woman in the kitchen wets a dishrag and runs it over the counter.

"Does that mean you didn't have to pay child support?" I say.

"I have the paperwork all right here if you'd like to see it," he says.

"No, that's okay," I say. I look at my hands. I wait for the man to ask more questions, but he simply sits, holding his glass of juice, looking at me. "I should probably go," I say.

"I can give you a ride to wherever you're staying," says the man. I think of our tent, pitched in the woods. Our peaceful tent, bathed in gentle forest light.

"No," I say. "No thanks."

Outside, the bright Alaskan evening sun casts the world in

long bands of light, and Joe and I walk down the busy boulevard, alongside the blowing traffic. I'm crying now. Joe has his arm around me. I'm crying like a bike tire deflating, all my fears and expectations leaking out through a small hole. *Psssss.*

The customs official at the Alaska-Canada border won't let us back into Canada.

"How much money do you have in the bank?" he asks.

"A hundred dollars?" I say. They've separated me and Joe, and they've got me in a little room. Joe is being interrogated somewhere else.

The man sighs.

"And you're not married?"

"No!" I say. "No, we're not married."

"But what if he leaves you?" asks the man, looking at me softly. "What will you do then?"

"Continue hitchhiking back to the Lower 48?"

The man stares at me.

"You don't have money and you're not married," he says. "I can't let you into the country."

I call my father, Bill, from a payphone. His voice is fake-cheery when he picks up.

"They won't let us back into Canada," I say. "And we don't have enough money to fly."

Bill meets us for Chinese food in Anchorage and hands us a paper envelope that contains five one-hundred-dollar bills, enough for both our plane tickets. He laughs in a forced way. I feel ugly and small. On the flight out of Anchorage, I look out the window at the receding mountains, the Pacific Ocean. Was that parenting? Is this what being parented feels like?

1993

The Christmas tree in the mall is bristling and festive and taller than a house. I am eleven years old, wearing my pink winter coat with the tear at the elbow and my snow boots that are a size too small and I am touching the boughs of the tree, which is hung with white paper tags in the shape of Christmas ornaments. The base of the tree is crowded with fake gifts wrapped in shining foil paper, and "The Little Drummer Boy" is playing on the mall's sound system. *Our finest gifts we bring, pa rum pum pum pum.* I upend a giant Pixy Stix and shake the last of the candy into my mouth. There's a comic book shop on the second floor of the mall that sells them for twenty-five cents, and I'm eating them for dinner a lot these days. The sugar makes me feel speedy and leaves me tired after, but it's better than nothing. The gifts under the tree wink in the light and looking at them makes my mouth water. I want to crawl under the tree and un-

wrap them all, even though I know that they are fake, just Styrofoam squares wrapped in glittering paper. What if a real gift has
been put under the tree, though, by mistake? I wish I could at
least shake the boxes to know for sure.

The paper ornaments on the tree have names written on
them—poor kids who need gifts. If you're shopping in the mall,
you can grab a tag, buy the gift on the tag, and then deposit it in
one of the barrels at the store exits. Jordan and I are somewhere
on the tree, I know. The counselor at school called us into the
office and had us fill out a sheet with what we wanted for Christmas. I listed three things: a new pair of jeans, a Discman, and
Alanis Morissette's album *Jagged Little Pill*.

Barbara is lying on the living room couch when I return
home, a comforter pulled over her, her black hair splayed on a
dirty pillow. It's quiet in the apartment. I still have "The Little
Drummer Boy" in my head as I push open the door to her bedroom, careful not to let the hinges squeak. Barbara doesn't want
me in here but I come all the time, to lie on her bed and smell
the pillow or rifle through her drawers, touching her things and
reworking a memory from when I was very small and she would
hold me on her lap while she rocked me in a rocking chair. *What
rocking chair?* I wonder, as I look at the room, with its piles of
dirty laundry and single bright overhead light. *Where has the
rocking chair gone?* She sang to me then, off-key. *You are my
sunshine, my only sunshine. You make me happy when skies are
gray.* Today I'm not here for that, though. I'm here for the contents of her closet. I slide the folding door on its track and peer
into the darkness. I find the cord for the light and yank, but
nothing happens. There's no light. Standing on the bed, I can
just barely reach the overhead light fixture and I unscrew it, and
then the lightbulb, which is too hot to hold and falls from my

fingers, onto the mattress. A moment later there is at last light in the closet. In the closet are wire shelves, and these shelves are piled with items: fabric remnants, cheap cologne still in its packaging, bags of expired ribbon candy that has hardened into bricks, a stack of identical, plain gray sweatshirts. Each of these items was on deep discount at the mall, and Barbara bought the whole lot and stuffed it here for some reason that only she understands. I often eat the ribbon candy, prying the bricks apart and sucking the shards, and I am slowly making my way through the stack of plain gray sweatshirts—they have become my school uniform. One can only wear so much Exclamation cologne, though.

Behind the wire racks is a cardboard barrel and I drag this out of the closet and down the hall, into the living room. Barbara is still on the couch, the splay of her hair undisturbed, the subtle rise and fall of the comforter the only sign of life. The lid of the barrel is tricky—a metal latch that has to be pulled on with a lot of force to loosen it. When I was smaller, it took me days of effort to loosen this latch, but this year I get it on the third try. Inside are Christmas ornaments, Christmas lights, and a small folded tree.

Bah rump a bum bum, I sing to myself, as I gently unfold each bough of the tree. I wrap the lights around the tree and then open the box of ornaments. Sitting on the floor, I lift out the small figures that I have known for as long as I have known myself. There's the little wooden horse with the red body and the white feet, the nutcracker with the jaw that opens and closes, the sparkling glass icicle with the missing tip. The girl with the shawl and the songbook, the green and white satin balls with the loose threads, the foil folding star. The God's eye I made in school from Popsicle sticks and yarn and the cloth-stuffed candy cane.

The wooden manger scene, which is missing two of the Wise Men. Tangled strings of plastic beads and, finally, the angel, a blond figurine in a voluminous white gown holding a small bulb that lights up when you plug her in. The bottom of the box is filled with strands of loose tinsel and the shards of glass bulbs. There were more ornaments, once, but a few are broken or lost each year, and there is nothing to replace them with.

I place each ornament carefully and then sit and lean in, until I feel as though I am inside a secret world. Here is a dense forest full of stars. I can smell the earth and the clear, cold night. I stand the girl with the songbook in the crook of a twig, where she can see the wooden horse with the red body and the white feet. She's lost her horse, and she is injured. She calls to the horse. She is fleeing the nutcracker, who hides nearby, watching. The strings of beads are walkways that help the figures move from branch to branch. The girl and her horse need to use these walkways to get to the top of the tree, where the angel holds her magic light. The girl moves cautiously toward the horse. The horse has seen the foil star and is spooked. The foil star is a portal to the dark world, from whence the nutcracker has come. The girl calls again to the horse. She steps on a twig, but the twig can't hold her weight and she tumbles out of the tree, falling thousands of feet to her death.

There are two boxes in our entryway when I come home from school the next day—one from the mailman and a larger one from the food bank. The food bank box has Stove Top stuffing, canned cranberry sauce, canned pumpkin, and a huge frozen turkey. I look at the instructions on the box of stuffing—we don't have margarine, but maybe it will still be good boiled plain. The cranberry sauce and pumpkin can be eaten as is, and the turkey just needs to be put in the oven for a long time. I open the box of stuffing and crunch a piece. It's actually pretty good dry. Like croutons, but more herby. The other box is from our grandparents in Colorado. Their yearly Christmas package is the only time we hear from them. I wonder if there was a time when they tried harder to know us, and if Barbara made it so difficult that they eventually gave up. Or maybe they are awful people, just like Barbara says, and we are better off not knowing them. Like all the stories Barbara tells us, I'm not sure what is real. I know what's inside the box from our grandparents without opening it: a kitten calendar for me, a remote-control car for Jordan, and a package of socks for each of us. I am most excited about the socks. I open the box and hold the calendar to my face, smelling the plastic wrapping. We visited my grandparents for a time when I was small, and I conjure the memory of their house: smooth wooden floors, a Formica table, the yellow cookie jar on top of the fridge. A box of Cheerios and a white sugar bowl. My grandmother with her hair the color of steel wool, wiping my face and cleaning the dirt from under my nails. That was years ago, though. Today, Colorado feels about as close as the moon.

There's a knock on the door to our apartment. I startle and drop the calendar, which tips over the stuffing. Outside, I find a third box, addressed to Jordan and me. Excited, I search with my fingernails for the ends of the tape. Inside are six wrapped gifts— three for me and three for Jordan. From "Santa." Christmas isn't for a few more days, but I don't care. I open my packages, the smell of the torn wrapping paper flooding me with feelings. A new pair of jeans. An Alanis Morissette CD. And, incredibly, a Discman.

"Yes!" I shout in the still apartment. There are even batteries for the Discman! I put the headphones over my ears and scoot to the Christmas tree with the box of stuffing. I press play and lean into the tree until I am gone again, in the forest with the lights.

And all I really want is some patience
A way to calm the angry voice
And all I really want is deliverance, ah . . .

Later that winter I am sitting next to the vending machine in the hallway of my junior high school, practicing calligraphy in my notebook, when I see her. She is pale, with freckled skin and a jet-black bob. She wears a velour dress with a lace-up bodice. She smiles at me as she punches in the number for Skittles and I watch the metal spiral rotate, dropping the bright candy into the hollows of the machine. I often fantasize about an earthquake that upends all the rows of candy, freeing them.

"I see you in calligraphy class," she says. "My name's Laura."

"Do you want to practice together?" I ask. I show her the page I'm working on. She slides down to the linoleum next to me. She tears the corner off the packet of Skittles and offers me a handful. She has a spiral notebook with a velvet cover that matches her dress and a pencil case of calligraphy pens.

"You're weird, you know," she says to me.

"Yeah," I say. I start laughing, and then she's laughing too. The laughter transforms her. Her face lights up, her spirit escaping via the gap between her two front teeth. It seems as though she can't stop laughing. Neither can I, and then we're both sprawled on the cool linoleum, gasping for breath. A few kids enter the hall, heading for the vending machine, but stop when they see us and reverse course. This makes us laugh even harder. I feel as though demons are being exorcised from my body. As though I am turning inside out, but in a good way.

"All clear," I whisper to Laura. We're in the Occult section of Barnes & Noble and I am posted at the end of the aisle, watching the people in the store. Laura opens her corduroy shoulder bag and stuffs in the titles we've selected together: *Wicca: A Guide for the Solitary Practitioner; Buckland's Complete Book of Witchcraft;* and *Candle Magick.* I feel like I am floating as we move, together, through the store exits, and in the parking lot euphoria almost lifts me off my feet.

So far in my life, I'd had access to library books and occasionally a seventy-five-cent paperback from the bookstore near my apartment. Now, I hold these stolen books to my face, smelling them, overcome with pleasure at their newness. So what if I don't have money to buy things? Money is, apparently, not the only way to get what I need.

Later we're sitting in the woods behind our school, in the warm light of afternoon. Laura pulls a citronella candle and a few jars of culinary spices from her bag and places them on the wet late-winter snow.

"Hopefully my mom won't notice I took these," she says.

"Here's a good spell," I say, smoothing a page in *Candle Magick.* "It says we should cleanse the space first."

"We need smoke," says Laura. She produces a tiny wooden box, from which she pinches a cone of incense. She holds a lighter to its tip until a red ember begins to smoke. "We should walk in a circle in the clearing. Counterclockwise. While asking for a blessing from the goddess."

"Can we do Isis this time?" I ask. I'd just discovered the goddess Isis. She's been around since ancient Egypt. Born of the earth and the sky, she listens to the prayers of both slaves and the most wealthy. She gave birth to the sun god, Horus. According to the library books I checked out, when Christianity was trying to assimilate paganism, they turned the mother and child images of Isis and her son Horus into images of Mary with baby Jesus, and images of Isis with the body of her dead husband on her lap were transformed into the crucified Jesus, lying across the lap of Mary.

The forest observes us silently as we walk around the candle. I imagine Isis, drifting like incense smoke among the bare winter trees. Keeping us safe.

The candle flame shakes in the breeze. I cup my hand around it.

"We close our eyes to make the spell," I say. "We don't have to say it aloud."

"I'm gonna think about Jeremy," says Laura. Jeremy is in eighth grade. He has greasy bleached hair and wears ball chain necklaces. He carries his skateboard with him to school and smokes cigarettes behind the gym. "Do you think I can get him to like me?"

I giggle, and then stop myself. "This is serious!" I say to Laura.

"I know," she whispers, moving her fingers through the candle flame. "I *am* serious."

I close my eyes. The world behind my eyelids is full of shapes, movement, flashes of light. What is the real world, and what is the world of the imagination? I picture my mother, alone in our apartment. Crouched on the floor of her bedroom, chain-smoking. Lost in the stories of her mind. What's happening in her mind is more real than eating, or sleeping, or any other functions of her physical body. More real than day and night and the passage of time. More real than me and Jordan.

Protect Barbara, I think. Isis is in the boughs of the spruce trees, under the sky that's waiting to rain. Isis is watching me. *Protect her. Keep her safe. Please.*

I'm changing for gym in the girls' locker room when I hear the laughing. I'm wearing the same gray sweatshirt I always wear and have just taken off my jeans. My changing spot is as far from the other girls as possible, an empty bench at the very end of the lockers, but it doesn't matter. There's no real privacy here. I look up, embarrassed, and the girls turn away. They're laughing at me because I'm not wearing any underwear. It's not that I don't own underwear, it's just that I don't have any laundry detergent, and there isn't any money to buy some. Isn't it better to wear no underwear than the underwear I'd already worn for a week? I don't say this to the other girls, though, don't tell them that my family can't even afford soap. That we also don't have towels, and that my shoes are too small. That our kitchen counters are cluttered with greasy Burger King bags and the trash can overflows onto the floor.

My head hot with shame, I fold my jeans carefully and hurriedly pull on my gym shorts.

That day after school I sit on the front steps waiting for Laura with my hands stuffed deep in my coat pockets and think about how badly I wish that someone would take me away. I want to be rescued. Protected. Fed regular meals. Where the fuck is my father? Why hasn't he shown up yet? Maybe he hasn't been in prison, like I imagined. Maybe he really is dead. It's breakup, that messy season between winter and spring, and the snow along the road is black and littered with trash. Winter is tired, worn out. Ready to be subsumed in the riot of spring. Laura and I have plans to ride the city bus together to the west side of town, where we'll hang out in a burger joint "doing our homework" until her mom gets off work and can pick her up. Laura will eat french fries and I'll fill a paper cup with free pickles from the condiment bar. After Laura's mom picks her up, I'll ride the city bus home. The thought of home turns my stomach. I don't want to hear the eerie laughter coming from Barbara's room, the way it echoes in the dark apartment. Laura knows nothing about my home life. She notices how hungry I am, how bad I smell, but she doesn't ask, and I don't offer. It's better this way. If she knew the truth, she wouldn't want to be friends with me. I don't deserve friends. I am trash. Nobody has ever wanted me. Not even my father, wherever he is.

Laura rushes out of the double doors of the school, breathless.

"Kurt Cobain is dead," she says, sitting beside me on the icy steps. "He killed himself." She's rifling through her bag.

"No way," I say.

"Come on." She grabs my hand. "We have to do something."

There's a bare patch of earth in front of the school, warm in the weak April sunlight, and we arrange our candles there.

"We're going to contact his spirit," says Laura. "To help his passing." We make a pentacle out of black Fimo clay baked to hardness in the oven, and Laura pulls this from her bag and places it in the center of the candles. She cups her hand against the wind and lights each candle. Her broomstick skirt pools around her, and her shiny black Mary Janes are tucked neatly under her body. I wonder where she got the money for her clothes. From her mom? I often wander the clothing stores in the mall, touching things, memorizing prices. There's a pair of black corduroy overalls that I want. How hard would they be to shoplift?

"Close your eyes," says Laura. I hold her warm hand in mine and do as I am told. "Our beloved Kurt Cobain. We bring you gifts from the realm of the living, into the world of the dead. Speak with us."

The ground is damp, but the air that moves across my face is warm. Laura's palm is soft against mine. I move my fingers over hers, feeling each one.

"I don't think he's here," I whisper.

"Shh," says Laura. "I feel something." I open one eye. Her brow is furrowed, her mouth turned down. She's wearing copper-colored lipstick. Wet n Wild. I was with her when she bought that one. "He's sad." Laura looks as though she might cry. "He *was* sad. That's why he shot himself. He didn't want to be sad anymore."

"Kurt Cobain, you can be at peace now," I say. The candles are dancing. They flicker and go out. I gasp.

"He's here!" I say.

Laura opens her eyes and we sit staring at the dead candles. I dip my finger into the wax and watch it harden on my skin. Clouds race over us. The air smells like wet earth.

"Does anyone want to go dumpstering later tonight?" I ask. I'm standing next to a fire in my friend's backyard. Someone I've never met before raises her hand. The light from the fire flickers on her face. She's wearing paint-stained Carhartts and a puffy vest. She's small, and her hair is cut short. She looks like a twelve-year-old boy. She tells me that her name is Finch.

After meeting my father, I returned to Portland, where I began to regularly harass him with emails. *What is my extended family like? What parts of the country do they live in? Do they want to be friends with me? Could I meet them?* I imagined them as writers, thinkers, creatives; interesting people who lived in historic houses in old cities and grew gardens full of dahlias. My father replied to my emails with short, cheery messages, but never answered any of my questions. *Why won't you answer my questions?* I finally asked him.

My family doesn't want to know you, he said. *You need to learn to let the past be past.*

I was enraged. *His* family? It was my family too. Right? Or maybe it wasn't. Was family something I was entitled to? Did my grandmother on his side, who I had never met, really have no interest in knowing me?

I stopped emailing my father. His cheery messages were a façade. He was afraid of me, thought I was someone horrible come to wreck his life. He didn't want a kid.

I felt lost and confused. My father—and, by extension, my entire family on that side—was a fantasy I'd constructed with nothing but my own hopes and dreams, longings, hot air, and ghosts. That side of the family was a helium balloon I'd lost hold of at a birthday party and now it was floating away, up toward the clouds. The balloon was a speck against the blue of the sky, glinting in the light. I had to squint to see it. Then the balloon was gone.

No one was out there, waiting to claim me as their own. No one was curious about me. No one wanted to know me.

My heart became the Grand Canyon. My heart was massive, yet contained nothing. The winds blew through it. Buzzards perched on the rim, waiting to feast on animals that had fallen to their deaths. Snow fell, muting the landscape. My heart was the loneliest place in the world.

I knew that if I allowed myself to feel these things completely, I would become untethered to the earth and sink into the blackness, where I would be lost forever. So I decided I wouldn't feel. Joe became another thing I couldn't feel, so I broke up with him.

Cold drizzle falls in the black street, but the inside of the Trader Joe's flower dumpster is warm and we pull armloads of bouquets, wrapped in paper, from under our feet and drop them into a milk crate on the ground. We strap the milk crate to my bike rack with an old inner tube and ride through the empty intersections, rain needling our faces. Finch lives in an old house with a wide porch, and the wooden steps are slick with mildew.

We drop the milk crate on the floor of her bedroom. The only items in the room are a futon pushed up against the wall, a handful of photos on the windowsill, and a small stack of books. Tall windows overlook the overgrown yard. "My housemates are never home," says Finch. She opens a Pabst Blue Ribbon and sits on the bed. The can gleams in the light from the streetlamps. I sit on the bed too. I'm wet from the rain but warm from riding, and my face feels flushed.

"You don't own a pillow?" I ask.

"Nah," says Finch. She picks a wilted paperback up off of the floor. *"Pilgrim at Tinker Creek,"* she says. "Have you read this?" I shake my head and she begins to read aloud, about the hundreds of bones in the mandible of a caterpillar. I lie back on the bed and let the dense prose work its way through my body. The natural world, the incredible unknowable ever-present machinations of the natural world. The wonder and the magic.

I pull off my shoes and wrap myself in the comforter on the bed. Finch stops reading and lies down next to me and I feel the warmth of her body, smell the damp scent of her hair. The comforter is just big enough for the two of us, as long as my arms are around her. Outside, the rain is ceaseless.

.   .   .

I don't hear from Finch for three days and then she leaves a message on the landline at the house where I'm staying.

"I just got back from riding to the coast," she says when I meet her on her front porch in the morning. "It took all night. I didn't sleep." It's springtime, and warm yellow light pools on the grass. Finch opens a beer. "Do you like Patti Smith?" she asks. She puts a CD in the stereo in the hall.

Every night before I go to sleep . . .

Finch turns the volume way up and slides across the hardwood floor of her bare bedroom, her arms in the air.

"Free money free money free money free money!" she's punching the air with her fists. The smell of roses wafts in the open window. I sit on the front step, laughing. Finch's copy of *Pilgrim at Tinker Creek* is there, resting on the warm wood. I flip through the book, stop at a paragraph about the negative shape of the air created by a standing longleaf pine.

Soon it's summer. We ride our bikes to the Willamette River and crawl through the brambles on its banks, pick blackberries until our hands are purple and bloodied. Finch tells me that she grew up in a small town in rural Utah. Her parents are Mormon, and when she came out to them at age fourteen they locked her out of the house. She lived on the streets for a while, where she discovered heroin. Then she moved to Portland to get away from those friends, those habits. The Willamette is flat and slow, the

Hawthorne Bridge vibrating overhead with passing cars. We eat so many blackberries we feel ill.

In September, my best friend, Willow, arrives in Portland, to make good on her promise to teach me to ride the Highline, the fastest train route from Seattle to Chicago. Willow's black hair is wild and she's wearing a skirt made from the hide of a roadkill deer. She smells acidic, like coffee, and she talks quickly, waving her hands around as she narrates the kaleidoscopes of information inside her head. She's been living in the old-growth forest outside Eugene, on a wooden platform in a Douglas fir tree that is hundreds of feet tall. That particular bit of forest was up for sale, and she and other forest defender friends moved into the tree to protect it from being cut down, taking shifts sleeping in its canopy for a week at a time. She hauled her food up in one bucket and lowered her shit in another. Wind rocked her sleeping platform, rainstorms rattled the tarps, and she threw stones to keep the black bears away.

"Living up in the canopy changes you," she says, as we sit in the sun on the porch, drawing the word SEATTLE in thick black marker on a piece of cardboard. "I've never felt so strongly the vibrations of a huge, living being. Of an entire forest." She tells me about the seedlings that sprout in the canopy of an old-growth forest, the topsoil that gathers on the uppermost branches. The insects and animals that live their whole lives up there. She tells me about the web of mycelium under the forest floor, the mat of fungal threads that connects the roots of every tree. The way a tree will use the fungus to send nutrients to another tree, or to communicate distress.

"Everything's connected," she says. "The forest, the earth—it's all one living organism. We're part of it too." She fills in the s in SEATTLE with careful, tidy strokes. "I can never go back to the way I saw things before."

In the end, they couldn't save the forest. The Feds used a cherry picker to pluck Willow from the tree. The stand of old growth was cut.

"My heart is broken now," says Willow. "I'm riding the train back to North Carolina."

Willow is really good at riding freight trains. She's brilliant with mileage and directions and maps and data and she never falls asleep, like I do when I'm supposed to be watching for a crew change—the brief stop in town when one has a chance to get off the train. Willow requires very little food and water, also, and she can fold all her gear just so, so that it fits in a daypack, and when she's in a town she passes for a regular person.

The Highline is the route that runs east from Seattle through Idaho, Montana, and North Dakota, all the way to Chicago, which is where I'll turn around and return to Portland, and Willow will continue south. I convince Finch to come with us to Chicago, even though she's never ridden a train before. I like Finch, and I don't want to be away from her. I'm not sure why I'm even going on this trip, except that the ghosts are following me again and movement is the thing that keeps me just out of their reach. If Finch comes with me on the train, maybe I can prolong this nice thing we have. Maybe I can keep her close to me, if only for a little while longer. Finch gifts me her battered copy of *Pilgrim at Tinker Creek* so that we can read it on our journey, and I pack it carefully in my backpack, among the warm layers—it's fall, and Montana will be cold—the cans of beans, the hard corn tortillas, and the bottle of hot sauce.

Willow, Finch, and I are outside Seattle, in a sprawling industrial neighborhood; in the distance we can see the lighted tower of the Starbucks headquarters, and we use it like a beacon as we make our way to the trainyard. None of us have cellphones or any sort of electronics with which to navigate—we have only paper railroad maps and written directions, passed along from friends. Our packs are strapped with empty gallon jugs and we search for a water spigot, finally finding one on the outside of a darkened building. We'll need to bring all our water with us onto the train, enough to make it to Chicago. There's a Krispy Kreme donut shop and we rip open the heavy plastic bags mounded in the dumpster and collect the glimmering donuts that spill out. At last we reach the edge of the rumbling, ticking trainyard, and we crouch in the shadows against a low stone wall, eating donuts as the moon rises. We eat until we feel sick and then we throw the remaining donuts at a string of railcars that are sitting silent, watch the little circles of cake break against the grimy steel.

A train sits on what we think is the correct track, and we climb onto one of the cars. The front of our train is out of sight; we don't know if they've hooked up the engines yet, or how many there will be. Whether this train will ever move, and when, is a mystery. We sleep a little, leaning against our packs, and stir when the train next to us lurches and begins to creep forward. We jump down onto the ballast and climb onto the moving train instead. A moving train is always better than a still train if you're actually trying to get somewhere. Our new train picks up speed, lumbers east out of Seattle, and dawn begins to break. Out come our bedrolls; we stuff in our earplugs against the sound of screaming steel, and sleep.

Willow is shaking me awake. It's dark. But it's daytime—*why is it dark?*

"The tunnel!" says Willow. "We're in the tunnel!" I sit up. The exhaust is so thick I can hardly see the car behind us. Finch is wetting a bandana and tying it over her mouth. I do the same. East of Seattle, I'd always heard, is a forty-five-minute tunnel, cut through the center of the mountain. The tunnel fills with diesel exhaust while you're being pulled through it. The exhaust is low-key poison. If the train were to stop moving, we would likely die.

Every so often there is a light bolted into the wall of the tunnel. We count these as they pass our car. One, two, three. *Please don't stop. Please don't stop.* I feel loopy, sort of sleepy. We don't speak, just sit in the car with the wet bandanas over our mouths, watching each other's frightened eyes. Every few minutes Willow leans over the edge of the car, to see what there is ahead. She does this carefully—leaning out of a train in a tunnel is dangerous. A metal pole can behead you. There is only darkness in the distance, and Willow sinks back down into our car. I close my eyes.

"Light!" shouts Finch. "There's light!"

The circle of gold is small, and then it opens like a fist unfurling. The thundering of our train changes pitch and we're launched into the open air, the world impossibly sharp and clear. We're being pulled on a narrow track along the mountainside, crisp green trees on one side and bottomless blue on the other, the wind like food. I'm breathing the sweetest oxygen I've ever known.

Glacier National Park, Montana, is cold—the forest dark and empty, the Flathead Lake milky blue with silt. We huddle in our sleeping bags as the train thunders east through the mountains, watch the stars rotate in the sky above us. The whole of me expands, out into the mountains, up into the stars. I let the rocking train hypnotize me until I'm empty inside.

The train slows to a crawl when we reach Whitefish. The storefronts glow yellow, the snow sparkles on the ground. The train picks up speed on the edge of town, and civilization recedes in the distance. In the morning the mountains are behind us and the plains are warm and golden—our train stops in Havre for inspection and we sprawl, languid, in the hot sun that pools in our car. Finch kisses me. *Pilgrim at Tinker Creek* is smudged already from our hands, which are black with diesel grease. I read aloud from the chapter called "Intricacy," about red blood cells streaming in the capillaries of a goldfish. There is no narrative structure—the book is organized by seasons and I am working my way slowly through the wheel of the year. The train is motionless, the day silent save for the beeping of work trucks as they drive up and down the string. I stick my nose over the lip of the car and see that across the street is a convenience store.

"Hot dogs!" whispers Willow.

As soon as the trucks are out of sight, I clamber over the edge of the car and onto the ballast. I jog to the store and then back, my arms full of hot dogs and cans of beans and grapefruit. Willow is waving at me, shouting something I can't hear.

"The brakes have already released!" she says, laughing, when I reach the ladder on our car. The car jerks a little as the slack in the string is pulled taut, and I yank myself aboard, dropping my armload of bounty onto our unrolled sleeping bags.

We're out of Havre, rattling through an endless sea of cornfields, sitting in the warm wind in our underwear playing Hot Dice. We're keeping score in Sharpie on the chipped paint of the car. Willow falls asleep on the floor, her dirty hands clasped over her stomach, a blue "Lake Tahoe" visor over her eyes. Finch and I sit on the porch of the car and watch the corn turn into North Dakota, the breeze almost as good as a bath.

The sun sets and the papery grass is an ocean with hills for waves. The moon rises. When a single track splits into two, a train will sometimes pull off onto this second track, or "side"—in order to let higher-priority trains pass or for reasons unknown—and presently our train does this, slowing and then stopping across from a field where a man stands next to his tractor, watching the last of the red bleed from the sky. I don't know if this man can see us, watching him watch the west; he stands there until the light is gone. The air turns crisp and we move, creep into our sleeping bags, and fall asleep.

In the morning we're in an Andrew Wyeth painting. The land is beautiful and iridescent, brown the way grass can be when it catches the light and waves. The trees are low like they're waiting for thunder; round yellow leaves drift slowly to the ground. I take a shit on a piece of cardboard in the car behind ours as the train rattles through Fargo. The train picks up speed and I fling the cardboard over the side, watching it collide with another track.

The ceiling drops in Minnesota; the sky is clotted with clouds. Vegetation crowds the stream banks and wetlands appear. Our train hurtles toward Minneapolis. Willow has a bottle of habanero hot sauce, and to entertain ourselves we try to see how much we can pour on the cans of refried beans we're eating. The three of us are so tired of eating beans, thick masses of salty brown. Like cat food, but for hobos.

The train slows as evening falls. We're entering a thunderstorm. We roll for ten minutes and then stop, roll for another ten minutes and stop. Lightning shears the sky; currents of water

pour into our car. Willow crawls into her bivy sack, which is waterproof. Finch and I don't have bivy sacks, so we stuff all our
things into the giant plastic bag I swiped from behind the Home
Depot in Seattle, put on our rain gear, and sit on the porch,
which is the metal lip of the car just big enough for our butts,
and watch the storm. To the north is clear sky and stars; to the
south is an impenetrable darkness, illuminated by sporadic
flashes of light. Eventually the rain lets up, but the lightning
keeps on for hours. Our train creeps through road crossings and
Finch and I are pinned in the headlights of the waiting cars, sitting on the porch in our dark rain gear, hoods over our heads, as
thunder rattles the air.

In the morning we wake in the trainyard in Minneapolis. The
air is humid and warm and flocks of Canada geese pass over us.
A worker appears above the edge of our car and stares down at
us; we can tell that he doesn't want to get us in trouble, but he
does want us to get off his train. We collect our things and climb
from the car, crossing the empty road next to the tracks, stumbling a little on our sea legs. We hitchhike to Chicago, arrive
exhausted, and buy a ticket for the commuter train, which will
take us to the outskirts of the city. At one A.M. we exit the commuter train and wander through the fog to a large, old cemetery.
Next to us are the tracks, with trains rattling by in the dark. We
find a hole in the fence and cross over the tracks to a flat, forested area, where we fall asleep in the drizzle against a huge
fallen log. In the morning there are Italian men in the woods
around us, gathering mushrooms in plastic grocery sacks. We
walk back to the Metra stop and there is a woman with a collie;
she looks at us and says, "Don't tell me you slept in those woods
last night!" So we say, "Okay, we won't."

"I know what to do now," says Willow. At the copy shop in

town, we buy an X-Acto knife and make some color copies; a little careful cutting and pasting and some lamination later, and we each have a fake Greyhound Ameripass. Willow will use hers to get the rest of the way to North Carolina; Finch's and mine will take us back to Portland. On the bus, I lay my head on Finch's shoulder and I sleep or don't sleep, the air stale and close. I stare out the window at the dull highway, eat french fries at layovers, and dream of North Dakota, the wild place that was everywhere and nowhere all at once, the way the wind would beat me so hard I could barely catch my breath.

There's a pounding on the door that wakes me from sleep. I lie stiff in my bed, listening for my mother, for her bedroom door to open. I wait for her shuffling footsteps in the hall. The pounding ceases, and there is silence. Then it begins again. I pull myself out of bed, feeling confused. Thirteen years old, in the same clothes I wore to school yesterday. The bedroom light is on, the way I like to sleep. The hallway is dark, and when I reach the front door, I find Barbara there, leaning against the wall. The pounding on the other side is rattling the door.

"Open it!" I shout. Barbara stares at me, then unhooks the chain and cracks the door. Cold air rushes in. I can smell snow. The clean, outside world.

Two police officers are standing in the dim concrete space in front of our apartment. They look at Barbara, and at me. The radios on their hips crackle.

It's Jordan. He's gotten himself in trouble again. They've taken him to McLaughlin, the juvenile detention center.

Barbara closes the door slowly after the cops leave. She walks down the dark hallway into her bedroom and shuts that door too. I follow her and listen outside the door. The radio plays softly. The door gives to my touch and there she is, crouched on the carpet, digging through a pickle jar lid of cigarette butts, looking for the one that has some tobacco left. There is the ammonia smell of her unwashed body. She's wearing the same green blouse and dark jeans that she's had on for weeks. The clothes hang on her loosely, as though there are wire hangers where her flesh and bones should be. Her thick black hair has begun to gray at the temples.

"What are we going to do?" I say. Barbara looks up at me and her eyes flash like embers, and then go dark again. She says nothing.

"What are we going to *do*?" I say again, louder. "Are we going to get Jordan out of juvie?"

She turns up the volume on the old radio, and classic rock thunders into the room.

"WHAT ARE WE GOING TO DO?" I scream at her, as loud as I can. Barbara leaps up and slams the door in my face. I jump back just before it catches my fingers. I slide down the wall to the floor and wrap my arms around my knees.

In the morning our apartment is changed. The air feels more still. Jordan disappears a lot, but he always comes back. This time, I know, is different. In his room, I lie on his bed, look out the window at the dark parking lot and the snowy forest beyond. I pull the *Hustler* magazines from under his mattress and flip through them. On the carpet next to his bed is a hunk of wood he's been whittling into the shape of a blue whale. His folded pocketknife rests on the carpet beside it. I pick up the whale. Anchorage sits on a spit of land where the mountains meet the sea, and in the gunmetal-colored water live all kinds of whales. The long tides and sucking mud beaches are a part of me, and I know they're a part of Jordan too. I wonder how they'll treat him in juvie. I've heard some stories. I wonder if he's scared, or lonely, or sad. The thought of him trapped in prison makes me feel as though I myself am suffocating. My own brother, and there isn't anything I can do to rescue him! I think of the time, when we were little, when Jordan wouldn't stop screaming, and Barbara tied him to the bed with a twisted sheet and extinguished her cigarettes on his chest. Then she ordered a pizza and ate it sitting on the carpet in front of him. She offered me a slice and I devoured it greedily. I start crying, my tears falling onto the pages of *Hustler*. I shouldn't have eaten that pizza. Jordan still has the scars of those cigarettes on his chest.

I remember the times Jordan set my Barbie dolls on fire. When he sat on me and tickled me, even though he knew I wasn't really laughing because I was happy, that I hated it. I remember how he showed me which dumpsters had food. He taught me to make a flamethrower from a can of hairspray and a lighter, and we burned black spots into the carpet. He showed me the forts he and his friends built in the woods, so that I could hide out there too, when I wanted.

Jordan isn't just my brother. He is also my witness. My confidant. The only other one who knows.

Winter loses its hold on the land. The ice crumbles, becomes chaos, and then is gone. One day I walk to Burger King for a sack of fries and hear wolves howling in the Chugach Mountains, their cries drifting over the city. The birch trees leaf out, heralding spring. Later, at home, the phone rings in our empty apartment. I put down the fries I bought with my last two dollars and pick it up.

"Hello? Jenni?" The line crackles. It's my grandfather. I press the plastic receiver, which smells like my mother's stale breath, closer to my ear. "How are you doing?"

"I'm fine, I guess," I say. I look at the paper Burger King bag. I can feel the fries getting cold.

"That's good," says Grandpa. He tells me that he and Grandma are adopting my brother. Barbara gave up her parental rights. Jordan will go to Colorado, to live with them. He won't have to be in juvie anymore.

Jordan will finally be free from juvie. My tears wet the receiver.

"We're being evicted," Barbara says. She's stuffing dirty laundry into a black trash bag.

"What?" I ask. It's summer and I've just come home from the woods, where I passed the day reading *Flowers in the Attic* in a grove of spruce trees and eating shoplifted cookies.

"We failed our inspection. We're being evicted."

I look at the broken blinds, the white paint gone yellow from cigarette smoke. The spilled food ground into the carpet. The overflowing trash can. Had we ever cleaned the fridge?

"Where will we live?" I say. Barbara doesn't respond. She's stuffing the laundry blindly, grabbing whatever is in front of her. The pile that's been accumulating in the hallway for years comes up to my waist. Lots of these clothes are too small for me now. Some of them are Jordan's.

We move into a women's shelter. The weather is mild and the world is a tangle of green and the days never really end, just bleed, gently, into each other. I'm not allowed to leave the shelter on my own, so I wander the quiet halls, open doors into rooms of supplies, folded linens, a well-stocked kitchen. I look in the fridge—vegetables, bags of shredded cheese, a chocolate cake. I pull a fork from a drawer and eat a piece of this cake. When we arrived, I was presented with travel-size toiletries and new, clean socks. The dorm where we sleep has bunk beds with stiff woven blankets that smell strongly of detergent. Each day, we make our beds, pulling the bedclothes tight and folding down the white top sheet. At night I lie in this perfect bed, the tucked-in sheet holding me fast, and watch the ceiling fan turn languidly. The midnight sun bleeds in around the edges of the blinds. Often I can hear a woman in the stairwell, crying softly into the payphone.

Barbara hates the shelter. She hisses at me about the other women there, about the staff who make the rules. Ignoring her, I return to the kitchen, where I eat another slice of chocolate cake. In the yard with its high chain-link fence there is a set of swings and I rest here, feeling the sun on my face. I can smell the loam of the forest and hear the seagulls crying and I know that the sea is just a few blocks away. I lie on the wood chips and stare up at the clean blue sky and think about whales, about my brother's blue whale, carved into a hunk of wood. The whale he never got to finish. We can stay in this shelter, but for how long? We have nothing, we are homeless. But I don't need anything when I have the sun. I can live in the forest. I can sleep on a bed of moss, I tell myself. The trees will be my family.

·   ·   ·

The apartment building sits alone, squat and with peeling white paint, on a busy industrial boulevard in an especially desolate part of town. Barbara unlocks the door to the stairwell and we drag in the two trash bags that hold our most important belongings—everything else is piled in a storage unit across the street. In the warm basement the dryer thumps companionably. The stairwell smells like miso and the neighbors' shoes are lined up neatly on the mat outside their door. I look at the neighbors' closed door and wonder about their food, their laundry, their lives. What is it like to live behind that door? Do they have matching sets of bath towels? Are there adults who become concerned if a child disappears?

Barbara pushes open the door to our apartment and flicks on the light. A bare living room, the carpet striped with lines from the rug shampooer. White paint, mini blinds, wall registers for heat. There is a couch, which is neat, since we no longer own any furniture, and there are three bedrooms: One for Barbara, where she can kneel in the dark and drink Mountain Dew while writing her manifestos about the Virgin Mary on paper grocery bags. One for me, where I will sleep on the floor curled against the wall, wrapped in an old comforter with the batting spilling out. If I leave the blinds on the window up at night, I can see the stars. The third bedroom is for Jordan. Barbara still sees Jordan, coming and going throughout the day. She speaks to this Jordan as if he is still with us. But Jordan is in Colorado. He's never coming back.

I wake at four A.M. in the dark apartment and pull on my Walmart winter coat and my boots; no hat or gloves, even though it's twenty degrees below zero outside. It'll take me an hour and a half on the city bus to reach East High School, where Laura and I are freshmen. Outside, I cross the wide frozen street, empty of traffic in this early hour, to the bus stop on the other side. The bus costs eighty cents, and today I have it. Last week I didn't have the change. Last week the bus pulled to a stop with a great diesel wheeze and the doors swung open with their sigh of stale, warm air and I told the bus driver I didn't have eighty cents, could I still come aboard. Just a fourteen-year-old in the bitter cold of early morning, standing on the side of the road.

"No," he said. The doors creaked shut and the bus lumbered away, leaving me alone.

Behind me at the bus stop is a shuttered restaurant, its neon sign promising hot soup. I have never eaten soup there, I've never had the four dollars for a small bowl of soup, but I think about that soup each day when I wait for the bus. Is the soup good? Does it come with crackers? How *many* crackers? What would it be like to walk into a restaurant whenever you wanted, and order soup?

Today, though, I have eighty cents—two quarters, two nickels, and two dimes—and when the bus jostles to a stop and the doors wheeze open, I climb on, accept my thin paper bus transfer, and take my place in comfort, sitting on my numb hands to warm them. Not having the money a few days ago felt like a rejection. Today, though, I have been accepted. I watch the driver nervously as we lurch along the icy street. My status seems tenuous. At any moment the bus could stop, and I could be asked to leave. I will my body to relax. I am safe here. Twenty minutes later we reach the intersection of Arctic and Northern Lights Boulevards and I hop out the back door into the dark and crunch across the street to McDonald's. I have a half-hour wait until my next bus and I like to pass it here, enveloped in the smell of cooking food. I usually don't have money for breakfast and my first meal of the day is the free school lunch at noon, which means fighting dizziness to stay awake in my classes, but today is a good day, an incredible day, because I have two dollars to buy two hash brown patties. I stole twenty dollars from Barbara when she got the small bit of cash that was left over after welfare paid our rent this month, and this is the last of it. I carry my hash browns on their plastic tray with four white paper ramekins of ketchup to an empty booth where I can watch the falling snow. The salt of the potatoes crackles like electricity in my mouth.

Laura is waiting for me when I get to school this morning, on the couch in the lounge area outside of our first class. We have a lounge area with a couch because we attend a smaller, alternative school that exists within East High School. The alternative school is for the weirdos, the gays and the poets and the cutters, people like me who are good at math and test well but can't really focus. Laura is wearing her blood-colored velour dress with the lace-up bodice and the bell sleeves, and her perfectly smooth bob is dyed a fresh shade of black. I sit next to her, close enough to smell her floral conditioner, and hold her hand. We take out our journals and swap them, open to a clean white page and uncap our colored pens and write stories for each other in the rune alphabet we like to use. When class starts, English, I'll sit at my desk but keep writing stories in my journal, and after a while I'll leave and return to this couch. Our alternative school has an open-door policy and we are allowed to leave class when we want to. I'm still barely passing, though, even by alternative-school standards. What is the point of homework? What is the point of paying attention?

"Do you want to come over to my house for dinner tonight?" asks Laura, as she closes my journal and hands it back to me.

"I think so?" I say. I run my fingers over the purple velvet of the journal, smoothing it. Fear rises in my throat. Fear tastes like McDonald's hash browns.

A split-level home on a quiet residential street. A tidy warm living room, a Christmas tree, piles of gifts wrapped in shining foil. The smell of onions sautéing. One of Laura's moms chops garlic in the kitchen. Her other mom tosses carrots into a colander and runs them under water in the sink. The swing of a cupboard door, a glimpse of shelves of packaged foodstuffs. An empty carton, dropped into the recycling bin. Laughter.

I am perched stiffly on a stool in the kitchen, trying to remember how to breathe. At home in my filthy apartment, I fit. I make sense. But here, I am suddenly aware of how bad I smell: like the ubiquitous secondhand smoke, plus mildew and unwashed armpits. There are stains on my sweatshirt, and I haven't changed my underwear in four days. I am aware of how hungry I am, not just for calories but for nutrients, for fresh living things and flavors other than fast food and ramen noodles. Watching one of Laura's moms slice open a carton of tofu, I feel like a feral cat that's been captured in an alleyway and brought home. My fur is matted with burrs and my face is disfigured from fighting. I have a limp from an injury that never healed right. My teeth are mossy when I run my tongue across them. When was the last time I brushed them?

One of Laura's moms, Sharon, is a social worker, and this makes things even scarier. At a very young age, I learned to fear social workers. I am sure that Sharon, more than the others, can see right through me, into my heart. She can see how full of shame I am, how undeserving of love. Any minute now she's going to drop the colander in revulsion and cast me out into the snowy street, where I won't have any money for the bus home.

There's an urge to run out of Laura's house and flounder through the deep snow into the forest, then crawl into the hollow beneath a spruce tree, the one place I know to be safe. But instead I grip the stool, willing myself to stay put.

Laura is kneeling under the Christmas tree, lifting the presents one by one and shaking them. The scent of wrapping paper is thick in the air. I wonder if I'll get a package of socks and a kitten calendar from my grandparents this year, now that Jordan is gone and I'm fourteen. How will they know where to send the gifts, since we moved?

At dinner I fork sautéed green beans into my mouth, trying not to seem too hungry. Laura's mom Brenda, who works for the phone company, smiles at me and I flinch. When will I have to run, or protect myself somehow? The food is very good. Maybe if I say as little as possible, I'll be able to finish my plate before things take a dark turn.

After dinner Laura and I retreat to her room and shut the door and I collapse on the bed like a starfish, relieved. It's a small room, the walls hung with tapestries and blacklight posters. Laura lights a stick of sandalwood incense, stolen from the mall, and places it in the small clay incense holder, made by me, that sits on top of her dresser. I reach my arm out and touch the clothes in her closet—flannel, crushed velvet, thrift store polyester. Laura flicks on the blacklight and we lie on the bed. I take her hand in mine. I can see the lint stuck on her dark shirt, the white glow of her teeth. Her eyes are closed.

"What's going to happen in the future, do you think?" she says.

"I don't know. Maybe we'll live on another planet. Instead of people, there will just be cats. The cats can talk, but only in sign language. We'll all speak in sign language."

"And we'll wear medieval clothing," says Laura. "It'll be on an island. The rest of the planet is water."

"We'll travel everywhere by boat," I say. "Except for when we're riding horses. There will be fruit growing all around us. The rain will always be warm."

"We'll live in a castle," says Laura.

I trace the lines in her palm, touch her bitten nails. Laura and I have made up so many worlds together—I have journals full of them. We've created alphabets. Languages. Galaxies. Since I was old enough to comprehend, I'd known the real world. Not the world that is shown on television but what exists under that, the bedrock of everything. And all I can think about is how badly I want to leave it behind.

2006

crouch in the alley with my pack against my legs and stare at the string of railcars, willing it to move. The string sits motionless, but I know that it is bluffing. In a moment, when the engines affix themselves to the front of the string, the trainyard will burst into life. Everything that was still will become noisy; everything silent will begin to lurch. I have only a few minutes in which to make my move.

I hoist my pack, heavy with cans of beans and several days' worth of water, and jog clumsily into the yard. The overhead spotlights hack the night into chunks of brightness and shadow, and I dart quickly from patch of black to patch of black. This string consists of UPS truck trailers on flatcars—piggybacks, as they're called. Mail trains are the second-fastest thing to Amtrak, and this one will cover the distance from Portland to Chicago in just three days.

Things with Finch didn't work out. Finch is like me, wild, and she would disappear for days at a time, or I would. I was never sure where she went. After reuniting, we'd curl on the futon in a friend's basement, where I was staying, and we'd fuck, and then we'd cry. Her heart beat to a rhythm that my heart recognized, but in the end, the mirror was too much. Finch started spending more and more time in Seattle, where she had another lover. She enrolled in trade school. She wanted to learn carpentry.

My intention is to make my way to North Carolina, on the train, by myself. I'm not so much heartbroken as I am running from the idea of being heartbroken. I'm running from Portland, from the rain, from a loneliness that feels like anemia; so deep inside that nothing can touch it, like a constant ache in my bone marrow. A month ago Willow wrote me from North Carolina, telling me about the sunshine. I'm hoping I can find something tangible there, something solid enough to hold in my hands. I'm not sure yet what that thing will be.

I've never ridden a train solo. The idea of it overwhelms me. I know that I have the understanding, the directions to lonely crew changes, the photocopied rail maps—what I don't know is whether I have the emotional strength to endure the challenges of the train alone. But what is my life if not an experiment in enduring challenges alone? I will be the sagebrush plateau, the glacial river. The open landscapes of the American West will be my mirror now.

I find a car that might be rideable at the back of the string and heave myself up onto the filthy steel, shoving my pack under the axle of the truck trailer that sits on the flatcar and then wriggling onto my belly after it. There is no graceful way to ride a piggyback, this truck trailer on a flatcar. Once under the axle, I

can crouch on my heels, my back hunched; hoses and metal con-
traptions, thick with road grime, hang around my face. There is
not enough room on the flatcar, under the axle of the truck
trailer, to lie down or stretch out completely, but I need to be
here until the train clears the yard; under this axle is the only
place to hide. Once I'm north of Portland, I can move out from
under the truck trailer and spread my bedroll in the open on the
flatcar. For now, I touch the hoses around me—to be curled in
the innards of a semi-truck's axle is something I imagine few
people have a chance to experience. I press the button that lights
up my watch and see that it's three-thirty in the morning. Beyond my car the yard is yet unmoving; blinking lights are distant
and slow, tracks gleam dully in the spotlights.

I close my eyes, aching for sleep. It's October, and the nights
are getting colder. I want to pull out my sleeping bag and wrap it
around me, but the bag is fluorescent orange, and besides, there
isn't any room. I think of the dusty futon I slept on in Portland,
in the basement of my friend's house, with the kitchen that
smelled of cumin and tea. I think of Finch, curled in my arms,
quietly weeping.

I don't know if I know how to properly give and receive love.
I understand the first bit, the early part when I feel euphoric and
unaffected by anything, but I don't know how to do the part that
comes after that. I wish I had a script, a template, some idea in
my head of how things should work. But I don't. The initial daz-
zle wears off and then there aren't any instructions, only the hot
nakedness of vulnerability, like a bad dream where you're in a
crowded room but you've lost your clothes. It's a sort of exposure
that feels insane to me, like someone could just hack me up with
a sword. I need armor to live in this sharp world; shining, heavy,

glinting armor. Anything else feels pathetic. Like a worm on the sidewalk after the rain. Like a slug about to be salted.

At four A.M. the train jerks and I startle; I didn't even notice the engines approaching the string. There are usually three or four engines, more if you're going over mountains, so that the train has more power; they hiss and click and make a thundering sound. I must be at the back, they must have added more cars to make the train even longer; that would make the engines far enough ahead that I wouldn't hear them. My mouth is dry, so I swallow some of the water in my gallon jug. And then my car begins to move.

Intimacy has always felt like a temporary stopover place for me, in between long stretches of being alone. I never hold it too tightly when I have it, and I am never surprised when it goes away. My solitude is a cabin in the woods I come home to again and again. The same pictures on the walls, the same comfortable chair. A small barrel woodstove that puts out a paltry heat. The cabin rocks in the wind, and the winter's cold seeps through the thin board walls. But it's mine.

I curl up as small as I can, willing myself invisible, as my train pulls deep into the heart of the yard. I'm wearing black Carhartts and a dark wool flannel shirt; nothing reflective, nothing white that makes its own light. There are dozens of tracks here, stretching away on either side; there are strings of cars everywhere; there are engines, crouched and spitting. There are workers in bright vests standing on both sides of the tracks; my car draws slowly past them but they do not look at me. I hear the *shhhhhht* of their radios, the crunch of their boots on the ballast. Overhead, a dozen massive spotlights thrum, banishing the shadows. And there, at a crossing, is the rail cop, parked behind the red-and-white-striped crossing arm in his unmarked SUV, inspecting each car as it passes. I hold my breath, the *ding ding ding* of the crossing arm overwhelming the air around me and then fading, and at last the heart of the yard is behind me.

And then my train is crossing the Columbia River, water growing lighter, reflecting the sunrise. The train turns in a great arc along the north side of the river, headed east. There are no more people around. I'm safe now. I let out my breath. Dropping onto my belly, I wriggle out from under the axle and yank my pack out after me. Out on the flatcar, I unroll my foam sleeping pad and sit, watching the great sparkling river. The wind thrashes my hair and face, but I don't mind. Piggybacks are windy—you're on a flatcar, which by definition has no walls; there is no protection. But the view is incredible; you're on a flatcar, being pulled across the surface of the earth.

I unstuff my sleeping bag and the black sleeping bag liner I use as a cover and arrange my nest in the wind. I scrunch down into it and feel the warmth envelop me. One of the best things about riding trains, for me, is the certainty that, while on the train, I will sleep. For the past several years, insomnia has followed me like a stray dog. At night I lie awake in my bed for hours, my mind full of thoughts, and in the morning I am exhausted, the world gone strange. This continues for months at a time, until my head is full of mud and my nerves are ragged, all light too bright and all sound too loud, and I curl up inside myself, wishing that I could disappear completely, wishing for my own death, anything but this numb, hollow place between existence and despair. On the train, though, I always sleep. The cold nights, the turning stars, the wind—I can sleep for ten hours at a stretch, wake for the morning, and then sleep the afternoon away. Rattling through the open spaces of the North American continent, I am finally soothed. After a few days of sleep, I become a new person, and the world is infused with candy-colored possibility again. Now I scooch farther into my sleeping bag on the flatcar, a wave of pleasure overcoming me at the thought of the rest I'm about to get. I am only halfway hidden, while lying down, by the short lip of the flatcar, and yet I am one hundred percent invisible, because no one is expecting to see me here. I reach down into the pocket of my Carhartts for my earplugs and push them into my ears. I close my eyes, feel the gentle rocking of the train, and let the weariness claim me.

I am woken by an urgent need to pee. Opening my eyes, I remember that I am on a flatcar headed east at sixty miles an hour, with nothing to protect me from the wind. Getting up to pee is easier said than done. I procrastinate for a while in my sleeping bag, sucking air through the small opening in the hood, and then finally I uncinch it and wriggle my way out. I lift my pack and place it carefully on my sleeping bag, so that my bed will not fly away, remembering the first time I rode a train and my sleeping bag was sucked through the hole in the floor, onto the tracks. I've learned a thing or two since then. My boots are tied to a metal rod that runs along the underside of the trailer, and I cross my fingers that they too will stay where they are. I crawl on my hands and knees to the far end of the flatcar, drop my pants, clutch the underside of the trailer, and pee. The flatcar is long enough that even if the wind changes directions, the pee will never reach my sleeping spot. After drawing up my Carhartts, I crawl back across the flatcar to my sleeping pad, the wind so strong in my face that it's difficult to breathe. Then, sitting with my back to the wind, I pull food from my pack, spreading it on the steel floor of the flatcar in front of me. Almond butter, brown rice bread, a package of nori. A head of celery. I work my keychain can opener into a tin of beans and pull a spork from my pocket. Out beyond the train the dun-colored gorge rises up, and the bright Columbia River shines like metal.

My plan was to ride the mail train all the way to Chicago, but a few hours later, in eastern Washington, I've had enough. The wind on this piggyback is too much; I can find another eastbound intermodal, with a rideable car that has more cover. "Fuck a piggyback," I mutter, as I pack my things away. Then I sit, back against my pack, and wait for the train to side. I don't know where it will, or when, but it has to eventually—every freight train must stop every eight hours to change crews, and usually it will stop another few times as well, to let other trains pass.

In the blur of afternoon my train begins to slow, then ceases to rattle, and at last slides to a stop. I climb off. I am dizzy and disoriented from the wind; I stumble away from the tracks. A moment later the train pulls away, growing smaller until it's gone completely. This is where I've ended up: a big open sky, brown dirt, the smell of sagebrush. Ahead a little ways is a highway overpass. And to my right, in a wedge of land next to the tracks, are a pasture and some tumbled buildings, everything hemmed in by a falling-down fence. There is the braying of chickens. In an enclosure, a young Latino man is roping a calf. A horse stands motionless in the shade. Directly next to me is a tree, its branches bending down to touch the grass. I drop to my knees and look under its branches. There is a space under there, shaded and cool, and I crawl in.

In my secret space, I am happy. I roll out my sleeping pad and stretch onto it, to wait for another train. Dappled shade falls over me.

I am asleep, I am awake. I am asleep, I am awake. My stomach lurches. The sun moves and my shade disappears; I cover my face with my hat and fidget in the dust. A train whistle blows in the distance and I sit up; the train does not stop. Then another train, going the other way. I shake my water jug; nothing. What the fuck am I doing? My morale plummets as the sun trolls the empty sky. I'll die here, I think. I'll either die here or I'll reach enlightenment. I open my worn copy of *Pilgrim at Tinker Creek*. Annie's at the rain-swollen river, which becomes a metaphor for many things. As I lie under this tree, curled in the dirt, Annie is my only friend. I feel like sobbing.

A few early crickets go off behind me, like car alarms in a parking lot. I put down the book. The sun is getting low; the blue of the sky is deepening; I can see a few stars. I finger the soft leaves of the tree, which look like boats as seen from underwater. The chickens bray. A door opens and closes; I feel the heat coming off the earth. Clutching my water jug, I stumble upright.

The embankment of the overpass leads to the road. After a time there is a city park, crowded with families barbecuing in the gathering dusk. Children gripping plastic cups of soda, their faces smeared with barbecue sauce, watch me pass. Their parents call them away, squinting at my tattoos in the half-light. Beneath a drinking fountain is a spigot and I stoop to fill my jug.

Back at my nest beneath the tree, the crickets are out in full orchestra and a porch light glows yellow on the farm. There are sounds of dinner and visiting. I have just gotten settled again when a train made up of the cars that carry grain—called a grainer—thunders up, headed east. The train slows and then stills. It's a long one, stretching in both directions farther than I can see. I quickly pack my things and run along the side of it, looking for a rideable car. The sand is soft and I stumble; the smell of sagebrush is everywhere. The stars are turning on, one by one. I reach the end of the train without finding a rideable car—essentially any car with a floor in which one is also hidden from view—and turn, look at the blinking red light affixed to the last car. I stumble back the way I came, toward the front of the train. Maybe there is something rideable up there. When I am nearly abreast of my tree-nest, the train begins to move; I have missed my opportunity, or the train has no rideable cars. I was slow or it was the wrong train. Parallel possibilities stretching out into the vacant night.

Some water from my jug consoles me, as does the softness of my nest beneath the tree. Movement keeps the ghosts at bay; my time in Portland allowed them to accumulate. North Carolina seemed like a fresh, clean place with sunshine, but instead I am here, next to these tracks in eastern Washington. Despair marches toward me across the open land; I can feel the reverberations of its many small feet. The crickets are deafening. I am going to die here, I think, again.

Barbara is straddling me as I lie on my back in the hallway. Her long fingers are wrapped around my neck. She is strangling me. I came home hungry this afternoon, to an apartment without food. I tried to talk to Barbara but she couldn't hear me, couldn't see me. She was far away, in a place where I couldn't reach her, a place in which she's been spending more and more time. I screamed at her. Suddenly she leapt up and shoved me onto my back on the dirty carpet and now she is strangling me. Her hair is wild, the stink of her body like a fog. The claws of her fingers dig into the soft skin of my neck. It's a curious sort of intimacy. Barbara wants to destroy me. She is a strong river current, a howling winter wind. I have to struggle against her in order to live. And yet, part of me thrills at her touch. At her acknowledgment of me.

Time is slow on the carpet with her hands around my neck.

Slow enough for quiet realizations to float across the surface of my mind. Little rafts that I can touch gently as they pass.

Barbara is a frail woman, weak from the long work of her illness.

I punch my mother in the face.

Barbara pulls back, her mouth twisted in horror. Never in my life have I fought back. Now, in this dark afternoon in a hallway clouded with cigarette smoke, the balance of the world has shifted.

I am fourteen years old, and my mother will never hurt me again.

And neither, I decide in that moment, will anyone else.

The next few weeks are a strange blur, a mass of time without shape. Barbara is getting sicker. I try to imagine the other Barbara, who existed in bright flashes when I was younger. Our current situation feels like a winter that has gone on so long that I can no longer recall the warmth of spring. I picture her reading or writing, the things she used to say in the moments that she was lucid. Now, I come and go from the apartment and she doesn't notice. She doesn't notice anything. She crouches on the floor of her bedroom in front of the muttering radio, mute. There is not even the loose scaffolding of delusions, anymore, on which to hang the fabric of her world. Gone is the urgency to scrawl prophecies on scraps of paper. She simply . . . exists. She inhales and exhales, and her body sways a bit. Her bones and skin and heart are all intact. Plastic soda cups surround her. She knocks the ashes from her cigarettes into them. Discarded tea bags litter the carpet like the heads of wilted flowers. Now and then she brings her shaking hand to her mouth and draws slowly from the cigarette clutched in her thin, yellow fingers. Often she forgets the cigarette and it burns down to the filter, dropping a slug of ash onto the floor. Her eyes are blank. Her lips move, but no sound comes out.

At night I lie on the floor in my empty bedroom, curled against the wall in my dirty comforter, and cry. I feel Barbara's fear, her despair, her solitude, and I cry. I long for her, for the mother I once had in that murky time before my memory begins. I long for her high, warbling voice. I wonder if, trapped somewhere inside her, is the nineteen-year-old girl who married my father and ran away to Alaska. I lie on my bedroom floor watching the snow stick against the damp windowpane, and I cry. What did that young woman who was my mother do to deserve this horror movie in which she now lives? I don't have a way to make sense of it; there isn't a room inside me that is large enough to hold it all. Mostly it washes over me like an ocean wave, and I inhale lungfuls of brackish water.

With Barbara gone, there is no one to fill out the paperwork for our welfare. We lose the last of our benefits, the money that pays our rent, and in February I come home to an eviction notice taped to our apartment door.

"I just, I just had no idea," says Sharon. We're in the living room of Laura's house after school. I'm in an armchair, staring at my lap, trying to disappear. "I had no idea how bad it was." Sharon reaches for Brenda's hand. Brenda is looking at me with wet, drowning eyes. I drop my head again, hear a rushing in my ears.

I've been staying with Laura for a week. When I told her about my situation, I made her promise that she wouldn't tell her moms. She did, though; she told them that Barbara and I were going to be homeless, and asked them if they would adopt me. Sharon, the social worker, then looked up my file with Child Protective Services.

"I had no idea," she says again. Brenda wipes her eyes.

"Once Sharon told me about your situation this morning, we actually did look into what it would mean to adopt you," says Brenda. "But then we learned that you have grandparents, who have your brother. It makes the most sense for you to go to them."

"We called your grandparents," continues Sharon. She smiles warmly at me. "They agreed to take you. We bought you a plane ticket to Colorado. You'll go next week."

The room tips. Laura is my one friend. The life I have here is the only one that I know.

That night, back at our apartment, I pack a few items of clothing, my journals, and a photo album I've managed to hold on to over the years, through every one of our moves. The album is covered in green cloth with white flowers, and the pages are yellow with age. There are photos of Barbara as a child, as well as a few pictures of me and Jordan. I open the album and touch a photo of me sitting on Santa's lap, wearing a dress and pinafore that Barbara had sewn, back when she could still sew. Here's Jordan in a cable-knit sweater, sitting for picture day in second grade. Barbara, doing a backflip on the trampoline in the bright desert sun as a teenager. Barbara standing against a Camaro with her three sisters, all four of them with long, straight hair. Sitting on the carpeted floor of my bedroom, I study these images, trying to imagine what her family is like.

Barbara hates her parents with the same fervor she directs at almost everyone. I imagine this is largely a result of her paranoia, which she can't help. But who are my grandparents, really? What will it be like to live with them, in the desert? Once, when I was eight and Jordan was ten, we were homeless and desperate, having exhausted all of the friends' couches that we could stay on, and our grandparents offered to buy us plane tickets to come visit in Colorado, and Barbara said yes. For a few months, Jordan and I stayed with these grandparents in their brick house in the desert, among acres of alfalfa and hay. I remember Honey Nut Cheerios and a yellow ceramic cookie jar that was always full of lemon wafer cookies. I remember my grandmother gently brushing my hair, dressing me in a clean denim jumper with a matching pink turtleneck. She gave me a gray-and-pink ten-speed bicycle, and summer storms would roil over the desert, flooding the streets. What will it be like, to live with them now?

I zip up my backpack and stand in the doorway to Barbara's room, looking in at her. What will happen to her? Where will she go? It's February, and the snow falls endlessly. Will she have to sleep on the street? How will she stay alive? A wave of dizziness overcomes me and I remember that I haven't eaten today, and that Laura's moms are expecting me back at their place in time for dinner. "Goodbye, Mom," I whisper, but she doesn't look up from the radio. I walk out of the dim apartment and into the bright hallway of the building, closing the door softly behind me.

2006

I wake in the night to another train. A grainer, again, sitting still in the moonlight. My cold hands pressed to my face bring me back to where I am. A random siding in eastern Washington, under a tree next to the tracks. I roll up my sleeping pad and strap it to the top of my pack, brush the dirt off my copy of *Pilgrim at Tinker Creek* and stash it away. The ballast crunches as I walk along the train. There are no rideable cars. And then, at the rear, there is the hissing and spitting of engines—slave units! "Slave units" are unmanned engines affixed to the end of a string. For extra power, like battery packs. For Montana, I think. For the mountains.

Cautiously I approach the units. They are rumbling and ticking, lit as if alive. I climb up the steep steel steps of the rearmost engine and try the door at the nose. It's locked. On the side of the unit is another small door. It's open. The moon has clouded over, and just now a little rain begins to fall. I duck through the short door and pull my pack through after me. And then I stand and marvel at what I have found.

Dark leather captain's chairs face the narrow windshield. There is a dash covered in blue-lit controls. All around me are switches and dials, panels and doors. The CB radio squawks, and I jump. *Am I safe back here?* Yes, at least for a little while, I tell myself. It's a good mile from here to the front of the train. No way is anyone coming back here now, at some random siding in the rain.

I drop my pack on the floor and check the mini fridge. Cold water in bottles. In the bathroom I flush the toilet, marveling as the water disappears. Where does it go? I pace the small room, anxious for the train to leave. At last it lurches forward, and the high desert slides away beyond the rainy window glass. My sleeping bag comforts me on the floor and I fall asleep, safe in the womb of the beast.

When I wake, the train has stopped. I jump up, stuff my things away, and cram myself into the tiny engine bathroom. My worn photocopied rail maps and the fact that it's morning tells me that we're most likely in Hauser, Idaho, so that the train can change crews. Will they check the slave unit now? Is it still safe to be in here? Can I ride this unit all the way to Chicago? What will happen if they find me? After a few minutes the train begins to creep forward and I open the door to the bathroom and peer out.

Through the windows of the unit, I can see that we're in a huge metal building, probably for refueling. *Shit.* I shut the bathroom door. Feet thud on the catwalk outside, the door on the nose of the engine swings open. Then the door to my bathroom pops out and I glimpse a white hard hat before it bangs shut again. *Shit.* A moment later the door opens again, daylight spills into the small, cramped space, and again the door is closed. A third time it opens.

"You have to leave," says a man in a hard hat. Two other workers stand behind him, looking down at the floor. I mumble something about wanting to stay out of the rain, and they mumble something about how they're sorry that I can't.

"How do I get out of this place?" I ask.

"I'll show you," says the first worker. I follow him off the train, out of the metal building, and he points me in the direction of the road. "Highway 53. Right over there." I set out across the yard, lifting myself over strings of cars, feeling disoriented in the bright daylight. When I get to the road, I turn and wave goodbye.

A ways up the road there are enough strings of cars between me and the workers that they can't see me anymore. There is no traffic. I turn back toward the yard and climb back over the cars; I'm south of the metal building now, abreast of a sandstone bluff that overlooks the main line, the track where the important trains, the trains more likely to go places, will be. The land shines in the sunlight; handsome pine trees move in the breeze. On top of the bluff I find a small spot of shade on its edge. My pack drops onto the soft pine needles. Breakfast is a can of beans and then I lie on my stomach, watching the yard below.

Finally, an eastbound intermodal pulls up and stops. This train, I imagine, is headed all the way to Chicago. I gather my things and sprint down the bluff. There are no rideable cars and the train hisses, releasing its brakes in preparation for departure. *Dangit!* And then, an unfamiliar car—it has a yellow painted platform, about four feet wide, on the rear, up against the freight containers. This platform seems like it could be rideable.

I climb the metal ladder onto the car and poke around. There is just enough space for my foam sleeping pad, and for me. There is a mess of machinery that I do not understand, but it partially hides me from view. The train begins to move and I lie back on the platform and look at the sky, willing myself to breathe. I am free again. Headed east. I will get someplace. I only wish I had a friend here, with me. Another human soul. These lands are too empty. I feel like I don't exist. I wish there was someone I could turn to and say, "How cool is it that we got kicked off the train but managed to catch another one?" I miss Finch. I imagine two people trying to hide in the tiny bathroom in that engine and laugh to myself.

Montana. I sleep through Glacier National Park. North Dakota, and the sky is a highway of wind. Clouds race over. The single track cuts through empty, rippling grasslands; shapes on the prairie move like shadow puppets on a wall. Old wooden houses stand empty next to the tracks. I'll move here, I think. I'll find a broth-colored creek; pull the stones from the ground and use them to build a hut. I'll watch the train blow through without stopping, no highways anywhere. It will be beautiful. How long, though, until I am crushed by my solitude? What would it feel like, to die from loneliness? Likely, I wouldn't die but live forever, haunted by my own demons. Below the known world is a world of loneliness so all-encompassing that not even the escape of death is allowed.

The train sides on the outskirts of Fargo. Only a few swallows of water remain in my jug. I try to read the train's stillness. There's a fast-food restaurant in the distance, baking in the hot sun. I hop off the train and jog to the restaurant, fill my water gallon, and run back to the train. It begins to move again, rolls a bit through town, and pulls into the Fargo yard, where it halts.

It seems as though we're just stopped for a crew change, which usually takes a few minutes, but after two hours we still have not moved. Night comes, and suddenly there are workers in little buggies, speeding to and fro along the train, and bright spotlights shine down into each car. *Shit.* I lie, frozen, hidden just so, behind the machinery on my grimy metal ledge. My legs are pressed along a metal pipe and my head is hidden behind a steel cylinder. My feet point skyward, against a square shelf. I am invisible. The spotlights sweep into my car and away, into my car and away. The little buggies pause and move on.

As I lie there, stiff, aching, invisible, the dark sky opens up, and rain begins to fall. I know what I need to do. I need to pull out the crackling, shiny blue tarp and spread it over me and my pack. I need to protect us both from the rain. But the buggies are still crunching up and down on the gravel and so I am frozen—if I move even an inch I'll become visible. So I lie, shivering, as the rain soaks my pants, dampens my flannel, and gathers on my eyelashes. The sound of the buggies recedes in the distance, and the trainyard settles again into its essential stillness. The rain stops; the sky becomes visible, the wind-battered stars. I pull off my stiff, wet jeans and crawl into my sleeping bag in just my long underwear. The hood of my bag, when cinched around my face, leaves just a small circle of stars in my vision. Sleep comes as dawn weakens the sky and my train pulls out of the yard, headed east.

Trainyards in big cities are complex, impenetrable labyrinths of steel, concrete, and concertina wire; their dirt roads lead into each other or dead-end in tangles of blackberry brambles; their bangings and screechings and stadium spotlights will drive you mad; they stretch for miles.

Trainyards in small towns are simpler; they have just a few

tracks, no workers, and often a small copse of trees in which to hide. On occasion, you can find interesting things as you walk along the tracks there: Sodden paperbacks, bottles of water, flattened bits of metal. Handfuls of wheat, spilled from grainers, that have sprouted into green grass between the railroad ties.

It is better to get on and off a train in a small-town yard, or, if you are going into a big city, at a random siding at its outskirts—a darkened field somewhere, or an industrial neighborhood. Sometimes, though, you have no choice where you end up—which is what happens to me when I wake in the incomprehensible hours of the night and find myself deep in the heart of the Minneapolis trainyard.

The trees are gone, the rolling pastures are gone, the moon is gone, the night is gone, even the wind is gone—instead, there is the screaming of steel on steel and the ticking of units as strings rumble past, the crunch of gravel beneath the tires of worker trucks, the hiss of CB radios, and the stadium lights, banishing all shadow. And in the distance, the beeping of cranes.

Also, it smells like oatmeal. For reasons I can't discern, the Minneapolis trainyard smells like oatmeal.

Eastbound intermodals sometimes go to Chicago, but sometimes they mysteriously terminate in Minneapolis. I figure that I've ended up on one of these trains, and so I pull myself stiffly from my sleeping bag, take a long drink of water, and pack my things away. I then poke my head around the side of the train—there's a white pickup driving toward me, the yellow lights on top of the cab flashing. A worker. *Shit!* I drop back onto the ledge and flatten myself. The pickup pulls up flush with my car, pauses, and then crunches away. The yellow lights wash over the wall of my car and then disappear. On the other side of the car is darkness. And then a bright white spotlight, making its way along the train. *Shit!* I lie down again and close my eyes. Gravel crunches as this vehicle approaches; I open my eyes into a squint and see that the shadows in my hiding place are gone; the grimy yellow steel, the twisted machinery, the lower half of my body— all of this is awash in blinding light. And then the light runs from the car like water, climbs the back end of the car behind mine, and is gone.

Out comes the breath I've been holding. I heave up my pack and, without looking, hop down onto the ballast. The narrow dirt road is cloaked once again in merciful shadow, and I run along this road, watching for a hole in the high fence that borders the yard. Up ahead I notice a gate, and I sprint for it; the gate is open and I see the truck with the spotlight beyond it, driving around huge puddles of water and mounds of gravel. There is a tower of concrete blocks and I duck behind these, where the trapezoid of dark shadow will protect me from the spotlights. A moment later a pair of headlights cuts across the puddle to my right, makes an arc over the piles of gravel, and disappears.

I sit on the muddy ground with my back against the concrete blocks. My rail maps provide no new information, nor do the handwritten notes I took while questioning train-riding friends about this route. There is some conflicting information, but as far as I can gather, my train is either terminating here or it's "working," and if it's just working then it should, at some point, continue on to Chicago.

The humid, oatmeal smell of the air pulls at my empty stomach. There's no way to know for sure what's going to happen with this train; there is only my best guess with the sprinkling of information that I have—like someone took a sheet of text and blacked out all but a handful of words. I can string them together, but they don't really make sense. Train riding is a thrift store puzzle that's missing half the pieces. You don't always know where you're going or how you're going to end up there, but you don't really care, either.

I know what I'm going to do. I'm going to get back on that train. I have a feeling that this train is only working, that it's continuing on to Chicago. I just have to find my car again, hide myself as best I can, and wait.

Somehow I make it down the shadowy dirt track back to my car without being seen; somehow I fling myself up onto my narrow metal shelf and down behind the twisted machinery before the next beeping worker truck passes by. Train riding is a video game, and I've dodged this round of zombies. Stretching out, I will myself deeper into the shadows. Then, carefully, I unroll my pad, scooch into my sleeping bag, and go to sleep.

Two hours later I am startled awake when the train begins to move. It's heading west. Backward. I don't know what this means, exactly, but I know that it's not good. I lie in my sleeping bag, wondering what to do, as my car is pulled beneath the rows of stadium lights. All around me are the beepings and clangings of industry, and it is difficult to ascertain, from my position, just what exactly is happening to my train. I should sit up, I think, but then my car comes to a stop directly beneath one of the giant stadium lights, and all the shadows in my hiding place are gone. There is the crunch of tires, the hiss of CB radios, and I know that I cannot move. It's not so much that I fear a trespassing ticket, at this point, as that I fear the humiliation of climbing down off my car into the very heart of the yard. I fear appearing, suddenly, before a whole audience of unsuspecting yard workers, who will turn away, who won't be able to look. Because I am an idiot. Because I am breaking the golden rule of train riding that binds worker to rider in a mutual pact of understanding—*be invisible*. Because if I am invisible, then the workers don't have to bust me. They don't have to turn me in. But if I show myself to a whole group of them at once, they do. And nobody wants that.

So I stay in my sleeping bag, peering at the washed-out night sky, and then, silhouetted against the stadium light above me, there appears the wide, rectangular arm of a crane, and this arm descends onto the next car down from mine and lifts that car's massive freight container, effortlessly, into the air above my face.

Oh. Fuck.

Moments later I am on the ground. I have never moved so fast, I think, in my entire life. One second I was on the train, in my sleeping bag, staring up at the red-lit fingers of the crane as they swung above my car after dropping the freight container from the one behind it, and the next my shoes were on, my sleeping bag was stuffed away, my foam pad was strapped to my pack, and now I'm here, on the ground, pinned beneath the blinding lights, surrounded by workers.

The spell of invisibility has been broken. The spell that was so strong I slept for hours, unnoticed, in a busy yard. A spell so strong I had almost been crushed, when the freight container I was sleeping against was lifted into the air.

A little white cart is idling next to me. The window comes down.

"Just where do you think you're headed?" asks the man inside.

"I'm trying to find my way out of here," I say.

"How'd you get in here in the first place?" asks the worker.

"I came in on the train."

"You were trespassing on the train?" he says, incredulous. "Where did you get on?"

I lie and name a crew change in Montana.

"You've been trespassing since Montana?"

Oh come on, I think. *Of course I was trespassing.*

"Look, are you going to give me a ticket?" I say. "You don't have to lecture me. It's late." A little rain is falling. I don't care, though. I've just cheated death.

"Wait here," says the worker. "I've got to call the rail cop. He can decide what he wants to do with you."

It takes a while for the rail cop to arrive, and meanwhile I stand, waiting, in the busy lot with my hands in my pockets, feeling like a fool. At last an unmarked SUV crunches over to me, and the rail cop steps out into the bright light, and I notice that he looks just like the man on the Pringles can.

I give him my ID and he turns it over in his hands thoughtfully. I study his tufts of silver hair and his carefully combed mustache, his tidy wool sweater. He looks up and meets my eyes.

"I'll take your information," he says, "and then you can go. This time. Next time I'll give you a citation. For theft of services."

"Theft of services? Really?"

He nods.

"Just like if you stole a ride on Amtrak." As if I have shipped myself across the country in a freight container without paying the postage. Which, well, I guess I pretty much have.

"And one more thing," he adds, peering down at me with his bleary, grandfatherly eyes. "Did you know that people have been riding freight trains since before you and I were born?" He nods again, looks out across the shadowed strings of trains, and rocks on his heels. "And they'll still be riding trains long after you and I are gone."

This is not the sort of rail cop with paramilitary aspirations, the kind who cuts his hair close to the scalp and treats you like a terrorist. This is the kind of rail cop who has a wood-paneled office in a trailer somewhere, where he sits drinking tumblers of whiskey and reading railfan magazines and out-of-print books on the history of freight trains, in between rounds of half-heartedly combing the yard with his spotlight.

He hands me back my ID and points me toward the dirt road out of the lot. "Thank you," I say. Workers turn the other way as I pass. I am a hobo, disgraced. *Be invisible.* Beyond the gates of the yard are gray, sleeping industrial buildings and a narrow bit of forest. I make my way into these woods, pushing aside the tangled branches, until I find a clearing, padded in fallen leaves. I spread out my bedroll, prop my pack beside it, and pull my tarp over everything. And then for a while I lie still, heart racing, listening to the gentle tap of rain on tarpaulin, and when I close my eyes I see the crane again, swinging over me with its red-lit fingers. Except this time I'm not fast enough: the crane grips my freight container and the freight container shifts, crushing me. I'll never sleep again, I think, and then, of course, I do.

In Minneapolis the next day, it mists, rains in fits, and then rains solidly, a heavy sheet that darkens the sky and sends torrents of water down the streets. The sky is no longer a warm roof but a crashing wave that sweeps over the city, into every small place that has once been bright and dry.

I may as well have jumped in the river with my pack on my back.

I trudge, senselessly, water dripping from my eyelashes, looking for a laundromat, some dignity, a meaningful life. But the outskirts of Minneapolis will not give me what I need. In the evening the rain stops, and a long bus ride delivers me, at last, to a laundromat, where I watch cable television and dry everything that I own. Then I walk back through the night to the trainyard, under a sky that has turned to clear stars. On a bluff above the yard there is a trampled-down place among the thistles, and I spread out my bedroll here, on a bed of flattened beer cartons, and lie on my stomach to watch the tracks. There is a train sitting there, but it's sitting where my train sat, the train that was unloaded of its freight containers, and I know that this string, too, is destined for the hungry maw of the great train-eating crane. Other trains come and go, and I consider them, but my Minneapolis trainyard spirit has been broken. Loneliness has crumpled me, my morale has bottomed out. I want to gaze upon a kindly face. I want to share this night, this bed of flattened cardboard, with someone. I can't muster the energy to try to catch another train. Not all alone like this. *I'll just sleep here,* I think, looking up at the glittering stars. *And in the morning I will hitchhike.*

On my second day in Minneapolis, it doesn't rain. I find a food co-op and eat dolmas and then spend the day on the bus, going this way and that, in the direction of what may or may not be the highway. The bus fills with people and then empties, fills and then empties. Nothing is where the map at the gas station said that it would be. The day begins to wane and I know that I have missed my opportunity, because no one picks up hitchhikers after sunset.

I find a payphone at a corner store and call Willow, in North Carolina.

"I'm trying to get there," I say. "I'm so exhausted."

"If you can get back on the train," says Willow, "you can ride it five hours east, to Winona. I've got a friend there you can stay with."

I hang up the phone and stare at the way the streetlights make patterns on the concrete lot. I'm not floating alone in space. Not really. I have a friend in the world who knows me. This friend has a friend who can be my friend. A train it will be after all, then. *I can do this.* I walk the three miles through winding industry back to the trainyard and climb atop my thistle-covered bluff. The yard is noisy below me, full of bustling workers and clanging steel, but I've watched it enough at this point to know that, in the early morning, the busyness will still, my train will come, and I will go.

My trip east began with the mail train, Chicago bound, fastest intermodal on the Highline, and now I catch that train again—at six A.M., when the sky is growing pale and the whole yard is asleep. A piggyback, that semi-truck trailer perched on a flatcar, that windy beast of a ride. I haul myself up and under the axle of the truck trailer just moments before the sun rises, the engines attach, and the whole yard comes awake. As the train thunders east along the Mississippi River I lie back and draw my hoodie over my face. I have a heat in my throat as though I'm getting sick, and the weariness that comes after days of travel; a hunger for vinegar and bitter flavors, an aversion to the wind.

Midday, when the train stops in a tangle of green beneath an overpass, I get off. The train passed a highway sign for Winona, Minnesota, just moments ago. I push my way to the road. At a gas station I call Willow's friend, whose name is Florence, and buy a banana and some gas station chili. My last meal was yesterday and I'm starving. I'm sitting outside on my pack, eating the banana, when a battered red pickup pulls up.

Florence is wearing a wide-brimmed straw hat and dirty jean shorts, and her hands are rough from work. She wrenches down the tailgate so I can throw my pack in the back of the truck. I am overcome with gratitude. *Who is this person, this stranger here to break my solitude?* She takes off her glasses and peers at me; her face is a constellation of freckles.

We drive past rolling green pastures and flame-colored oak trees to Florence's farm, where we park alongside a little red house. The interior of the house is one tall room, with a wood-stove and high windows and sunbeams puddled on the floor. A ladder leads to a loft for sleeping, and Florence points me to the laundry room so I can wash my grimy things.

I sort my laundry and then discover Florence's good-smelling peppermint soap, which I use to scrub the diesel exhaust from my face. When I emerge from the bathroom, I find that she's made us a salad of kale and tomatoes from her garden, with turnips and black pepper. We eat it sitting at the little table looking out at the sprawling land, which is weedy and dry at the end of the season.

"Do you want to see the boathouse?" asks Florence.

We drive over a bridge to a small island in the Mississippi River. The island is crowded with ash trees and the air is heavy with the screeching of insects. A soft dirt path takes us to a sandy shore where a wee house rocks gently in the current. The walls are fashioned from oddly shaped pieces of wood, and inside, Florence strikes a match and touches it to the wick of an oil lamp. The gold glow reveals a counter cluttered with purple plums and taper candles stuffed into wine bottles. A row of theater seats is bolted to the wall. Upstairs is a bedroom with a view of the river, and a little closet with a four-gallon bucket full of sawdust.

"That's the shitter," says Florence. "There's a smaller boat-house too. We call it the raftshack." She leads me outside and around the worn wooden deck, past some tomato plants in hewn plastic barrels, to where a one-room cabin sits bobbing in the water. The raftshack has its own tiny deck, to which a wooden park bench has been bolted. Florence hops carefully from the boathouse to the raftshack and I follow, feeling its front end dip down into the water. There is a plywood door and screen windows, and inside is a heavy dresser, a futon on a wooden frame, and some shelves.

"I just got it two days ago," says Florence. "Some kids built it. They floated it down the Mississippi from Minneapolis. They didn't want it anymore, and they sold it to me for two hundred bucks." She runs her hand along the doorframe. "I've got to take it apart and shorten it," she says. "Make it less heavy. And I've got to get an engine."

There are voices in the distance: Florence's friends. They've built a fire in a clearing in the trees. Florence has an old fiddle and someone else has brought a case of beer. I make a pot of lentils in the kitchen and then stand on the deck, listening to the music and eating the lentils with a wooden spoon. The night grows late and the fire flickers low and my weariness overcomes me; I put myself to bed in the raftshack, fashioning a nightstand from a plastic bucket and setting an oil lamp on it. There's a sleeping bag and a book of train graffiti to read and I lie on the futon, feeling myself rise and fall with the gentle movements of the water. Later I get up to pee and everything is still; the sky is black, stretching out over the Mississippi, the stars like handfuls of broken glass. I hang my butt off the edge of the porch and pee in the water. I fall asleep and dream that Florence and I are playing in the water like muskrats, that we have bicycles we ride across its surface.

"Tomorrow is the farmer's market," says Florence the next morning as she pilots the truck along the rutted dirt road, a mason jar of coffee clutched between her knees. At the farm, we harvest tomatoes and I battle the yellow jackets in the apple orchard, collecting enough apples for pie. I make ten tiny pies to add to her farmer's market stand, and Florence puts them in a metal case for display.

I stay in Winona for four days. I feel as though I have been gutted by the solitude and peril of my journey, and I do not want to leave this happy place where I can eat heirloom tomatoes and help Florence polish vegetables for the market. But I know that Greensboro, North Carolina, is waiting for me, the gentle southern winter, the brick house where Willow lives that will be my home. Florence is busy and I have no purpose here, really. This is a stopping-over place, a place to rest, but not a place where I can belong. I call our friend Bob, who is in Ohio visiting his family. Bob is six feet tall and has a huge copper-colored afro. Just out of college, he travels the country via freight train, whittles wooden spoons, and harvests acorns to make acorn flour. Bob is kind. He never talks down to me or tries to explain things to me that I already know. He says that if I can get to Ohio he will join me; we can attempt to ride trains the rest of the way to North Carolina together.

The next morning I walk to the roadside, a Tupperware of gifted tomatoes stowed carefully in my pack, and put out my thumb. I think about Florence—the way she frowns when she plays the fiddle, the freckles on her shoulders. In the evenings she told me stories while we sliced vegetables for salad—about Winona, her teen years, her grandparents who started the farm. I like Florence's world. I like Florence. I wonder if I'll ever see her again.

1997

step out of the plane into the high Colorado desert. Red dirt, red mesas, the sun coming up over everything. I shade my eyes with my hands. I have never seen light this bright; it feels as though the rays are piercing my skull. And the air is so dry! I peer out from behind my fingers. Frost glitters on the tarmac. Tumbleweeds edge the blacktop. The mesas have a dusting of snow at their rims. The sky is a cold blue.

Grandma and Grandpa pick me up in a white Oldsmobile. They are just like I remember them: Grandpa in his Wrangler jeans, his shining pate, Grandma with her button-down shirt and her helmet of steely gray hair. They are the same but I am different. I have grown, from a guileless child into an unkempt, feral teenager with an ocean of grief inside me. Grandma smiles tightly and gives me an awkward hug. She smells like dryer sheets and Dove soap.

"There are wild horses up there," says Grandpa, pointing at the tops of the mesas. We're driving north on an empty road. Fields, both overgrown and cultivated, surround us. We're in Grand Junction, where the Colorado and the Gunnison Rivers meet. A faded town in the lonely desert thirty minutes from the Utah border. We've already passed through downtown, where a meat-rendering plant makes the air smell of roadkill.

"Peaches," says Grandma. We're passing an orchard, and the rows of trees spin like the spokes in a bicycle wheel. "In summer there will be peaches. Do you like peaches?"

"I've only had canned peaches," I say, trying to imagine summertime. "There aren't fruit trees in Alaska." If I ate ripe fruit off a real living tree when I was here before, I don't remember it.

The house is true to my memory as well—one story, half brick, surrounded by acres of dead winter corn. We park next to Grandpa's huge pickup. *Two cars*, I think. *A whole house*. This is unimaginable wealth. In the gravel next to the driveway is a much older vehicle, a rusted brown Ford.

"Jordan's fixing up that one," says Grandma.

Jordan.

Jordan is in the kitchen, standing at the sink washing his cereal bowl in the light from the window. He's wearing a crisp white T-shirt with a gold chain necklace and his hair is combed and wet. He's sixteen now. His jaw has squared and veins cut his ropy forearms.

"Hey," he says.

"Hey."

"I gotta go to school," he says.

"All right. See ya."

He ducks through the doorway without meeting my eyes. I

watch as he walks to his truck. My chest is a hot fist of anxiety. I look around the kitchen. The Formica table with its four chairs upholstered in vinyl. The scuffed linoleum floor. The tins of flour and sugar, glinting in the light.

"You can have the room at the end of the hall," Grandma is saying. "That was Barbara's room." I startle. *Barbara's room?* I didn't sleep last night, on account of the red-eye flight out of Anchorage, and the world feels strange. I carry my suitcase—given to me by Laura's moms—down the narrow hallway, the wooden floorboards creaking under me. I pass Jordan's room; the door is ajar and I see that the space is tidy and bare—white bedspread, no decorations, like a hotel room—then there's Grandma and Grandpa's room, with a big bed and a wooden armoire cluttered with antique perfume bottles and face creams, two nightstands, a dresser with Grandpa's handkerchiefs and watches on top. At the end of the hall is my room, next to the cupboard that holds Grandma's canned goods: dozens of quarts of peaches, salsa, pickled green beans.

I open the bedroom door and peer inside. There is a window that faces the backyard, with its clothesline full of sheets and pillowcases, and beyond that, the fields. Light from the window pools on the bed, where a handmade quilt is pulled taut. There is a dresser with a mirror. A single chair. On the wooden floor, a rag rug. Grandma slides open the closet door. One half of the closet is filled with cardboard boxes, shoeboxes, clothing.

"Some of Barbara's childhood things," says Grandma. "The rest of the closet is yours."

I sit on the bed. I am exhausted and yet my whole body is buzzing. I can see myself in the mirror—tired eyes, brown hair pushed behind my ears.

"I'll make some breakfast," says Grandma. I look up at her, as if for the first time. "You want sausage and eggs?"

"Yeah, okay," I say. It's hard for me to speak.

I am standing in the pantry off the kitchen, running my hands over all the boxes, jars, and cans of food. Soup. Pasta. Pasta sauce. Bread. Bagels. Tuna. Peanut butter and jelly. Macaroni and cheese. Tortilla chips. Salsa. Four different kinds of cereal, including my favorite, Cap'n Crunch's Crunch Berries. There is also a chest freezer full of meat, frozen vegetables, a gallon tub of ice cream. In my head I tick off what I know is in the fridge, because Grandma and I went grocery shopping earlier—milk, cheese, lunch meat, pudding, cucumber pickles that Grandma canned herself. I heft a loaf of bread in my palm, feeling its weight, and then return it to the shelf. Today was the last day of my first week at the local high school, Central High, and after school Grandma and I went to Costco, where we bought much of this stuff. Grandma raised six kids, shuffling them all through the three bedrooms of this small house, and she knows how to stock a pantry. She also lived through the Great Depression, so she likes to keep a lot of food on hand. And she is careful. She clips coupons, studies receipts, looks for deals. I've only ever seen this much food at friends' houses, never at my own. *Is this my house, though?* I touch a plastic package of chocolate muffins and think about Central High.

The high school is different from the alternative school I attended in Anchorage, where the classes were small and the teachers were kind. Central High is a huge school with wide corridors that echo with the cacophony of over a thousand voices. The classes are large, and the teachers seem worn out, their enthusiasm used up. The textbooks are shabby and dog-eared, some of them missing covers, and there aren't enough to go around. In my science lab there isn't enough equipment, and a good deal of what we do have is broken. Most of the girls straighten their hair, and many of the boys wear cowboy hats. The parking lot is crowded with dented Camaros and pickup trucks that spit blue exhaust. Most days I hardly speak to anyone. I have decided to become invisible.

I look at the chocolate muffins again. The phone rings in the living room. It's Laura, and I take the cordless to my room. I shut the door and lie on the bed in the afternoon light and cry while she tells me how difficult things are now that I'm gone.

"I'm so sad," she says. "I want to die."

"I want to die too!" I say. "But don't die. Neither of us can die, okay?"

I trace my fingers along the stitching of the quilt on my bed. It's a starburst pattern, and each ray of color is a scrap of fabric from a piece of clothing that Grandma sewed for one of her six children. I imagine all six kids in this small, three-bedroom house. Yelling, fighting. My uncles Dave and Brian, the young-est, shooting prairie dogs in the field with their BB guns. My aunt Pat on the back of her boyfriend's motorcycle on the lonely country road. My aunt Cathy, the oldest, and her sister Christy quietly sewing this quilt with Grandma in the living room while *Wheel of Fortune* played on the wooden swivel TV. And my mom, Barbara. What was she doing? I've been told that she played basketball in high school. That she got excellent grades in everything but math. In the faded family photos on the wall in the living room, she smiles widely, showing too much gum. Was she happy here? If she was happy, why did she leave?

Grandma told me that her grandparents came over on a boat from Northern Ireland in the 1800s. She was one of seven siblings raised in a small log house in Bonne Terre, Missouri. Her father was laid off from the railroad during the Great Depression, and after that, he worked for the Army Corps of Engineers, digging ditches. They had a wood-burning stove and a chopping block out back where they cut the heads off chickens. Grandma's dad died of a heart attack after the kids were grown, and her mom lived alone. She and a neighbor woman, who also lived alone, would hang their rag rugs over the porch every day to signal that they were okay. One day, the rug wasn't there, and the neighbor woman called the police. Grandma's mom had had a stroke and died.

Grandpa grew up on a farm in Parachute, Colorado. For generations his family had been homesteaders on the Front Range, between the Rocky Mountains and the High Plains. His mother had hallucinations and religious delusions, and disappeared when he was five years old. An older brother found her in an apartment in California. She wasn't eating. He took her back to Parachute and cared for her for the rest of her life.

Maybe, in the beginning, Grandma and Grandpa tried to take care of Barbara. But she went to Alaska, and she won't speak to them. If they still love her now, they don't say so. They don't mention her at all—it's as though she doesn't exist.

No one knows anything about my dad's family. When I bring him up, the room falls silent. He worked for the railroad, says Grandma. He was into conspiracy theories. They got married. And then Barbara was gone.

I look more closely at the starburst pattern on the quilt. Tiny, faded flowers. Red and brown stripes. Sky blue. Grandma pushes the door of my room open and stares in at me, lying in the bed curled up on my side, my face puffy from crying, the phone pressed to my cheek.

"Dinner's ready," she says.

A Pyrex dish of gleaming roast beef. A ceramic bowl of mashed potatoes. Sliced sandwich bread, still in the bag. A head of iceberg lettuce, hacked into chunks. A bottle of Hidden Valley ranch dressing. A glass bowl of sliced cucumbers floating in vinegar and sprinkled with salt. A tub of margarine with a butter knife stuck in it. A gallon of milk. Even after a week, this spread of food still feels unreal to me, and I stare a bit warily at the mashed potatoes on my plate. What did I do to deserve this? If I eat this, will it become a debt that I owe? If so, how will I repay it?

Grandpa fixes himself a screwdriver—vodka from the bottle under the sink and orange juice from concentrate—and sits at the head of the table spreading margarine on his bread. Grandma fusses with the napkins. I can smell Jordan's cologne.

"Elbows off the table," Grandma snaps at me, and I startle. "Let's say grace." She extends her hands. I take one warm palm and close my eyes for the prayer. Grandma and Grandpa are devout Catholics, and they pray before each meal. "And please bless these two and help them to be good," finishes Grandma, and she drops my hand.

"How was school this week?" she asks as I cut into my roast beef. Jordan frowns. I look sidelong at him, trying to get a read on his mood. We've barely talked; many nights he goes out and doesn't return home until the wee hours, the sound of his truck tires on the gravel drive shattering the still dark. He is edgy and hostile when I pass him in the hallway, and we don't laugh together like we did when we were both in Anchorage.

"School was fine, I guess," I answer for both of us.

Grandpa finishes his drink and pours himself another.

"You didn't pick up your tools in the drive like I asked you," he says to Jordan. "And where in the hell do you go at night?" Grandpa's hands are red around his drink glass, permanently irritated from a lifetime handling caustic chemicals. Jordan quietly cuts his meat into chunks, his face inscrutable. Grandpa turns to me. "What's this crying in your room this afternoon? Is there something wrong with you? Are you on the pot?"

I laugh, and spit the food back onto my plate.

"On the pot?" I repeat.

Grandpa bangs his fist on the table. The silverware jumps.

"George!" says Grandma.

"There's something wrong with her," shouts Grandpa, louder now. He stabs a finger in the air in my direction. "She's gonna end up on welfare, just like her mother."

I put down my fork and focus on the Formica of the table. The lights seem to dim.

Far away, like a radio station turned down low, I can hear Grandpa yelling at Grandma. Something about the place she took the car in for repairs. Grandpa is retired but Grandma will never retire, really; she still works to make their home, the same way she always has; each day she fixes his meals, cleans up after him, runs the household errands, does his laundry. And yet she's fucked it all up, somehow. *Like she always does.*

Grandpa's face is flushed, his lips wet with spit. His anger becomes expansive, and reaches out to include the larger world. The wetbacks are stealing all the jobs. There's a goddang subdivision being built across the street, where pumpkin fields used to be. I focus my gaze on the thick hair of his forearms, the backs of his hands. I suddenly realize how lucky I am to have never had a father.

Jordan pushes back his chair. I hear the slam of the kitchen door. The roar of a truck engine starting. Flying gravel.

After dinner I lie in my bed in the dark, waiting to hear the television click off, Grandma's slippers in the hall, water running in their bathroom. Moonlight from the window illuminates the far wall, where my mother's childhood things are stacked in the closet. On the chair next to the dresser is my school backpack, with my homework inside, which I haven't done. I don't care, though. When have I ever cared? What did Barbara think about, when she was my age, lying in this same bed? When she was young and healthy and strong? When this was all that she knew? I wonder where she is now. I haven't heard from her since I arrived in Colorado. Is she homeless, in Anchorage in the wintertime? Is she dead? My head has gone hot and fuzzy. Oh God. The blackness is going to return and swallow me. I am going to float in the universe alone again, untethered. The floorboards in the hallway creak, and then the house is silent. I switch on the reading lamp on my headboard and extract my journal from its hiding place behind the other books on the bookshelf. I page through the notebook to a blank page, and uncap my pen.

I want to die, I want to die, I want to die, I want to die

I jog north, along the dirt track that follows the fields. Once, I pause to look back at the small brick house and then I keep running, pushing through the stitch in my side. *Away. I need to get farther away.* I run until I am surrounded by open space, the sky, the sun. The smell of sagebrush in the warm afternoon. At the end of the field is a ditch, choked with tamarisk and wild asparagus, and I crouch in the shadows there. I am still getting used to this sun, this light brighter than anything I have ever known. Like a noise I can't turn down. I am from the land of black-dark winters and cool overcast summers with frigid lakes. The place where the sea washes up against the high mountains. I am damp moss, I am delicate lichen, I am the loamy forest floor.

I draw myself up and keep running, out of the ditch and across the neighbors' fields, to the road. The road carries me past the faded corner store and I turn left and climb into the dirt-colored hills. The houses are larger now, gated. Estates. I reach the horse pasture and lope up the snaking drive, out of breath by the time I pound on the huge wooden door.

It opens. A woman in a turquoise terrycloth robe stands holding a glass of white wine.

"Is April here?" I ask. The woman hollers into the yawning cavern of the house and then April appears, six feet tall with long red hair, and gathers me up into a hug.

"Is this your new friend you were telling me about?" says the older woman, in a Louisiana drawl. "I'm Frankie." She extends her hand. "April's mother. I was just headed out to the pool. Do y'all want some food? There's snacks in the kitchen."

I met April a week ago, in first period—she rushed into class late, flustered, her hair in sheets around her face, her arms full of books, wearing a patchwork skirt that swept the ground. "Do you know there's an article in the school paper about me?" she said, after sitting in the seat next to mine, at the back of the class. "They say I'm the oddest kid in school." I checked, and it was true—the school paper had written about April—about her cheesy jokes, her propensity for talking too loudly and laughing at the wrong moment, her extremely good grades, her strange flowing clothing. I decided then that we would be friends, a suggestion that April agreed to enthusiastically since she didn't have a friend at school, either, and we ate our cold pizza and paper boat of french fries together at lunch, at a table all by ourselves, while April listed off to me, loudly, the things that she liked—*Star Trek*, her cat, swing dancing, and Renaissance festivals.

"I live near you!" she said, after I told her where my grandparents' house was. "You should come over! We have a pool!"

I'd felt happy that afternoon, in the passenger seat of Jordan's truck, on our way home from school. I had a friend! Jordan was silent, watching the road, his gold chain glinting in the light. Nas was playing on the stereo, from a mixtape that Jordan made. We listened to this same cassette each morning—me bleary with sleep, my coat zipped up because the truck didn't have a heater, trying to remember if I'd done my homework, or what my homework even was, a twenty-dollar bill in my pocket to buy lunch for the week ("There's no Santa Claus," Grandpa always said, before pulling the bill from his wallet)—and again on the way home, when I was spent from disappointment and the exertion of maintaining my invisibility (some of my teachers still hadn't even realized I was in their classes).

That day I was smiling, though. A friend! I held on to the bench seat as we jostled over the train tracks in town. I cranked the window down, letting in the fresh spring air. Jordan turned up the stereo.

If I ruled the world . . .
I'd free all my sons . . .
Black diamonds and pearls . . .
If I ruled the world

I accept some carrots and hummus from April in her huge kitchen. The appliances are stainless steel, like in a restaurant kitchen. There's an island in the middle with a rack above it from which hang gleaming pots and pans. On the island is a bowl of pomegranates, a bottle of balsamic vinegar, a large wooden pepper grinder. This is my first time eating hummus—it's good.

Grandma was fixing dinner when I left the house—meatloaf, the top shiny with ketchup. When I walked through the kitchen, Grandpa grabbed my wrist and squeezed, hard.

"You look like a slut!" His breath stank of vodka. I was wearing a tank top with no bra. It was spring in the high desert, and the days were warm. And I didn't really have boobs yet, anyway.

I wrenched myself free and ran out the kitchen door. Grandpa hollered.

"Let her go," I heard Grandma say, through the open window.

"Let me lend you my extra bathing suit," says April, returning the hummus to the fridge. "We can swim!"

April leads me through the dining room with its long oak table, the library with its walls of leather-bound books, to a set of French doors beyond which is the pool, clear blue in a concrete patio. Frankie is in a bikini on one of the lounge chairs, smoking a cigarette and reading a magazine. April drops her shorts and hands me a small bundle, her other suit.

"What's your house like?" asks April. "Where you live with your grandparents?"

"It's small," I say. "Not like this. But it's really nice." I try to find words. "Do you think I can stay here tonight?"

"Of course you can, honey," says Frankie. "But why? Do your grandparents know where you are?"

Shame makes the deck recede. I talk around what feels like a sock in my mouth.

"I don't know. It's . . . complicated. I just moved in with them a few months ago. Before that I lived in Alaska with my mother. She's schizophrenic. She used to beat the shit out of me. We didn't have any food. Anyway, I told myself that no one would ever hit me again. My grandpa got pissed at me today after school, called me a slut and grabbed my arm. I freaked out and ran up here. I don't think my grandparents even like me. I mean I'm pretty sure they don't like me. I don't know." The world is rushing white noise. Everything is too much. I sit on a pool lounger and close my eyes against the sun.

"What's your grandparents' number, honey?" says Frankie. She disappears inside the house, closing the French doors behind her.

"Fuck your grandparents," says April.

The pool is incredible. We do cannonballs, stand on our hands under the water, run off the end of the diving board. We drop quarters to the bottom and dive for them, holding our breath as long as we can. *Is that the sound of Frankie shouting in the kitchen?* I can't tell. Our hands and feet are prune-y and we reek of chlorine by the time we pull ourselves out and lie like seals on the warm concrete in the sun.

"Dinner!" Frankie calls from the doorway. "Don't worry about your grandparents," she says, as she spoons spaghetti onto scalloped white china.

April hands me a fluffy towel to wrap around my dripping suit. "I'm glad you're staying with us tonight."

I'm not sure what to do with all the pillows on the guest room bed—what are they for? Do people really sleep with this many pillows? I shove them off, onto the floor, and climb into the tall bed, burying myself in the blankets. On the walls are framed portraits of April over the years—April with big hair and heavy eye makeup as a young child, April wearing a leather jacket, a caricature of April bought from a street vendor while on vacation, maybe. The house is silent except for a clock in the hallway that ticks softly and persistently. I wish I could call Laura and tell her about this house, about the stainless-steel kitchen and the hummus and the pool. I close my eyes before the blackness can come and carry me away.

hitch thirty miles from Winona to the next town, where the train I want will stop to change crews. I set up in the trash-strewn weeds along the tracks and eat Florence's tomatoes. When a train arrives, the rail cop materializes as well; parked in his SUV, lights off, on the access road. He's probably napping in there and not really keeping a lookout, but there's no way to be certain, and I am directly in his line of sight. My maps show another catch-out spot, where the train stops; I can probably walk there. It's six in the evening and creeping toward dark.

I traverse the sprawling outskirts of the town, across a vast industrial sea. There are no sidewalks and the starry sky expands above me, the occasional bright lights of a grumbling semi-truck pin me to the road. Four hours later I still have not found my spot. I'm standing at the edge of a field, facing a dark intersection. There's a merry little house with a jack-o'-lantern in the window. I'm tired and lonely, and everything seems impossible.

Down the road a bit is a gas station. The doorbells jangle and I am enveloped in the warm, cloying air. The clerk lets me study a map. I turn it upside down and right side up again. My head is hot and there's a rattling in my lungs; maybe I'm a little delirious. And, of course, I find that I am impossibly far from where I need to be. Of course I have, in my attempt to go one direction, walked in a great circle instead. I rotate the map again. There are highway overpasses between me and my catch-out spot, and gray chunks of map that represent unknown lands. I fold the map carefully and hand it back to the clerk. I buy a banana. I'll go back to my original spot, then. The rail cop has probably moved.

This is train riding. There is the bit on the train, and before that there are days and days of this.

An hour later I heave my pack over a tall fence, climb over after it, and wade through a field of dry grass beneath a power line. It's dark but I'm near the trainyard, so I don't want to use my headlamp. I flick the light on now and then, shading it against my palm, to reassure myself that I'm going the right direction.

A forest of hardwoods edges the trainyard. This forest is dark and open, the leaf litter heavy and soft underfoot. Through the trees, I can see the tracks glinting in the moonlight. I'm in the spot I was in earlier but on the other side of the yard, away from the access road, so if a train comes it will obscure me from the rail cop.

My bedroll is comfortable but I toss and turn, warm enough but too keyed up to really rest. In my imagination are Florence's hands, her strong palms, the crow's-feet around her eyes that soften her smile. I picture her in her sleeping loft, wrapped in a tangled white sheet, the heat of the woodstove gathered around her. I wish I'd told Florence that I like her. I wonder if she likes me back.

In the morning I'm on a train, but it has not yet left the yard. When this train arrived, I thought it was headed to Chicago, and so I'd climbed aboard. But instead of leaving the yard, it had split, while I was asleep, into two neat pieces, and my piece had been left behind. I lie on my bedroll, dawn breaking over my face, while flocks of pigeons beat the grainers with their wings. The sky is a cold, autumnal blue.

Another train rumbles up and stops on the other side of the trees. I throw my things together and sprint through the tall grass down into a mucky ditch, scramble up the ballast and over an unrideable car and down the ballast on the other side, to where I am once again hidden on the edge of the forest and can walk along the train, looking for something rideable.

But I find nothing. The train leaves.

I'm thirsty. I have to take a shit. In the forest I rest on the ground, quiet. The leaves on the trees are just beginning to fall. My pack stashes neatly in the lee of a tree and I leave the forest for an old residential neighborhood, blank houses steeling themselves against the coming Wisconsin winter. At a fast-food restaurant I order chili cheese fries and then find the public library and use the bathroom, after which I stand in front of the mirror for a long time, staring at my face.

I pass the rest of the day and another night in the hardwood forest next to the trainyard, sleeping and reading and lying on the ground, watching the sky. It's cold, and I think of the roar of the woodstove in Florence's red farmhouse. The way I'd wake in the night and feed it split wood. What would it be like to have a home like that? With someone like Florence? The clouds roll over and away again, stack up like houses of playing cards and then tumble apart. At night a creature makes its bed in the thistles around me, and spiders crawl over my sleeping bag. When I'm hungry, I eat salted kidney beans rolled up in the leaves of a red cabbage from Florence's farm; when I'm thirsty, I have water in my plastic gallon jug.

Trains come and go, slow pounding power with their lights reaching into my nest. The engineers lean out the windows of the units. Do they see me? I can't tell.

On the third day, I abandon the hardwood forest and hitchhike. After a period of waiting, I am on my way east. A dude in a pickup truck stops for me, and then an aging hippie in a crumbling Subaru. And then, in Illinois, a man named Mark picks me up and says he will take me all the way to Ohio.

Mark makes his living buying and selling things on Craigslist, which he tells me about as we drive through the night, stopping once for gas station nachos and Diet 7Up. At five in the morning we are finally in Ohio. Bob meets me in the darkened driveway when I arrive.

"Last night was my little brother's birthday," he says. "We played cards and drank Old Crow until late. I fell asleep on the couch."

After saying goodbye to Mark, I stumble into Bob's parents' huge house, with hot and cold running water, soft beds, lace curtains, and all sorts of other things. I drift off under smooth pink blankets in the guest room and sleep until noon, waking to find the house empty and warm sunshine coming in through the curtains. My dreams were full of death and heterosexual sex, weeping, and men.

.　　　.　　　.

Sixty years ago, in the woods behind Cincinnati Union Terminal, hobos waited in the cottonwood trees on nests of rain-soaked cardboard boxes for their trains. They drank liquor from green glass bottles, trampled paths in the weeds, and built fires to cook their stew. The woods were busy with comings and goings and the sounds of shouting. Now, Bob and I are in this same jungle, under the trees that shake in the wind and catch the last of the light, and it's quiet. The air is fresh and clean, and October leaves drop over last year's flattened beer cartons. These days the jungles are mostly abandoned. The cold trains blow through unridden. We'd pored over our maps at Bob's mom's house and decided that this would be the spot to catch a train. Trains come through here headed to Chattanooga, Atlanta, Louisville, East St. Louis. They do not go to North Carolina, which is where we want to go, but we figure that the first step in getting to our destination is just getting out of Ohio. After that, we'll figure it out.

We watch the trainyard come alive in fits and starts as the afternoon lengthens, and then the activity dies down again and everything is still. Honeysuckle bushes and boughs of half-naked box elder shield us from the tracks. Surely, if we wait long enough, our train will come. We overturn a couple of four-gallon buckets as chairs and play cards in the leaves.

At night while we sleep under the moon, there is a *crunch, crunch, crunch.* A groundhog on his rounds. "Bob," I whisper. "This is the enchanted groundhog forest." In the morning we explore the land: A chain-link fence shapes the northern terminus, and a tall brick wall defines the back. And here, where the forest meets the wall, there are two old cisterns—deep holes lined in brick, filled with dark, leafy water. I follow the wall, kicking up the surface of the leaves, and there I find a steady trail of glass bottles. Old, dirt-caked glass bottles. Brown beer bottles, pale green Pepsi bottles. Bottles engraved with peacocks, bottles with stamped tin caps. Bottles half buried in mud, bottles stuck in the bases of the trees. I fill my arms with the unbroken ones. They were here, I think. They waited for trains. In the thirties, in the forties, in the fifties. Headed to California, to pick peaches. Headed south to work in the coal mines. West for logging work. They were here, waiting, and they left these bottles.

I carry the bottles back to our camp, to our white buckets upended in the leaves. I show them to Bob and he goes to the wall, fills his shirt with bottles too. There's an old fueling station of sorts next to our camp, a pump and some rusted pipes grown into the forest itself, shackled in box elder. Here, we arrange the bottles along a wide flaking pipe that runs horizontal through the branches of cottonwood trees. The sun is dipping on the other end of the trainyard and the light shoots through the forest, setting our bottles of green and brown and amber on fire. Bob retrieves his white paint pen, and on the face of the rusted pipe, in bright cursive, he gives our installation a name: *The Cincinnati Union Terminal Hobo Museum.*

On a mission for water, we climb a fence to a wing of the massive, sprawling train terminal, and there we find a sort of secret garden, a row of cabbages and a brittle tomato plant. And through the glass, a history exhibit: plaster businessmen at broad oak desks. We unscrew the garden hose and fill up our water jugs, pick a few yellow fruits from the wilted tomato plant.

After dark we grow bored, so we play cat and mouse with the yard workers. Walking in and out of the trainyard, climbing ladders on strings of cars, ducking yellow lights. Bob teaches me the things he learned as a boy, from a children's book about sleuthing given to him by an aunt. Duck low when you look around a corner; no one expects to see your head way down there. We pet stray cats, we count the groundhog holes. I'm not sure what time it is when I finally fall asleep, in my bed in the leaves, with the rumble of trains so close to my head. *Are we ever going to get out of this yard?* Maybe, maybe not.

In the morning we leave the patch of woods for a few hours, a sort of field trip. We walk out of the hobo jungle and find ourselves suddenly in Cincinnati—hungry, humid Cincinnati. We find a cluttered brick grocery store and buy ridiculous things: sugar beans, beef stew that smells like cat food. Bob finds a root beer float for two dollars.

All day we wait again, and the trains that come through our yard, that rattle our jungle with their bright lights, are but the dregs of trains; slow, junky trains, trains that crawl through without stopping. Still we wait; surely our train will come. The day passes, each hour laid out plain in the warm October light.

And then, at dusk, a compromise. We have come to accept, at this point, that there is no way for us to know which way our train will go. We have also come to accept that we'll have to ride something other than an intermodal, that fast and trusty beast that goes anywhere you would want to go except, apparently, away from Cincinnati. We let these truths into our hearts, and then climb aboard the next junk train that stops. The train is carrying empty coil cars. "Hot" is written on the sides of the cars. Neither of us has ever seen a coil car before. What is a coil, and from where does it come? And why do the cars say "Hot" when they are, in fact, cool to the touch?

We drop our packs on the floor of the car and lie back against its rusted, sloping floor. The sides are very low, and so we'll only be completely hidden while lying down. Because of this, the views, we know, will be incredible. The train stirs and begins to drag itself forward. It picks up speed. "Goodbye, enchanted groundhog forest!" I scream into the wind.

There is, incredibly, an elevated track in Cincinnati that stretches over the city. And we are being pulled onto this track, now, as though onto a roller coaster. We rattle past the great downtown buildings and over the Ohio River into Kentucky. We trundle slowly through people's backyards, into the forest and finally east, along the river. Night has fallen and the warm wind rushes around us, flinging metal flakes into our hair. Pillars of light rise from the darkness, as though from cities on the river's banks. Steel mills. Coke plants. Coal power plants. Thrumming with life and spewing great mushrooms of exhaust. Hulking. Dystopic. Smooth.

Our train sides in the middle hours of the night, on a residential street in a small Kentucky town. Twenty feet away from us a woman sits on her porch, talking on the phone. Loud music plays from behind her screen door. Neighbors on either side come in and out of their houses, slamming porch doors, the cherries of their cigarettes glowing red in the dark.

In the cool, damp hour before dawn, our train pulls into a massive complex of steel mills. The train starts, stops, jerks. I have been half sleeping, my head bouncing on the cold metal, the wind rushing over my face. Bob has been sitting up, alert to the rolling night. A train passes us, rattling west, coil cars like our own, but these ones are full; long, gleaming cylinders are stacked inside. And they actually are hot. We can feel the warmth radiating from them.

Oh shit. Is our train headed to a place where hot cylinders will be loaded onto our car? We pack up fast and jump down, onto the ballast. "I'm exhausted," I say. Castles of industry are clustered all around us. We walk out of this sprawling place, feeling small and slow, like ants. There are towering concrete mounds. Plumes of dust. Lights.

There isn't a town to be found at this early, empty hour, but there is an intersection with a few fast-food restaurants, and beyond these—what luck!—a sprawling field of wet grass, a bluff of rock, a dirt path. Mist hangs in the air, heavy like cobwebs, as though you could claw it down with your fingers. We spread out our bedrolls behind the bluff, me with my foam pad and Bob with his cardboard, side by side in the grass. A bit of day is weakening the night sky, revealing a creek on one side of us, and trees with yellow leaves. It begins to rain. Softly at first, and then harder. Bob unrolls his camo-print waterproof bivy sack, bought secondhand for cheap on the internet, and scoots down inside. I toss open my tarp and drag it over my bag, then curl into a ball underneath. As the rain falls, I drift in and out of sleep. Puddles form on the tarp, and the seams begin to drip. I wake a few hours later, soaked and angry.

We pack up camp, stuff our sodden things away, all our gear heavy with rainwater. Rubbing our eyes in the gray light, we study our maps and have a realization: There are no trains that go south from here. Trains here only go east or west, along the Ohio River. To and from steel plants. We can wait here until we turn blue in the face, but no train will take us to North Carolina.

We'll have to hitchhike.

April convinces me to go swing dancing with her, at a small church in the part of town where all the sweet corn is grown.

"You'll love it!" she says, smiling wider than any other teenage girl would dare to smile. We're in first period, whispering over the announcements, which are broadcast on a black-and-white television bolted to the wall. I haven't eaten any breakfast, and the Clorox smell of my desk is making me dizzy. I've decided to mostly stop eating, which is turning out to be harder than I thought. At lunch I'll allow myself one Taco Bell bean burrito, and whether or not I can eat dinner depends on how big that burrito makes me feel. I've been getting dELiA*s catalogs in the mail, and although I don't have any money for the clothing therein, I like to use the models as a yardstick for how I myself should look. So far I haven't measured up. As far as I can tell, the dELiA*s models make no shapes inside their clothing at all; it is as though someone laid the clothing on the ground, smoothed it flat, and then photoshopped in the models' heads, hands, and feet. At home I take off my shirt, stand in front of the mirror in my bedroom, and suck in my stomach as hard as I can, but my body still makes a shape. This is unacceptable. I am grotesque. I am the most disgusting person who has ever existed. A failure in the most basic sense of the word.

The blackness tugs at me, and I lay my head down on my desk.

"Did you study for the history test?" whispers April.

"No," I say. I try to remember what we've been studying in history, but I can't.

I've also recently started counting. I count on my fingers, tapping them against my leg. I count lines in the linoleum, panes in the windows, streetlamps that pass the car when Grandma and I drive to Costco. I count seconds. I count calories. I've memorized the calorie content of every single food that I like to eat. I count each food item again and again throughout the day, like beads on a rosary.

Besides counting, I also touch my hair. I have a deep feeling, like an itch, that my hair should be a certain way at all times. The problem with hair, though, is that it shifts constantly, so I have to touch it a lot to make sure it's how I want it to be. I surreptitiously touch my hair several times a minute. It annoys me that touching my hair so much makes it greasy faster, which is ultimately counterproductive to my goal, but still I can't stop. Recently I've begun to grow pubic hair, just a handful of individual hairs, and this itches at my brain as well. Each night I lock the bathroom door, sit on the sink, and dutifully pluck out these hairs. Sometimes they're ingrown, which makes them even more

satisfying to remove. I also pluck out my lower eyelashes. This is
painful but feels incredibly relieving, as though each eyelash is a
foreign object embedded wrongly in my body. I have mild acne
on my upper arms, and I pick at this until my arms are covered
in scars and I can no longer wear tank tops. This picking is the
most euphoric release of all—removing literal wastes from my
body, manually, in small white spurts.

April and I are not like the other kids at our school. The other
kids drive their pickups off-road into the desert for keg parties.
They shoot prairie dogs with high-powered rifles, hoping to see
the elusive "red mist." They smoke meth. The girls iron their
hair and tan at the mall. April and I wear thrift store clothes and
we don't do our makeup very well. We listen to Rob Zombie and
we don't play a single sport. We read a lot of books and write
poetry in our journals. We don't smoke weed, but we hang out
with the kids who do. The kids who wear Korn shirts and know
all the words to Rammstein's "Du Hast." The kids who see Insane Clown Posse every time they tour through Grand Junction,
which is a lot. The kids with wallet chains and JNCOs. I want a
pair of JNCOs so badly, but I don't have the money. After school
we hike into the hills behind April's house and cast spells, pre-
tending to be witches. April shows me her collection of corsets
and elaborate dresses that she wears to Renaissance festivals.
Although she is only fifteen, April has a boyfriend, Jared, who
is twenty-five. She met him at one of these festivals, where he
was playing the part of a knight. Jared has a mullet and wears a
T-shirt with a howling wolf on it.

I keep not caring about my classes, because not caring at all
is less embarrassing than caring a little bit and failing. I'm bright,
so I do well on tests, and because of this I pass most, if not all, of
my classes. I skip class often to sit with the stoners in the field

behind the school. I let a boy finger me in the ditch there, among the wild asparagus. It feels terrible. We walk to the apartment where he lives with his mom and try to have sex, but he can't get hard. We're bored and disinterested in each other, but I guess we're not virgins anymore? Afterward we watch a Doors documentary and his mother microwaves us corn dogs. I carefully eat one single corn dog. That painful feeling of hunger in my stomach is the only thing that I own.

I feel as though I don't know how to be a person. I watch the other kids at school, taking note of their easy way of speaking to each other, their warm smiles. I can copy their mannerisms, and this seems like a useful skill to have. But mostly I keep to myself. Humans are wildly unpredictable, I've decided. I'm not sure when this idea that people can't be trusted became an integral part of my core self. I probe it, following the threads of my thoughts down toward my heart, and find that the idea is so interwoven with my bones, tissues, and organs that the two can't be separated. I grew in a certain soil, and the contents of that soil became a part of me. Barbara's fear became my fear.

At night I lie in the bed that once was my mother's and watch the white curtains move in the moonlight, wondering how I can kill myself so that I don't have to go to school. So that I don't have to hear my grandpa ranting at the dinner table, telling me I'm a fuckup. So that I am no longer pulled, at inopportune moments, into the infinite aloneness that lives inside me. It is a parallel universe to Barbara's universe, in which she is also alone, and I want to be free from it.

Laura's not doing so well in Alaska, either. That skater boy who looked like Kurt Cobain who we thought was so hot in junior high, with his long, greasy bleach-blond hair parted down the middle and his baggy jeans with the wallet chain and his piercing blue eyes? He broke her heart. She'd even taken up smoking.

I miss Laura so much. *I should be with her.* I should be watching the way her blunt dark bob swings across her pale face. I should be holding her hand. We could have eating disorders together. We could become cutters! I would do that, for her.

"You've got to take the sacrament." The bedroom feels small and close and yet too large, too bright. I'm under a hundred blankets but I can't get warm. Am I dreaming? Time has ceased to be linear, the hours of the day irreparably tangled. The curtains over the window billow, and the sun dances on the bed in bright patches. "You've got to take the sacrament." It's Grandma, standing over the bed, holding something in a paper napkin. The Communion wafer, from church. It must be Sunday.

"I can't really eat anything right now." My voice is hoarse. All I've kept down in the last few days is some chicken broth and a few chunks of sugar-free green Jell-O.

"You have to eat this, though," says Grandma. I can smell her breath mint.

"No."

"Yes." Her lips are a tight pink line.

"Fuck off, Grandma!" I roll onto my side and pull the pillow over my head. The bed shifts as she stands, and I hear the door of my bedroom shut. How did she get that Communion wafer? Did she let the priest put it on her tongue, and then take it out and save it for me? Grandma tries every week to get me to go to mass with her, but I hate mass. The boring sermons, the sitting and the standing. Riding in Grandma's Oldsmobile with the Freon smell of the air conditioner. Donuts in the church basement afterward, which I can't even eat.

I know that Grandma is sitting in the kitchen now, at the Formica table, staring at the damp Communion wafer on its white paper napkin. Clutching her hands together. Wondering what to do about the matter of my soul. I don't care, though. I just don't fucking care. Last week she found my birth control, which I'd gotten from Planned Parenthood. I've been sleeping with Tristan, the stoner who lives in the trailer with his hoarder mom, every room full of old magazines and the carpet reeking of cat piss. Tristan smells like socks, and I don't enjoy the sex, but it feels good to be worth something to someone. I'm not stupid, though, and no matter how many times Grandpa tells me that I'm going to end up like my mother, a single mom on welfare, I know that isn't true. I'm not ever fucking getting pregnant. Ever. And if I do by accident, I'll have an abortion *stat*. Because *fuck that shit,* I think. And then Grandma found my birth control— she went through all my things, actually, and found my birth control and my journals of dark poetry about wanting to die— and was more upset about the birth control than any of it, including the fact that I was having sex. Because birth control is abortion, according to the Catholic Church. So now I have the flu and she's sitting at the kitchen table, staring at the Communion wafer, clutching her hands together and trying to figure out how to get me to swallow it. Because of the birth control.

Last week I saw my aunt Pat, the one who was wild as a teenager—her boyfriend had a motorcycle—and who is now a mild-mannered special education teacher and married to a sullen, absent man. Pat told me that growing up, Grandma and

Grandpa's policy was to never say anything positive or encouraging to a child's face.

"They figured that would give the kid a big head." She smiled down at me as she cracked open a can of Diet Coke.

"Oh," I said, not knowing what else to say. *Was that supposed to make me feel better?*

She has the biggest, thickest mane of brown hair I've ever seen (*like a Disney princess*, I think), long gangly limbs, and feet that seem too big for her body. We're standing at the edge of a cornfield in the cool night, the muffled sounds of swing music coming from the small church nearby. My face is flushed and my skin is damp from how hard and clumsily I've been dancing in that warm, crowded room. Her name is Nicole and she smooths her dress, her hands bright against the dark. She pulls a pack of cigarettes from a pocket and shakes one out, offers it to me.

"You smoke?" I say.

"Just a few a day. It's a terrible habit. Nobody knows."

Nicole and I are both sixteen, but she doesn't go to my high school.

"I'm homeschooled," she says, as I swat at the smoke from her cigarette. "You ever just drive around in the desert for hours, for fun?" She tilts her head back toward the church. "I've got a car."

The desert is warm, open, full of strangeness and yet familiar. The night is a balm for my sadness. Nicole's Subaru has a CD player, and she owns two CDs—Bloodhound Gang's *One Fierce Beer Coaster* and Cake's *Fashion Nugget*. She slips *Fashion Nugget* into the stereo and rolls all the windows down, letting in the smell of earth and freshly irrigated fields. Nicole tells me that her father was killed when she was four years old; he was shot during a mass shooting at an Albertson's where he was manager. The life insurance money from her father's death allowed her to buy a house, where she now lives with her mother, Beverly. Beverly dresses like a teenager and drinks too much, and sometimes she loses touch with reality.

Nicole becomes my best friend. We drive in the desert almost every day, letting the open space carry our worries away, singing aloud until we've memorized all the lyrics to Bloodhound Gang's "Fire Water Burn." We travel in either her car or mine, the 1984 Honda Prelude my grandparents are letting me buy in installments. It's 1998, and gas in western Colorado costs eighty-seven cents a gallon. We follow the straight smooth country roads past the stubble of cornfields, soothed by the smell of sun-warped vinyl, Melissa Etheridge songs on the radio. Since finding my birth control, my grandparents have forbidden me from going out in the evenings, so after the house quiets I pop the screen from my bedroom window, climb down onto the grass, and reverse my little car out of the drive, headlights off. When I return after midnight, I shut the car door as quietly as I can and stand looking up at the cold stars, stretched wild and abundant across the desert sky. I listen to the crickets and smell the new alfalfa growth and feel held by the sky, the stars, the earth. Sometimes, when I gently open the kitchen door, I find Grandma and Grandpa sitting at the table in the dark drinking decaffeinated instant coffee. They've waited up for me. I walk past them, through the thick fog of their disappointment, none of us saying a word.

One weekend, Nicole and I drive through the night to Las Vegas, arriving just as the sun is rising. Another day, we go onto the mesa and jump off cliffs into deep red-rock pools of cold, churning water. We take mushrooms and strip off our clothes and draw flowers on each other with colored markers. I bury my face in Nicole's heavy brown hair. April is busy with school— with her AP classes, with the yearbook committee, with all the important things that are setting her up for the rest of her life. She decided years ago that she would study to be a doctor. When I actually attend my classes, I mostly sleep at my desk, and I see April less and less. I stop returning her phone calls asking me to come swim in the pool. I remember how alien I felt, standing in her beautiful kitchen while her loving mother butchered a head of romaine lettuce and they discussed April's future together.

I have two jobs. One of them is bussing tables at a buffet for $5.15 an hour. The buffet serves canned corn, spaghetti, and popcorn shrimp, and teenage girls vomit in the bathroom. It isn't a great job, but my four-hour shifts fly by pretty fast and it's the only place that would hire me when I was fifteen. My other job is running documents to the courthouse for a lawyer whose name is—I kid you not—Dick Gurly. I like driving the documents to and fro for minimum wage, but sometimes I am tasked with making huge stacks of photocopies and the sound of the photocopier going through its machinations for hours on end makes me want to die, so I eat the paralegals' stashes of Dove chocolates and lie on the carpet, staring up at the fluorescent lights.

I think about Barbara often. I still haven't heard from her—no one in the family has. When I left Alaska, Barbara couldn't speak, or hear, or read, or write, or eat, or sleep. What happens to a person like that? Did the police come and force her out of the apartment? Was she taken to an institution? How did she stay alive, in Anchorage, in the winter, when she couldn't even talk?

When I'm rolling silverware at the end of my shift, when I'm driving home from work, when I'm in the shower, I think of her. I wipe the tears from my face and make myself focus on the traffic lights. The water stains on the soup spoons. The smell of my strawberry shampoo.

One Saturday afternoon I'm helping Grandma unload the car after a trip to Costco while she scolds me for not cleaning out the garage and dusting the living room like she asked. It's hot outside and I'm hungry and cranky—I haven't let myself eat anything yet today.

"Don't be such a bitch," I snap at her.

Grandma slaps me.

I punch her in the face.

Just like that. There aren't any thoughts, only instinct, the same one that overtook me that day with Barbara in the hallway. The right lens pops out of Grandma's glasses. She pulls them off, and I can see a small cut on her nose. She looks away, out the window at the stubbly fields. I watch her shrink into someone small, weak, and elderly. My skin crawls in horror. *Dear God.*

I decide to move out of my grandparents' house. I have a boyfriend, a cook in his twenties named Kyle, who works at Outback Steakhouse. I don't love him but he's kind to me and has his own apartment, and since I'm only seventeen and unable to get a place on my own, this feels like an important alliance. My grandparents forbid me to go; shacking up before marriage is a major sin. *Since when have they given a fuck about me, though?* They don't love me, they just love their stupid rules. I miss the hallucinatory, mystical Catholicism of my mother; it's far preferable to this dry, soulless one. I pack my things, my journals and CDs and flared jeans and cardigans, and I go. The next morning, my car is missing from Kyle's apartment; they sent Jordan in the night to take it back. I lived with my grandparents for three years, in their warm quiet house with the smooth wood floors and well-stocked pantry. In this time, I learned that hunger for food was not the only kind of hunger. Hunger for love will starve you in its own time, no matter how much you have to eat.

I still have the job running documents for the lawyer, but now it seems like I'll lose it, on account of not having a vehicle. One of the paralegals, who is kind and pretends not to notice when I eat her stashes of candy, offers me the 1980 Mazda hatchback she had been saving for her teenage son but that he has summarily rejected, and I am so grateful for this act of kindness that I cry. The car, which smells pleasantly of dust and old plastic, has a hole rusted in the floor and the driver's-side door is stuck shut. It billows blue smoke when it starts, and if I take my foot off the gas, the engine dies—so at stoplights I have to put the car in neutral and rev it, with one foot on the brake and one foot on the gas, until the light turns green again. But it goes. *It goes!* The car is manual transmission, which I don't know how to drive, so Kyle teaches me in a parking lot dusted with snow. Within a day I am lurching my way through intersections and stalling in awkward places.

I move on from the second job at the buffet to Denny's, where I work graveyard shifts, pouring milkshakes and serving Moons Over My Hammy sandwiches to the drunks, goths, and gays as fast as I can until four A.M., at which time the restaurant empties and there is a pause in the bustle of human life. Then, for an hour, it's only me in my apron restocking the ranch dressing and scouring the coffeepots and the cook banging around in the kitchen, and then the elderly folks in their perfectly neat clothing and coifed white hair climb onto the stools at the counter for their toast and single egg. My shift ends at seven A.M., when the desert is a soft pink. I throw my mustard-stained apron that stinks of fryer grease into the backseat of the Mazda and smoke my way out of the parking lot, into a world that has made itself new again, somehow.

By midwinter of my senior year of high school, I've missed so many classes that, the school counselor warns me, I might not graduate. I'd been flirting with failure but the knowledge that it might actually happen lights a fire under me, and I manage to pull my shit together for the last few months, dragging myself daily to the hell place that I hate, and after all is said and done I do graduate—with a 2.8 GPA. No one in my family comes to the graduation ceremony, although April's mom is there, cheering for both of us. April graduates at the top of her class; she got into the college of her choice. I tested in the ninetieth percentile on my SATs, so in spite of my bad grades, I am awarded a partial scholarship to the local state college. I don't really want to go to college—I hate school, I always have, and I'm not sure what I would even study if I did go—but I take the packet of financial aid information home to my boyfriend's one-bedroom apartment and look it over on the couch, trying to understand it, with a bag of Doritos open on the coffee table in front of me. A familiar wave of shame washes over me as I attempt to navigate another grown-up thing without an adult to help. As far as I can tell from the packet, I can apply for financial aid for the half of college tuition that my scholarship doesn't cover, but I'll need my grandparents' tax information to do so, as they are still my legal guardians.

I could be the first person in my family to go to college. Why not?

"No," says Grandma. We're standing in her kitchen with its spotless linoleum and shining Formica, its cracked vinyl chairs

and wooden bread box, its dish towel folded neatly over the faucet. She's scrubbing a spot on the stove.

"College ruins women," says Grandpa. He's sitting at the
table with the funnies section of the Sunday paper on his lap,
drinking instant coffee.

"You won't fill out these forms?" I hold up the packet.

"No!" spits Grandma. Her face is red from the effort of scrubbing.

I look at the yellow ceramic cookie jar on top of the fridge. I
try to remember when I was too short to reach that jar. I try to
remember those months I lived here as a little kid, when
Grandma bought me ruffled white socks and taught me to brush
my teeth. She'd stand me on a stool and wash my hair in the
kitchen sink. I try to remember the careful feeling of her hands
in my hair, working the suds around, dodging tangles.

There are other memories too—eating a ripe peach for the
first time in my life the summer after they adopted me, off
the tree in the yard. Tearing the fruit open—bigger than my
fist and warm from the sun—picking out the live earwigs, juice
running down my arm as I swallowed what tasted like the sun,
only sweeter. Grandma teaching me to make my bed. "You
should make it every day!" she said, snapping the sheets taut—
a movement I at first resented but later learned to appreciate—
smoothing the starburst quilt just so, making a place for the
sun to gather. The crickets at night through my open bedroom
window, hollering in the fields. The slate cat, Ms. Kitty, who
Grandma and Grandpa had fed since she appeared one day
from nowhere, but who wasn't allowed to come in the house. I'd
sit on the back stoop in the sun with Ms. Kitty, listening to her
raspy meow and watching the sheets on the clothesline move
in the still afternoon. Canning tomatoes from the garden with

Grandma, dozens and dozens of quarts of tomatoes. Lifting the mason jars from their steaming water bath and arranging them on clean dish towels, hearing the lids *ping* shut as they cooled. Grandma teaching me to peel a clove of garlic—"You smash it first, under the flat part of a knife, and then the skin comes off easy."

I wait for Grandma to speak again but she's turned away from me, working the stovetop with a piece of steel wool. I can't see the spot she's scrubbing; the stove looks clean to me. Grandpa shakes the paper and grunts, flips to the next page in the funnies section. I shut the kitchen door softly as I leave.

Bob and I are huddled in a plastic booth in McDonald's. Tiny elderly people file past us, clutching red trays of breakfast sandwiches. A smell of hash browns and acidic coffee fills the air. I am stiff and cold inside my wet clothes, and I hunch over my hand of gin rummy, the cards damp in my fingers. We want to hitchhike but we can't, not until the rain stops. So for now we're stuck in this McDonald's in eastern Kentucky.

The rain does stop, though. We walk the broad pavement, which hardly seems to move for us. The rushing car-wind hurts my eyes. It takes us a hundred years to summit a low hill, another hundred years to extract a bit of cardboard from the sterile landscape. How, I wonder, will we ever get anywhere significant without our good friend, Train? Train is a steadfast, forward-moving, down-the-tracks sort of friend. What else is there?

A man in a little red sedan picks us up. He's headed five

miles down the road. He pronounces "Ironton" "Arnton," which sounds like music. "Let me take you to Huntington," he says. "There are free bus tickets there. Just tell 'em I sent you."

He drops us in the crumbling downtown of Huntington, Kentucky, where the only people around are strange, with empty eyes. We say, "Free bus tickets?" but no one has any idea what we're talking about. We plod the streets. Our packs, it seems, have grown at least twenty-five pounds heavier.

A bus circles the town, and eventually leaves us at a laundromat. We dry our wet, stinking sleeping bags. I buy a candy bar from a vending machine, but it gets stuck. I shake the machine while staring at the sticker that says, DON'T SHAKE THE MACHINE. I keep an eye on the proprietor, who is pacing the front-loading washers, nodding his head.

An angel appears a few blocks from the laundromat. A man across the road, screaming at us. *"Do you guys need a ride to the highway?"*

The man has clear blue eyes and crooked teeth. As we speed away from the curb, he tells us that he's a drug addiction and mental health counselor.

"Where do y'all sleep at night?" he asks us.

"We camp," says Bob. "In the trees."

"Ah," he says, nodding.

He ferries us to the highway in his flaking ship of cat hair, the heater turned to maximum. The distance to the highway is several unfathomable miles. An ocean of concrete. We never would've made it. Gone, is what we would've been. A tarp, blowing in the wind. Caught on a thorny bush. A crushed paper bag.

Our next ride, Thomas, is a giant man in blue coveralls driving a faded pickup truck. He's just gotten off work at the steel mill. He stayed late today, until six o'clock. Usually he's up at four A.M., drives an hour to work, is out at four P.M., and home by five.

"It's good I worked late today," he says, nodding. "I was helping this guy out. I'm the one to help somebody out, if they need it. God meant me to work late also so I could give you two a ride." Thomas talks slow, his voice low, big fingers rubbing together, making a sound like paper rustling.

"You got any kids?" asks Bob.

"Got ten kids. Oldest one thirty-four, youngest fifteen. Got ten grandkids too." He tells us he's been shot, stabbed, and nearly decapitated. He "fried his brains" with drugs and alcohol. Then, fresh out of prison, he found Christ. He was saved. Now he's married to his second wife. He works six days a week at the steel mill. His wife is in grad school, studying to be an addictions and domestic abuse counselor.

"It was God meant for me to pick you two up," he says again. "God, he take care of you. The birds, they don't think, 'How we gonna make it? How we gonna live tomorrow?' The birds, they know God will take care of them. And me picking you up, that's God, taking care of you. Every time a sparrow touches the ground, God know. Ain't anything on this earth that he don't know."

Thomas pulls off into a bright gas station parking lot on the edge of his town, somewhere in Virginia. He has us bow our heads while he says a prayer for us.

"Take care of these two. Watch over them. I don't know how well they already know you, but whatever problems they have, and I know we all have them, right now, you take care of all those problems, whatever they might be. Watch out for these two, they're your image, we're all your image, I know everything on this earth is yours. It's your property, you control it. Send your angels to watch over these two."

Thomas laughs a weary laugh and hugs us goodbye. He'll have to be up at four A.M. tomorrow for work, and it's eight P.M. now. Bob and I stand under the lights of the gas station, watching his truck disappear into the night. Thomas wished for angels to protect us. He prayed over us. But *he* was that angel, I think. *He* was that good luck. The God that he prays to, who takes care of the sparrow—Thomas is that God. He is what makes that God real.

Inside the gas station, Bob buys a slice of pizza and I fill up my water bottle, browse the shelves of food. A man is mopping, and he smiles at us. It feels good to be here in this nowhere town, where everyone will smile at you, no matter how dirty you look. Even late-night gas station clerks. Angels. Bruce Springsteen is playing on the stereo in the back.

Born down in a dead man's town
The first kick I took was when I hit the ground
You end up like a dog that's been beat too much
Till you spend half your life just coverin' up

Across the highway is an old, leaning board fence and beyond that a patch of woods. In the woods we find a graveyard, tombstones peaceful in the low-hanging mist. We spread our bedrolls under a flaming orange sassafras tree and drift off under the clear night sky. I wake up once to pee and hear a coyote howling in the hills. *Am I ever going to have a home?* I wonder, staring up at the boughs of the tree. *Have I ever had a home? Does home even exist? Or is the concept a construct, a thing to aspire to but never reach? Do we search our whole lives but never arrive?* I imagine myself living here forever, under this sassafras tree. *How long until the ghosts catch up to me? Until they crowd around me, shouting away anything wonderful in my world. Until they grab my ankles and attempt to drag me underground, back into the darkness.* I think of Barbara, and then stop myself. *Don't think of Barbara.* But the thoughts return, I cannot fight them. *Where is she? Is she still alive? Does she suffer alone, endlessly, in some dark room thick with cigarette smoke?*

Sometimes the side of the highway is not your friend. There's a bad wind flinging dust at you, highway cones, no shoulder, everyone's speeding anyway. The drivers frown apologetically.

Can't stop. Can't stop. Can't stop.

Bob and I have been standing on the road with our thumbs out for hours. I'm having menstrual cramps and we take turns slouching against the guardrail, letting our eyes go soft. Our cardboard sign says NORTH CAROLINA. This morning we were dropped here by a smiling man in a cluttered pickup.

"Used to go down to North Carolina," he said. "Unloaded lots of bud down there. Pounds and pounds."

When you hitchhike, people tell you their secrets. You exist in a liminal space between what is real and what is not, a sort of leaf come unstuck from an eddy. The driver feels as though talking to you, the hitchhiker, is like stuffing a note into a bottle and tossing it into the sea.

Bob and I play the only hitchhiking game we know—we guess how many cars will pass before one stops and offers us a ride. One hundred, two hundred, three hundred, everyone loses and then your heart is broken. We decide that a car is a capsule of energy, hurtling down the road, and that maybe it's better to be where we are, in the fresh air, where feelings are free to come and go with the wind.

Morning melts into afternoon. We are going to die on this highway shoulder. Morale dries up and blows away, leaving just our barren souls behind. Bad posture, aching backs, tired thumbs. Hunger.

Suddenly there is a car there, stopped in the road.

There are rules and rhythms that govern hitchhiking, just like every other thing. For example, sometimes no one will stop. Other times, a car will stop within minutes. In the first instance, sometimes there's a reason people will not stop, a reason of which you, the hitchhiker, are unaware. A blind corner, maybe, or the shoulder seems sketchy. In this situation, if you have the patience to wait long enough, a second rule applies—someone truly wild will stop.

Andrew drives a sleek silver SUV. He opens the back for us and we stuff our packs inside as cars rush by all around us. Once we're inside the car, he wrenches the steering wheel and we tear back into traffic. He shakes a cigarette from a pack of Marlboros and lights it. He's a Marine, he says, on leave in Indiana. Now he's headed back to North Carolina. Or maybe he's stationed on a base in Indiana, and he's going to North Carolina to see his family. I can't catch all the words, mumbled around the cigarette. He's got a fresh crew cut and a hard, smooth face. He's speeding. A pink scar runs through his eyebrow, breaking it into two slightly uneven pieces. "They sewed me together crooked," he says, pointing to it. He opens a Monster energy drink and pounds it.

"How old are you guys?" asks Andrew, turning back to look at me, swerving toward the median.

"Twenty-four" and "Twenty-five," we say.

I'm only nineteen," he says. "Be twenty in November!" He tosses the empty can from his energy drink into the backseat. We ask him if he's been deployed yet. "No. But I want to be! I might go to Afghanistan in a year." He pokes at the stereo, but it won't turn on. The glass face is cracked. "I forgot," he says, glancing at it.

"I have a brother who's considering the Marines," says Bob. "Would you recommend it?"

Andrew shakes his head. "No, especially if you're like me. I go on leave, I find someone to be with, then I gotta go back. Shit!" He clutches the pocket of his polo shirt, swerving into the right-hand lane. "Where's that pink piece of paper? I need that pink piece of paper!" He lifts a stack of CDs and finds it underneath. A small pink slip, bright against the gray dash. Andrew smooths the paper clumsily and stuffs it into the visor above his seat. "I need that slip of paper. That's her phone number, address, everything."

Andrew swivels his whole body to look at me in the backseat.

"So, what do you guys like to do?"

Bob says he likes to garden. I say I like trees.

"I like to hunt," says Andrew, facing the road again. "But not just deer. I like to hunt coyotes."

"Oh," I say. "My brother likes to hunt coyotes too. In Colorado. It sounds pretty hard. How do you hunt them?"

Andrew shrugs. "I bait 'em. With meat. Then I wait. It's easy!"

"You bait them?"

"And I wait for them to start a feeding frenzy. And then I just blow them to pieces. It's not the hunt I like," he says, watching my face in the rearview mirror, grinning. "It's the slaughter. I've got an anger problem," he adds, squinting at the road.

"It sounds like it would be fun," I say, "to bait them and then when they show up to eat, to just watch them. I bet it would be fun, to watch coyotes eat."

Andrew holds up his forearm, where a scar snakes from elbow to wrist.

"I tried that once. And then this happened." He shakes his head. "I almost bled to death. Called my dad before I passed out. Would have died."

Right.

"Where did you grow up?" asks Bob.

"On a military base," says Andrew. "Both my parents were Marines."

"Do you have siblings?" I ask.

"Yep, younger ones. I was born with a briefcase in my hand. Never got to have a childhood. Both my parents went to prison when I was a kid, so I had to take care of my siblings. Started my own business when I was fifteen. Graduated high school the next year. Made fifty thousand dollars a year, with my business. Then, because I'm an idiot, I sold my business and joined the Marines." He shrugs. "When I get out in a couple years, I'm going straight to Fort Bragg. I want to train to be in the CIA."

Andrew changes lanes aggressively, throwing me against the wall of the SUV. "What I really want to do, I want to start a family. And I finally found someone, too. Just when I find someone, I have to go back."

"You better make it back from Afghanistan," I say. "If you want to start a family."

Andrew frowns, and then he smiles.

"She's not even old enough yet," he says. "She's only seven-teen!"

"Old enough for what?" I ask. "To have sex? Or to have kids?"

Andrew laughs. "To get married! My fiancée! We want to get married! And the funny part is, her family, they want her to marry me too."

We stop for gas, and then drive on. Andrew, it turns out, is headed straight through Greensboro. We'll make it at last.

Andrew asks us if we're hungry.

"I've got some MREs you could eat." He reaches under the passenger seat and hands us the prepackaged military dinners. I tear one open. Hamburger patty meal. It isn't half bad. I eat the "western beans." There is a tiny bottle of Tabasco hot sauce.

"Cute!" I say. "Look at the little Tabasco!"

"That comes in handy," says Andrew. "Sometimes you gotta drive thirty-six-hour convoys, and you need to stay awake."

So you put it on your dick, I think.

"So you put it on your dick," says Andrew. "That shit burns, but it keeps you awake."

After eating, I crack the window, drowning all sound in the rush of air. I space out, leaning against the glass, until Andrew drops us on the curb in Greensboro. As he pulls away, relief floods over me. Evening has come, and with it, a sort of misting rain. Bob relays a story that Andrew told him while I was spacing out. The story started with "I don't believe in hitting women, but . . ." and ended in the broken car stereo.

"feel so good. I can't believe how good I feel." I'm lying on the carpeted floor of Nicole's guest bedroom, where I've been staying since moving out of Kyle's apartment. Kyle wanted to get married. He bought me a gold bracelet in a white box. He wanted to take me back to Newark, New Jersey, to meet his family. He had a kind smile and smelled of rancid fryer grease and took me to my senior prom, but I didn't love him, and so I had to go. Now I have my blankets and pillows on Nicole's guest bed and my fiber-optic lamp on the nightstand and the lamp makes a small whirring noise as it turns blue, then purple, then blue again.

"Mmm-hmm," says Nicole. She has her head on my shoulder and my arm is around her waist and I am breathing her in. I had my first orgasm a month ago, alone in my car in a dark parking lot, with a vibrator I bought from a tacky sex shop, and this feels kind of like that, only longer.

"Did we buy Gatorade?" I say. "I feel so thirsty. What flavors did we get?"

The walk to the kitchen is a surreal parade of tactile wonders: the cool wall under my fingertips, the soft carpet beneath my bare feet. The rooms of Nicole's house radiate safety. The lighting is soothing and low. The Gatorade—red flavor—tastes like the wettest, sweetest, most refreshing drink that has ever been consumed in the history of all beings, anywhere. I pull Nicole close to me in the kitchen and we kiss, and her lips are the most alive thing my lips have ever touched. I can't believe how long I've wanted this, to kiss her. It doesn't seem strange; doesn't everyone feel this way about their best friend?

We bought the ecstasy in Denver, from a friend of a friend. The drug makes me feel exactly how it sounds, and I am overjoyed by this simple, literal truth as I lie on this deep carpet that Nicole vacuums regularly, in this spotless house that looks as though it has just been built. I have the urge to go upstairs to Nicole's room and open her dresser drawers, touch all the clothing there. To open the curio boxes on her shelves and handle their contents. The walls of the house are hung with Nicole's black-and-white pencil drawings, framed: Her mother, in profile. Her older sister, and the daughter her sister had at sixteen, a toddler now.

Later, we are wearing just our underwear; at some point it became unbearably hot. The night has aged considerably. We are in that indeterminate time now that I know from working graveyard shifts at Denny's, when, for just a moment, the whole world is still. I trace my fingers across Nicole's hips, wishing this strange long night would last forever. The room is full, absolutely full, with the whirring of the fiber-optic lamp.

I wake the next day; *did I sleep, though?* Sitting up, I discover that my blood, brains, and all the soft tissues of my body have been replaced with dry, coarse sand. The world is harsh, the sunlight angry and too bright. I take a shower, repulsed by the acid smell of my own body, and sit in the tub, watching the water swirl around me. The sound of the water is like faraway, mumbling voices. I try to recall the flood of feeling last night, the goodness of embodiment. I can't. *Did I eat yesterday?* The thought of food brings a wave of nausea. I stare at my belly, legs, and feet. How is it possible for a physical form to contain so much ugliness?

"We should make out sometime . . . when we're not on drugs," I say. It's four A.M., and Nicole and I are in her parked Subaru in front of the donut shop, pulling still-warm glazed twists from a waxed paper bag. This is one of our special dates, getting up early and buying donuts—they're forty cents each—from the donut shop the minute they open. Nicole turns to face the window, avoiding my eyes. We've been taking ecstasy every weekend. I work at Applebee's now, where I average ten dollars an hour after tips, and that feels like more money than I can possibly find ways to spend. Once, when we had a thousand dollars between us, we drove to Denver on the icy highway over the Rocky Mountains and spent it all on ecstasy, which is cheaper to buy in bulk. We use the drugs to have parties at Nicole's house, with all of the "friends" we suddenly have—snowboarder bros who work as lift operators in Vail and promise to pay us for the drugs but rarely do.

"Seriously, though," I say. "Don't you want to? Make out, I mean?" Nicole frowns and starts the car.

"Are you done with your donut?" she says. "Let's get out of here."

I am eighteen when I fall in love with Chris. There is the love I have for Nicole; my longing to touch the broad plain of her stomach, my obsession with her hair, her brown eyes, the angles of her elbows, her melancholy frowning, her shy laugh, my need to comfort her, the way I ache when she is sad. I dream that she tells me all her secrets, that I get to sleep holding her in her perfectly made bed.

And there is the love I have for Chris. This love is different, because Chris loves me back.

I've been living in a rented room in a house with a couple of nice twenty-something dudes who work as line cooks and spend their evenings drinking Mountain Dew and playing Dungeons & Dragons. The carpet is dirty; the shades are always drawn; the furnishings are one loveseat and five cardboard cutouts of *Star Wars* characters. None of us knows how to cook. Besides my shift meal at Applebee's, I eat mostly peanut butter sandwiches. Chris was a friend of these gentle nerds, and one day he showed up after his shift at the Home Depot carrying a case of Budweiser and a fistful of pop-punk CDs. He was wearing a white T-shirt, jeans, and work boots, and his eyes were the color of ice. His ears stuck out and the words STAY GOLD were tattooed on his right arm. His Honda Acura with its stick-on racing stripes and loud muffler was parked at the curb. Before long I knew the sound of that muffler by heart.

Chris is kind and eccentric and has just a bit of a country way of talking. He says "I seen" instead of "I saw," as in "I seen a coyote crossing the road on the way to work this morning." He listens to Bad Religion and Anti-Flag and rides a dirt bike in the desert, flying fast over hills, flinging red dust. Now and then he crashes the bike and dislocates a shoulder or bloodies his face. Sometimes he wears a cowboy hat, and eventually he'll trade his Acura for a shining white pickup truck.

I try to learn to skateboard to impress Chris. At the skate park I watch him do ollies with his shirt off, body flexing as he reaches the top of the ramp, jumps, spins the board under his feet, and drops back down. But I am too scared of the ramp, the board, the feeling of falling, of everything. I can skate on flat pavement and turn around; sometimes I can go down a bit of a slope. But that's it. After the skate park, we always go through the McDonald's drive-through. What we eat together consists almost entirely of fast food; I still have my eating disorder and so I obsessively count and recount every little thing that I eat, drink gallons of Diet Coke, am painfully hungry almost all of the time. At McDonald's, I order one hamburger with the dusty hole on the bottom of the bun and the melting slice of cheese and eat it slowly. I'm tired a lot, never exercise, can barely walk uphill, and seem to be always fighting a cold. But I am thin. So, so thin. Chris thinks I am naturally this way. He thinks I'm perfect and that the way I look is the way all women should look. I love Chris. He loves me back, and it feels like starving myself is a sure way to guarantee a continuation of his love. The way my body doesn't fill out my clothes makes me feel safe. *Safe safe safe.*

Chris and I drive to Denver for punk shows, eat pizza, sleep in the back of his truck. We listen to the Bouncing Souls. *I'm a hopeless romantic / You're just hopeless.* He takes me fishing and hiking in the bright, scrubby desert. We drive to Glenwood Springs and eat mushrooms in the hot springs—not at the developed resort, but at the place where the extra hot water is diverted into the Colorado River by way of a huge, busted concrete pipe. Hippies have built pools here using river rocks, and while we soak, the mushrooms work in me until the sky splits and the stars fall and the boulders in the river are singing me songs. I get bad tattoos to impress Chris, and I rip his entire music collection onto shiny blank compact discs. In the afternoons, I put on my apron and join the other servers at Applebee's, the young mothers who chew gum and wear tiny silver cross earrings and unilaterally dislike me. I am in love and yet I am desperately unhappy, here in this desert town that time forgot, so much so that I feel like I might break.

Chris tells me I am wild.

"You're wild, Jenni," he says, putting his hands up like hooves and neighing like a pony. "Wild Jenni. You're gonna leave me someday."

After not seeing Jordan for months, I visit him at the apartment he's moved into, which he shares with three friends. The lamps have no shades on them, and the only thing in the fridge is milk. Jordan's handgun sits on the kitchen table, next to a crack pipe. His truck is parked outside.

"The pipe is Dustin's," says Jordan. He smells like Old Spice and his hair is wet from the shower. I've brought Taco Bell, and I set the paper bag on the kitchen table. "I enlisted in the Marines," Jordan says. "I leave for basic training in a week."

His words swirl in my head.

"Oh," I say. "Okay. Really?"

On the drive home from Jordan's apartment, I remember the way he would parade my Barbie dolls around when we were children, making them talk in funny voices. His freckled cheeks when he was little, the absurd length of his eyelashes. We both had such long eyelashes when we were kids. The thrill of depressing the hairspray nozzle while he held the lighter, the *whoosh* of flame that charred the living room carpet. The way he would stand up to Barbara, fight back when she went after him with the belt, the plastic rod from the window blinds, whatever she could find. Jordan holding my hand as we walked through snow flurries to the bakery thrift store, watching him climb up onto the dumpster and throw back the lid, rip open trash bags, the warm smell of bread. "You can always find food here."

In our dark apartment in Alaska, stomach pinched and empty, I would watch Jordan eyeing our mom as she paced, her words rapid-fire, nonsensical, syntax collapsing in on itself, her eyes far away. I'd watch Jordan watching her and tell myself, *This is real, because Jordan sees it too. This is really our life.* Walking the streets of Anchorage, my scarf wrapped seven times around my face against the bite of the wind, I'd look into the eyes of strangers and tingles of shame would run up my spine, down my arms to the tips of my fingers. *Nobody knows.* But Jordan knew. I rocked alone on the bathroom floor after one of Barbara's violent rages, my mind full of static. *Nobody knows.*

Jordan knew.

When I arrived in Colorado after our year apart, Jordan was agitated, strange, hostile. I didn't recognize him.

"You're weird," he said to me once, when we were eating lunch at Applebee's after my shift. His voice was controlled but I could hear the disgust, and the fear. "Being weird is not okay. You should be medicated." It was the same disgust and fear I saw on my grandparents' faces, when they looked out at the larger world. The face they made at anything they didn't understand. The face they made at me. It was a look that made me want to curl up inside myself until I was so small I ceased to exist. I left the restaurant without finishing my mozzarella sticks.

A few months after my brother leaves for boot camp, two planes fly into the World Trade Center in New York City and the war machine rumbles to life.

War is incredibly dangerous.

There is a plane of existence on which Jordan and I are the only living beings. We are the two bearers of an experience so heavy it cripples me.

Don't leave me alone, I whisper as I watch the news coverage in the weeks after the attack on the twin towers. *Please don't leave me alone.*

They say that if you want to move away from Grand Junction, you have to fill a jar with dirt and take it with you, or else you'll be sucked back and you'll never fully escape. I drive past the faded strip malls and the "Faces of Meth" billboards on the way to my job at Applebee's, where my coworkers talk about church and their young children's birthday parties. There's a big world beyond these sun-crumbled mesas, I know. What is in this world? Are there places with less sadness and heartbreak? Or is it the same amount of sadness and heartbreak everywhere that you go? After work I park my car on the side of the highway and walk into the desert. I fill a pickle jar with sandy, loose soil and stash it in my trunk. I've been saving my tip money for a year, and I think about that money when I wake in the quiet hours of the night and the blackness unfurls around me, threatens to pull me under. My head fills with images of my mother, alone in Alaska, of my brother in his barracks, curled under a wool blanket. I count the bills in my head like rosary beads.

"Maybe we should move away together," I say to Chris over pancakes at the Village Inn on my day off. His mouth scrunches up and he pulls his baseball cap low over his face. I start to laugh, and then stop myself when I realize that he's crying. Chris doesn't travel at all—he was born in the high desert and wants to live here until he dies. Later on in life, I'll think of Ennis's line in the movie *Brokeback Mountain*, when Jack asks him to run away with him to Wyoming, where they can start a ranch together. Ennis declines, saying, "You know me. 'Bout all the travelin' I ever done is goin' around the coffeepot, lookin' for the handle."

I have two cousins who are brothers, the children of my mom's sister Patty. Nathan and Jason are three and five years older than me, real adults in their early twenties, and I've met them only in passing, when they were in town for holidays. Nathan has dreadlocks, loves beautiful women, snowboarding, and psychedelics. Jason is tall, spectacled, thoughtful, and teaching himself to write code. Nathan recently moved to Portland, Oregon, and Jason is planning on joining him there in the fall. I've never been to Oregon, but it sounds nice; forests and green things and rain. Like Alaska, but not so lonely and not way up in the middle of nowhere. I ask Jason if I can make the drive with him. He agrees, and Nathan offers me space on his couch when we arrive. I pack everything I own into my small car and one morning Jason and I set out, the red mesas receding in the car mirrors, *Fashion Nugget* on the CD player.

It is November of 2001, and I am nineteen years old.

t's so green. I'm standing in a city park in the fog, wearing several pounds of thrift store wool, as the dew on the grass soaks through the thin fabric of my shoes. The wide trunks of Douglas fir trees hulk around me in the mist, their boughs suspended in the cold white. These trees are hundreds of years old, I've learned. They are the tallest trees I've ever seen. I take a deep breath and draw the wet air into my lungs. I breathe again, trying to tug the air all the way into my heart. Moving to this dim sodden corner of Oregon called Portland, with its coniferous forests, damp wooden buildings, and air so close to the sea that it never quite dries out, has felt like coming home.

The drive from Grand Junction, Colorado, across Utah, into Idaho, and finally Oregon—first high plains dusted with snow and then the wet Columbia Gorge and, finally, rainy Portland—took us eighteen hours. My cousin Jason, a worldly twenty-four-year-old, perched his wire-rim glasses on his sharp nose and leaned forward to squint at the road, which was often icy, his pale hands wrapped tightly around the wheel. I was too high to drive; we'd both taken Adderall, which I'd never tried before, and once the drug overcame me I resigned myself to the passenger seat, clenching and unclenching my jaw as we drove through the night, my thoughts racing as Jason recounted to me the entire premise, chapter by chapter, of Howard Zinn's *A People's History of the United States*.

"Our government can't be, like, bad, though," I said, as dark, unknown open spaces wheeled themselves past the warm crowded capsule of our little car. Silhouettes of landforms approached us and receded, and out beyond everything there were stars, impossibly bright. Although I knew that things were bad in the world, I'd never thought to question the systems and institutions that made up the scaffolding of our society. I'd never heard that idea spoken out loud, that our government could have anything but our best interests in mind, had never known anyone who believed it. Or if the idea had been floating around, I hadn't been paying attention; I'd never given it any thought.

Jason replied by recounting the careful, systematic process of genocide and colonization on which the "United States" was originally founded.

"The generational wealth and power of white Americans is a direct result of the exploitation of indigenous peoples and African slaves, over a few hundred years of American history," he said. "The richest white people didn't get to where they are by hard work. They got there by stealing from others. Meritocracy is a myth. The system is built on oppression. It's a pyramid of oppression. A Ponzi scheme. In order for rich people to exist, there must be many, many poor people, working for such low wages that they are essentially performing slave labor. There is no other way."

The wheels in my Adderall-racked brain were spinning.

"It's called capitalism," continued Jason.

Jason was different from the other men in my family. The men in my family were stocky and muscled, loved driving lifted trucks in the mud and worked the sorts of manual-labor jobs that eventually broke you. Jason was delicate and spoke softly, preferred books to TV, and had been teased by my grandparents and uncles his entire life.

"He'll never have a good job," my grandparents would whisper with my aunts and uncles in the kitchen after church. My grandpa's mouth would turn down in disgust. "He acts like a faggot. He'll never find a wife. All he loves is computers!" They didn't know, though, about the way the world was changing. They didn't know that Jason had more of a chance of making it in this new world than almost anyone.

"But why were Europeans the ones who were able to colonize the U.S.?" I asked. "Why was it so easy for them?"

Jason then explained to me the premise of the book *Guns, Germs, and Steel,* by Jared Diamond. Europeans had access to metal. Because of this, their weapons were more efficient and wreaked more havoc than those of the peoples they were colonizing. The Europeans also had immunity to certain infectious diseases; their presence alone visited a plague on every new shore on which they landed. Also, there was the Anglo-Saxon Protestant idea of Manifest Destiny: an entitlement to and sense of ownership over the land, an insatiable need to extract resources at a rate so reckless it would eventually destroy the land itself, and then the entire earth—but no matter; that's what the Rapture was for. At the very last instant, when the earth had been run into the ground, God would appear; a god who loved only these exploitive white folks and no one else. This god would spirit them away to eternal life in heaven. The earth was just a stopping-over place. It was here to be destroyed. That was its only purpose.

"Wow," I said, as the black night began to purple and the stars dimmed. The sun would be up soon. "I . . . I never thought about that."

We arrived in Portland midday and my cousin Nathan put a Pabst Blue Ribbon in my hand as we stood in the drizzling rain outside his apartment. Nathan told us that his apartment was so damp the landline had stopped working because it had molded, and the clothes and shoes in his closet had also molded. I tried to enjoy my beer, but I had that deeply tired, gritty sensation in my brain. I fell asleep on the couch that night feeling as though I had left one world behind and entered an entirely new one; as though I had traveled through space and time. As though I had experienced a rapture of my own.

The park in which I walk now is so large that, in the very middle of it, I can pretend that I am lost in a forest. Then I am out of it, crossing Powell Boulevard with its swell of traffic, and then into the quiet of the neighborhoods north of Powell, with their peeling Victorian-style houses sitting wet in the rain and small coffee shops with mismatched chairs and the People's Co-op, where Jason, Nathan, and I buy black beans, brown rice, and peanut butter in bulk. Twenty minutes later I arrive at the Bread and Ink Cafe on Hawthorne, where I work as a busser. I hang up my wool layers, now steaming, and tie on a black apron, soon to be marked with flour handprints. Nathan works here too, and he helped me get the job. The Bread and Ink Cafe makes its own challah, bagels, and garlic bialys, and the tables are spread with clean butcher paper. My shifts pass quickly; I compete with myself to see how many glasses and plates I can carry in one trip, and before I know it, the day is done. On slow afternoons I stand behind the server station eating buttered toast, dreaming, and watching the rain fall. I've been reading the book *Evasion*, which is published by an anarchist press called CrimethInc. Jason found the book at a punk house when he was traveling across the country on his bicycle. Originally, *Evasion* was a zine, or more accurately, a stack of xeroxed pages that were re-photocopied and passed from hand to hand. Then it became a book, and now I have a copy. Anarchists, I've learned, think that the system is fucked, the whole lot of it, and that for any real change to happen, the entire system must be dismantled. *Evasion* is the story of a young man who quit his job to squat in a utility closet on a university campus. He eats dumpstered bagels for every meal (forty percent of the food produced in the U.S., he writes, ends up in the trash), and rides freight trains across the country just for the poetry of it, and because it's free and doesn't use any fossil fuel. I've never met someone like this young man, and I hadn't realized that people rode freight trains in this day and age. And I've never thought about eschewing systems entirely, but it makes a lot of sense. If everything is busted, why participate? I know that things are broken. I've seen it. I've seen more than most of the people around me in this fancy restaurant have seen, combined.

Someone got into my car the first week I was in Portland, and everything I still had in there was stolen: my clothes, a box of checks, my fiber-optic lamp. I sold the car for a few hundred dollars and began walking everywhere. On these walks I felt my spirit expand, as though it could fill up the sky. I bought a vintage cruiser bicycle for thirty-five dollars and rode the heavy bike with great effort up hills, my lungs and muscles burning. On the bike I could go much farther than on foot; I could pedal west to the gunmetal river or across the Hawthorne Bridge, with its cars singing on the metal grating. I could ride all the way to downtown! At Nathan's apartment I learned how to cook for the first time in my life, feeding myself burritos from the huge pots of black beans we kept bubbling on the stove. I drank dark coffee that tasted like the earth. My eating disorder began to feel less useful. There are so many things, now, to look at and think about and talk about and do. It's much harder to starve myself when I feel so hungry from all the exercise. And it's hard to remember what I've eaten when there's so much else going on in the world!

One day in January a letter arrives from Jordan. The letter is pencil on lined sheets of notebook paper. The envelope looks as though it's traveled a long way. Basic training is awful, he writes. They are woken in the middle of the night and berated. He is often hungry. He worries about going to war. He's also heard from Barbara—she called our grandparents, and they used caller ID to get her number. He called her on that number, and she answered. Jordan said she spoke clearly for a moment. She told him she loved him and missed him. And then her speech disintegrated and she turned strange and cruel, monologuing about Satan and the demons that possessed Jordan and me. He asked her where she was staying and she hung up the phone.

I read the letter three times, smell the envelope and then fold it, trancelike, and tuck it into my journal. So Barbara is alive. Barbara still exists. Barbara. I go into the bathroom of Nathan's apartment and close the door. No one else is home and the apartment is still, the patter of rain on the window glass the only sound. I sit on the bathroom floor next to the tub and draw my knees to my chest. I rock back and forth as the blackness whooshes out of that very small hole in my heart, the hole that connects me with the Great Dark Nothing, the hole that often overwhelms me. My guts are cold seawater; my head is television static. I am outside of myself, floating alone in space again. I've worried about Barbara since I left Alaska, but hearing nothing from her, as well as my recent move to Portland, has allowed me to distance myself from the darkness; the darkness has receded and occasionally I've been able to pretend that it is gone. It isn't gone, though. It waits. The darkness is a part of me.

Later that afternoon I pull myself up off the bathroom floor and walk to the kitchen, where I numbly put the kettle on to make tea. I have to put Barbara out of my mind. For the first time in my life I have a hold, however tenuous, on another way of being. I am finding good things in the world. Ideas that enchant me. There are moments of possibility. I want to grasp this rope in my two hands and follow it to sturdier ground, until it no longer feels as though I am standing on thin ice that might fracture at any moment. I don't want to be afraid. I don't want to be that little girl, standing on the side of the road in the dark of a winter morning, waiting for the city bus, hoping that the driver will let me on even though I don't have money to pay. The little girl who hasn't eaten for three days. The little girl whose only parent speaks in tongues, when she speaks at all. That little girl who belongs nowhere, and to no one. The one who can't imagine a future, much less how to survive another day.

"I can't go back there," I say to myself, as I pour steaming water into a mason jar of dried nettles. "I can't go back there." I wrap the jar in a dish towel and sit on the couch, clutching it like a hot water bottle. The darkness is in my bloodstream now, has disseminated all through my body. I close my eyes and shake my head, but the feeling remains. I feel like I've been drugged. How long will it take for this terrible intoxication to pass? Days? Jordan wrote Barbara's number in his letter, but I know I won't call her. If this is how it feels to hear that she is alive, what would happen if we spoke? "I can't go back there," I say again.

"'m leaving to hitchhike across the country," I tell my coworker in the spring. We are watching the rain fall. He laughs.

"You are? I'll believe it when I see it."

"I am," I say. I spread butter on a hunk of warm baguette. I've gained twenty pounds since moving to Portland six months ago, but I don't care. I have muscles for the first time in my life. I can ride my heavy cruiser up hills without having to get off and push.

"When I was your age," says the eighty-year-old mother of the restaurant's owner, when she stops by with our freshly laundered tablecloths, "I wanted to be free too." She puts her hand on my shoulder. "I think that's just great."

I buy a discounted external frame backpack at an outdoor gear store, and put things inside until it is full. I make a cardboard sign like the guy in *Evasion*, whose sign said, simply, EAST.

One morning I ride the city bus to the freeway on-ramp and walk partway up it while cars hurtle past. My heart shakes in my chest. I have no idea what I am doing. I don't really feel scared, though. I feel oddly safe. No one can hurt me. I am harder than any motherfucker. I lift my thumb in the air and wait.

With incredible luck, I am picked up by a couple in a VW bus headed all the way to the East Coast. I let out a sigh of relief as I climb into the vehicle and shrug off my heavy pack. Hitchhiking alone as a woman is genuinely dangerous, and lonely besides. I'm glad I won't have to actually use my toughness now. My kind saviors are a younger woman and a much older man, and they say they can take me all the way to DC, which is my vague destination. I know only that there is a large protest planned for DC, and I have never been to a protest. It's a march against the International Monetary Fund and the World Bank. To prepare, I've cut my hair into a long Mohawk. I'm an anarchist now. Capitalism blows. Let's all get free! Now I just need . . . some friends.

Three days later I say goodbye to my hitchhiking ride. They're headed to a Rainbow Gathering, which is another sort of way to be free. While together, we camped under the stars on dirt roads off the highway, the two of them in the van and me on the ground in the army surplus sleeping bag I bought for cheap in Portland. Before drifting off, I gazed up at the Milky Way, my heart stammering, and thought about what a big world it was, and just how little of anything I knew.

The groups that organized the march in DC have set up all sorts of infrastructure, including a website that leads me to a gathering space in an old church, where I am able to sign up for a place to stay, a volunteer shift cooking meals, and which arm of the march I want to join. Do I prefer to march on foot, or would I like to be on a bicycle? If I want to bike, there's a separate sign-up sheet to borrow one. I hold the Sharpie in my hand and hesitate, looking at the paper taped to the walls. I read the names already on the sheet—Milk Crate, Yarrow, Warbler, Spindle. Does no one here go by their real name? I look at the bag of baby carrots in my other hand, which I grabbed from the cardboard box in the corner labeled FREE FOOD.

"Carrot," I write on the sign-up sheet for the bicycle contingent. Carrot is as good a name as any. I wander into the adjacent room, which is crowded with people, and that's when I see her.

The woman is short, with crooked teeth and huge, tangled black hair. She's unpacking a box of zines and arranging them carefully on a table. A man with face tattoos approaches her and they engage in conversation. The woman's hands fly about like wild, angry birds. I walk over to the table and pick up one of the zines. The cover is a beautiful illustration of a freight train, some mountains, trees.

"Did you make this zine?" I ask, after the man is gone.

"Yeah," she says. "My name's Willow. I need to go help prepare lunch." She's looking at her watch. "Do you want a zine? Here, take one." She waves as she hurries out of the room. I turn the zine over. Her email address is on the back, as well as her mailing address: a P.O. box in Charlottesville, Virginia.

The march is permitted, which means that there's a police escort and intersections are closed off so that we can pass through the city without blocking traffic. The day is gentle and warm; I slept last night on the couch of a local politician who volunteered to house protesters, and he also lent me my bike. Breakfast was from Food Not Bombs: tofu scramble and oily potatoes in the park where everyone gathered before beginning the march. Now we're wending our way down a large, empty boulevard, waving signs and clanging our bike bells. I've never been to a protest before, and the energy of all the people around me is flowing through my own body, a current that feels like it could lift me off the ground. I am overcome with wonder. *Look at all of us here!* I can't think of a time when I've felt this alive, when I've been such a part of something so large. Then the bikes ahead of me stop; there's something going on just out of view. I wait, but the march doesn't continue forward. What's going on? The people around me are murmuring, jumping up and down, trying to see. We just arrived at a park, Pershing Park.

Then I can see it—a row of riot police, dressed in intimidating black body armor and helmets. They're carrying assault rifles and they're making their way through the crowd. Soon they've encircled the entire park. They turn and face us and then go completely still, as though they've been turned to stone. Those at the edge of the crowd move toward the riot police in an attempt to pass through, but the riot police just raise their shields and push the marchers back. It appears as though we are now trapped in the park, in this circle of police. But why?

The crowd mutters to itself. Groups have been separated, and those on either side holler back and forth, trying to figure out what's going on. Fear moves through the crowd in waves.

I am sitting on a city bus, resting my head against the window glass. The bus is parked on the street outside Pershing Park. It's been parked here for the last ten hours, since a fleet of these repurposed buses arrived and we were forced into lines, our wrists were zip-tied together, and we were herded aboard—all four hundred or so of us who were in the park. Some buses rumbled away, to who knows where, and some have simply been sitting, like mine. It's dark outside now. The plastic zip ties cut into the skin on my wrists and I rub them against each other, trying to loosen them. The others on the bus—there are about twenty of us in total—are in the same shape as I am—tired, demoralized, hungry, and thirsty. They lean against the windows, and against each other. Some of them doze off and then wake, then doze off again. When I was first loaded onto the bus, I was excited, almost high; *our march has taken a wild turn! What will happen now?* We weren't given any food or water, but I had a bagel and a package of tofu in the pockets of my puffy vest, and I got a lot of laughs from my comrades on the bus when I was trying to open the package of tofu with my wrists zip-tied together, after which we passed the tofu and the bagel around until they were both gone. The hours had dragged on, though, after that, and no additional food and water had been forthcoming. None of us had been allowed to contact anyone on the outside, and no one could tell us how long we would be here, or where we would be taken after. Eventually we all fell silent and just stared out the windows at the empty street, or slept. There's a cop sitting in the driver's seat and if someone hollers at him that they need to pee he'll begrudgingly lead them off the bus to a porta-potty and shut them inside, where they have to figure out how to get their pants down, and then back up, with their wrists zip-tied together.

Sometime in the night there is a squawk of radio and the bus rumbles to life. I feel relief. We're going somewhere. Anywhere is better than this, right?

Rows of gymnastics mats have been arranged on the floor of a school gymnasium. We are herded into this room, instructed to choose a mat, and a third zip tie is added, joining our wrist restraints to one of our ankles. Thus hobbled, we lie in the fetal position while guards pace between the mats, barking questions.

What are our names? What are our addresses? What are our phone numbers? The banks of fluorescent lights on the ceiling of the gymnasium are blinding. Okay. This is worse than the bus.

It is impossible to sleep. I have no idea what time it is. I shut my eyes. Some people are crying and the sound echoes off the walls of the gymnasium, adding to the din.

It's dark outside again when we are finally taken out of the gym; it must be the evening of the next day. We are each given a bologna sandwich in a paper bag that we can attempt to eat with great difficulty. Our ankle zip tie is removed, leaving just our wrists tied, and we are again loaded onto the buses.

We are moved to a cold metal holding cell. I sit on the floor, my back against the wall, and watch the heavy door with its small glass window latticed with wire, waiting for something, anything. There are many other women crowded into this cell with me, all from the protest. Some of them are crying, some are talking quietly. A woman in a long brown skirt is hollering and banging her fists against the door, demanding to speak with someone. She's been yelling for a while, and her voice is hoarse. I'm so hungry, and we still haven't been given any information: where we are, why we are here, how long until we will be released. At least we have a toilet—a steel contraption bolted into the cell—and we can pee whenever we need to.

The door wrenches open, and two guards grab the woman who was pounding on the door. They drag her into the hallway by her hair. She screams and then the door slams shut, muffling her sounds. I close my eyes. All the fun and excitement of this wild turn of events has worn off. Now I just feel terrible and very, very trapped. Being in a holding cell makes me think of my mother. Is this where Barbara has always been? In a cell, alone?

Hidden from the rest of the world? With no idea how she got there, or what she did to deserve it?

A few hours later I am standing in the sunshine, weak with hunger and relief. I've just been released. People were called out of the cell one by one, until it was just me and two others. Finally the guards came for me and I was led through a network of cold cinderblock hallways and heavy locking doors to a foyer and a glass door bright with sunlight and then out, into the open air. And now I am free.

Why am I free? I think, as I stand blinking in the light, looking at the way the trees move in the afternoon breeze. *What have I done to deserve to be free?*

The community center is still open; there are still boxes of dumpstered food lined up against the walls. I fill a grocery sack with sprouted bread, hummus, juice that may or may not have gone bad. A huge sheet of butcher paper is tacked to the wall: a rideshare list.

Carrot, I write, in black Sharpie. *Looking for a ride to Charlottesville, Virginia.*

Willow lives in an ancient house at the top of a long hill. The house is three stories and she shares it with five other people. There is a peeling porch with a couch on it, and bikes are stacked in the hallway. In the kitchen is another couch, and Christmas lights are tacked in the corners. Flyers from shows, protests, and gatherings paper the walls. A huge pot of soup is bubbling on the stove, steam rising into the humid air.

Willow is pulling everything out of my backpack and tossing it onto the kitchen floor. "You don't need this," she says, looking at my full-size hairbrush. "How many pairs of pants did you bring?" I don't really know what's in that backpack. I just packed it until it was . . . full. Willow shows me the backpack she uses when she travels. It's a daypack. All of her things are rolled neatly, and everything fits together like pieces of a puzzle.

"I ride freight trains with this," says Willow. "And hitchhike. When your backpack is this small, it's easier to move around. And you don't look as sketchy. You can get away with a lot." Willow tells me stories as she tosses aside my sewing kit, my extra pair of shoes, two paperback books. She spent the summer riding freight trains across the country until her Carhartts were shiny with grease and stank of diesel exhaust. She navigated massive inner-city trainyards and ran from rail cops. Willow doesn't have a job, and she spends her time making art and zines, organizing protests, reading dense political theory, fixing and building bikes, and sourcing discarded food. Sometimes she works the beet harvest in Minnesota in the fall, feeding sugar beets into giant machinery in the bitter cold for six weeks at a time for minimum wage. Between that, dumpstered food, and her low rent in this small town, she is able to get by.

"But what about everything else?" I say. "What about the food you can't dumpster—olive oil, almond butter, honey . . ." I touch the jars on the kitchen shelves. "How do you live?"

"Shoplifting," says Willow. She's absentmindedly folding my extra T-shirts for me, pressing them flat. "There's a way to shoplift everything."

Willow and I push the cart through the aisles of the upscale grocery store on the other end of Charlottesville. Jars of olives, fancy cheese, small cartons of berries. Tofu. Three containers of hummus. Fresh apple juice. Bell peppers and spinach. A pie. It all goes into the cart. This morning Willow traded her ripped jeans and pit-stained, sun-faded tank top for a clean pink T-shirt and slacks, and her wild hair is bundled into a neat ponytail. I'm wearing a long-sleeve shirt to cover my tattoos. We're in the toilet paper aisle, which is a relatively quiet aisle, and as soon as the man loitering over the baby wipes makes his selection and disappears around the corner Willow explodes into action: her messenger bag whips around to the front side of her body, the flap comes up (the Velcro is covered with duct tape so that it doesn't make a ripping noise), and the things in the cart begin to fly into the bag. I stand at the end of the aisle, idly fingering the paper plates. A woman with a basket approaches.

"Hey, Willow," I say casually, as if I am about to ask her which paper plates she wants. The flap on Willow's messenger bag closes and the bag swings around to her back. A serene expression settles on her face. She contemplates the price of a jumbo pack of recycled toilet paper.

"You know what?" I say. "I think I left my wallet in the car. Let's leave the cart here and go get it."

We approach the sliding glass doors at the front of the store. There had been a small rectangular magnetic tag stuck to the bottle of vitamins I wanted, and I had pulled it off while we were shopping, holding the bottle in my hand and picking stealthily at the tag with my fingers until it transferred to my palm. I had then lifted a box of pancake mix and attached the tag to the box, replacing the box on the shelf afterward. The alarm towers stay silent as we make our way through the sliding front doors and out into the bright sunshine, and I let out the breath I've been holding. In the parking lot, everything is still and calm. We force ourselves to walk slowly. Normal. Casual. We reach our bikes where they are chained to a stop sign at the corner, and I fumble with the lock. I drop my keys and have to bend over to pick them up from the ground. This store has a no-chase policy, which means that even if we set off the sensors or they suspect us of shoplifting, no one will run us down. We know this because Willow found an online forum where professional shoplifters share all the information they've gleaned in their research. The employees might yell at us, ask us to come back inside, or ask to search our bags. But we can just say no, and keep walking. We're safe.

On the bike ride to the shopping center this morning, Willow explained the other rules she lives by: She only steals from large chain stores, never from independent businesses. The larger the chain, the better. This is called "victimless crime." We aren't stealing the jar of almond butter; we're "liberating" it. I am exhilarated as I finally fumble the key into the bike lock and free our bikes. We pedal out of the parking lot, into the warm sunny street. The stores with their prices no longer have any power over me. I'm rich!

A few days later, on a busy Saturday, we return to the same store. We fill an empty cart with everything that catches our fancy, everything we can think to eat. And then we simply push the cart out of the store.

"People only see what they're expecting to see," says Willow. "It's the same with freight trains. Part of it is white privilege. You can be right in front of someone, breaking the law, but if you're white, and a woman, and you look clean and like you have money, they won't see you. They just won't see you."

In order to look clean and like she has money on our shoplifting trips, Willow needs specific clothes. She steals these clothes from the mall.

"Just take a whole armload of stuff into the dressing room," she tells me, as we lock our bikes outside yet another huge shopping center. I'm sweaty from the ride, and already looking forward to the burritos we'll eat after. "But only in stores where they don't count what you take in." In the dressing room, Willow pulls a multi-tool from her pocket. She shows me the white plastic sensor fixed to the hem of a shirt that she wants. "This sensor isn't an ink tag," she says. "There's no ink inside it. It's just a magnet that sets off the alarms at the store entrance. You can tell the ink tags because they say WARNING, INK TAG! all over them. The ink is meant as a deterrent, so they really want you to know that it's there." Willow works the pliers of the multi-tool around the metal pin that attaches the two sides of the plastic tag, and begins to wiggle the pliers back and forth. A moment later, the pin snaps with a small popping sound. "Always bring something into the dressing room that has pockets, like a pair of pants," she says. "Then, after you break off the tag, put the tag in the pocket of the pants that you don't want, and hang the pants back up on the rack as you leave. But do it in a tidy way, like put the pants back where you found them, so no one will have to mess with them and the tag will stay undiscovered for a while." Willow opens her messenger bag and folds the shirt neatly inside, along with the hanger. Together, the shirt and hanger barely take up any space; Willow's bag looks just as empty as it did on the bike ride. "If you're getting something larger, you can fill out your bag somehow at home, like with a cardboard box. And then you can fold the box flat when you're in the dressing room. That way your bag is the same size when you leave as when you came in."

We eat our post-shoplifting burritos on the floor of Willow's room, which is a kaleidoscope of colors: one yellow wall, one magenta, one blue. She has a futon on the floor, sourced from the curb, rumpled blankets, stacked milk crates for shelving. In the milk crates are hundreds of marker pens in every imaginable color, organized in rainbow order. Stolen, a handful at a time, from craft supply stores. And her drawings, in small piles all over the floor.

"My mother is a painter," says Willow, as she hunches over one of these sketches, her black hair in a huge, messy ponytail, adding a few more intricate lines to a drawing of a tree. "I grew up in New York City." I'm lying on Willow's futon, digesting my burrito and watching her draw. I have never met anyone like Willow. She doesn't make herself small. And she's not afraid to not know something. She asks questions constantly and I can almost *see* her brain working, cranks and wheels turning, weaving it all together. I feel like I can learn everything I need to know secondhand, just from hearing her stories. Here is a person, finally, who can show me a way to *be* in the world.

A week later Willow is packing up her zines; she's leaving for an anarchist book fair in the Northeast. It's time for me to go home, to Portland. I can't just hang around her house forever, trying to absorb her vibes. At night I dream we're on a train; the wind is whipping her hair around, and she's teaching me to read maps. Willow moves her fingers over the black lines in an atlas. *This is how we know where we're going,* she says.

My savings from my restaurant job in Portland are mostly gone and I find a young punk woman, a recent college dropout from Florida passing through Charlottesville, who's down to hitch with me back to the West Coast. After a long wait in the cold, and a couple of rides that take us just a few exits, we are picked up by a pair of truck drivers piloting a rig to Texas. The men chain-smoke and drink Red Bull but are kind, and they hardly speak. My friend and I ride in the dim top bunk, drifting in and out of sleep and listening to bursts of radio chatter and breathing in the stale smoke. Time unspools into a long ribbon of dark highway and after twenty-four hours they drop us at a truck stop in El Paso, Texas, in the care of another pair of truck drivers, who are headed to Oregon.

"These are good guys," our rides say.

Again, we are not harassed. We arrive in Portland a few days later, in the rain.

It's at an anarchist conference in Eugene, Oregon, called Against Patriarchy that I meet Sami. She's taller than me, cheeks rosy from the sun, wearing stained overalls and a shirt that looks like it was dug up from a riverbed. Her hair is wild, like she got in a fight with a pair of scissors. I am too awkward to talk to most people—I don't know how to be cool—and it seems like everyone at the conference was born cool, with their screen-printed band shirts and their knowledge of obscure radical theory and their sardonic senses of humor. I only just learned what anarchism *is*. At the conference my heart shakes and I talk too quickly or forget what I'm saying in the middle of a sentence. I look people in the eye for too long or don't make eye contact at all. I smile too readily, and know nothing about hardcore punk, Paul Zerzan, or bicycle touring. I can't skin roadkill, tune a banjo, or make acorn flour. Mostly I am ignored. Sami talks to me, though. She corners me outside after lunch, lights a cigarette, and tells me about her estranged father in Burbank, California, who works for Disney, her chaotic mother who loves vintage dresses, is a palm reader, and has married seven times.

"I don't really have parents," I say. "My mom is homeless in Alaska, and I don't know my father. I lived with my grandparents for three years in high school, but we don't speak anymore."

"I'm sorry," says Sami. She stubs out her cigarette and takes my hand. "Here, let me read your palm. My mom taught me how when I was a kid." She carefully studies the lines etched in my skin. "This says you're going to be all right." She squeezes my hand. "Let's be friends."

And so I have a friend. Together, Sami and I attend workshops on female ejaculation and zine making and eat expired tofu sandwiches provided by Food Not Bombs.

"There's a room open in the house I live at, in Portland," says Sami, at the end of the second day. "The front yard has this giant elm tree. You should totally move in!"

The Wych Elm house is on a narrow street of moldering craftsmans, boarded-up storefronts, and warehouses. There are only two bedrooms in the house, so the nine people living there have made space for themselves in creative ways: Wej, who is studying to be an environmental lawyer, lives on a ledge he built under the stairs that's just big enough for a futon mattress and a stereo but not tall enough to sit up in; Abe, who spends the days teaching himself Madeline Adams songs on the guitar, has used a curtain to section off a corner of the dirt-floored basement whose brick walls are always weeping moisture; Lisa shares the loft above the dilapidated wooden garage with a number of spiders. A camper van doesn't run but, parked next to the garage, provides another living space, and Nico, one warm summer, builds a shack in the backyard from scrap wood. Rose and her four-year-old daughter, Yosha, live in the attic, in which they've installed a woodstove, and I take the office-turned-bedroom off the small living room. Sami has the other room, which opens onto the single bathroom in the house—the bathroom that, in my year of residence at the Wych Elm, is never once cleaned. Since I have an actual bedroom, twice the size of my stained futon, which I found in the street, I pay the highest rent—two hundred and fifty dollars a month. In the living room is a couch on which visitors often sleep, their train-dirtied packs propped against the wall. There is a record player in the living room, and Against Me!'s *Acoustic EP* often spins on repeat, or Neutral Milk Hotel's *In the Aeroplane over the Sea*.

Exchanging labor for capital is not something that we, the residents of the Wych Elm, have much interest in; we jealously guard our labor, choosing to squander it on our own projects—zines on DIY abortions; elaborate shadow puppet plays on the history of the North American Free Trade Agreement; bicycles built from salvaged parts; gathering tea from the tea dumpster that smells of bergamot and rose, and hummus, fizzy with fermentation, from the hummus dumpster; wild travels south on freight trains to escape the winter rains. Because of this, of course, we have little money. When we need money, we work in manic spurts, going to North Dakota for the sugar beet harvest, or to southern Oregon in the fall to trim weed. You can offer up your body for drug trials, or pick old clothing by the pound from the Goodwill outlet, model it yourself, and resell it on eBay. You can hawk your dirty underwear online, let a strange man watch you get a pedicure, or wrestle with your friend in a baby pool of Jell-O while this same strange man jerks off. When you have a couple thousand dollars, you quit, because you can; you are young, healthy, and you need very little. You can subsist on day-old bread from the trash and boiled pinto beans. Life is breathtakingly short, and Western civilization is definitely going to collapse in the next five to eight years. Paid work is a sort of death.

"You can't change the system," says Sami. She's standing at the stove in the Wych Elm house's damp kitchen, stirring tofu in a cast-iron skillet with a wooden spoon. Condensation drips down the windowpanes. We haven't turned on the heat yet this winter—we can't afford it—and cooking lends a modicum of warmth to the drafty space. Sami lifts a jelly jar of curry powder, unscrews the lid, and pours a heaping amount into the skillet. "You can't change the system. It has to be destroyed."

I nod as I dip bagels into a bowl of water and arrange them on a cookie sheet to toast in the oven. This is how you revive stale bagels. A black trash bag of assorted bagels sits on the kitchen floor, in the corner, next to the four-gallon bucket of tahini from the nut butter dumpster in Ashland. At least we think it's tahini. There's no way to know for sure.

The idea of living outside of societal systems and corrupt institutions that serve no one but the rich intoxicates me; it's as though we can imagine a parallel reality to exist alongside the everyday one, invisible to the naked eye. If I try hard enough, maybe I can slip inside this other reality, and live the rest of my life there.

It isn't enough just to live outside of capitalism, though. We have to actively work to overthrow it—or rather help it along on its own inevitable decline. EMPIRES FALL—I saw this phrase on a sticker in Eugene, Oregon, and I think of it often. A week ago I got the phrase tattooed on the inside of my forearm. All that's busted will eventually end, and something new will be born. Right?

We aren't entirely sure how to hurry along the fall of Western civilization, though. Shoplift more? Make banners? Ride our bikes? There aren't any clear answers. But in the meantime we're getting ready as best we can to survive in the world that will come after. Production of goods will end, so we'll need to relearn earth-based skills. In the wooden garage a couple of deer hides salvaged from roadkill hang from the rafters. Next to this is a half-tanned raccoon skin, belonging to God knows who, that has begun to mold. On the bookshelf in the kitchen are yellowed paperbacks on beekeeping, DIY boatbuilding, fermentation. Zines on how to sew a western shirt on a treadle sewing machine, the legalities of squatting on public land, how to weave a pack basket from invasive ivy. No one who lives at the Wych Elm owns a vehicle, and there is only one computer in the house—Wej, who lives under the stairs and who is in law school, has a laptop. It's 2002, and none of us own a cellphone. A white plastic landline sits in the kitchen next to a notebook made of scrap paper and bound with dental floss, in which whoever answers the phone writes down a message for the intended recipient. This plastic landline, smudged with dirty fingerprints, rings often—many people live at the Wych Elm, and even more pass through each week, carrying wax boxes of cabbages and saying they're headed to Fargo on the train, does anyone want to come along? The notebook is scrawled with doodles, love notes, missives from moms, and when the last page is filled it joins the others, lined up on the bookshelf like well-thumbed school yearbooks, and a fresh notebook is made from paper found in the trash. There are always piles of scrap paper around, in the living room and the basement, left over from zine-making projects, screen-printed band flyers, puppet shows. If you have a skill, you're obliged to share it, via zine, hand drawn or pounded out on the typewriter, copied at Kinko's with a stolen key card and then passed along hand to hand on your travels or through the mail.

"Do you think this needs more curry powder?" asks Sami, pausing with her wooden spoon in the air. I look at the bright yellow tofu in the skillet.

"Maybe a little more?" I say. Sami unscrews the glass jar and sprinkles more powder out. I peek in the oven—the bagels are steaming. Perfect. The back door bangs open and a small woman, Madeline, appears. She's wearing a ratted fur coat over a leopard-print bodysuit and stonewashed jeans. Madeline is visiting from Olympia, where she's been attending Evergreen State College. She carries a milk crate of bruised apples, which she hefts onto the kitchen counter with a sigh.

"Let's make apple butter," she says as she picks through the apples, which are wet from the rain. "And pie."

Madeline has been staying in the camper van out back for a week, each day joining the bike posse of unemployed punks who scour the city for free goods, and she is considering staying for-ever. She brought her violin with her, and in the evenings she and a group of folks climb up onto the roof of the warehouse next door and play old-time music well into the night, some-times sleeping, if it's clear, under the stars, on a futon they hauled up. Madeline is from a small town in rural Idaho—she was raised by a single mother who worked as a housekeeper, and they lived in the homes of her mother's employers. Her father, who is from Mexico, died when she was very young. Evergreen State College was her escape, but she's bored with school. What is the point of it, when the world is ending?

.   .   .

A keg of root beer means we're having a party. It's Trish's birth-day. Trish plays the accordion, wears layers and layers of tattered petticoats, and paints murals. The keg of root beer was acquired, rolled in on a dolly, and left in the living room in anticipation of this night. Everyone in our house, and most people we know, are straight edge, meaning we don't drink, smoke, or do any drugs, and so parties consist of sugar in great quantities, games that are similar to charades but with more emphasis on hating cops, and, sometimes, group sex.

This party will be a dance party. The furniture is cleared away and Christmas lights are strung on the walls. There are slices of stale baguettes, some grapes someone found in an alley, and tubs of fizzy hummus. A Cyndi Lauper cassette alternates with a Ma-donna tape throughout the evening, and the walls begin to trickle with moisture as people, packed tight in the small rooms, work themselves into a sugar-fueled frenzy. For some reason, about a dozen people are wearing roller skates. In the backyard is a bon-fire of pallets, with a wax box thrown on now and then to make the flames shoot up, charring the lower boughs of the wych elm tree, which is so large that, although it's in the front yard, its boughs shade most of the backyard as well. People in Carhartts and flannels stand in the flickering shadows of the fire with their mason jars of root beer, sharing train stories, or they run from the house, overheated, and tear their clothes off, releasing their wet skin to the misty night. The familiar refrain of "Black Jack Davey" floats down from the roof of the warehouse; everyone who can pick out a chord on a banjo is up there.

I sit on a milk crate next to the bonfire, listening to people talk about trains. I haven't yet ridden a freight train and the idea fascinates me, makes my heart stir with a longing I can't explain. One woman at the fire, Kirsten, just rode solo from Salt Lake City to Portland. There was snow, but she snuck into the rear engine, with its heat and captain's chairs, to stay warm. When the train stopped to work or change crews, she hid in the unit's tiny bathroom, and she was never caught.

Andrew and Gabriel just returned from an old-time music festival in Idaho, where they caught a boxcar "on the fly," which means jumping onto the train while it's moving. They did this carrying a banjo, a fiddle, and two bikes. And not only was the train moving, it was going over a trestle at the time. Trestles are train bridges, airy frameworks of metal and railroad ties that stretch above rivers and canyons. There isn't usually any place to walk on a trestle, and if you're on one when a train comes you might have to climb up the supports of the trestle to get out of the way.

I want to ride a train so badly, but all I know of freight trains is what I've heard from my new friends. I have no real experience of my own. I can't ride solo without any previous experience—it won't be safe. A few weeks ago I met a young woman who rode a train without knowing what she was doing and lost both her legs below the knee. She'd jumped from a moving boxcar, not understanding how dangerous that was or how to do it safely, and was pulled under the wheels. I try to imagine what it must've been like, in the moments after falling under the train. Was she in pain? Had she felt anything at all?

Maddy, who has face tattoos and whose hair is a mullet that ends in a single long, flat dreadlock, lifts a wax box from a pile and tosses it onto the fire. The flames rise ten feet, and everyone gasps. Maddy announces that he just rode through the longest railroad tunnel in the U.S., on the train heading east out of

Seattle. He was in the tunnel for forty-five minutes, and the exhaust was so thick he could hardly see his hand in front of his face. If the train had stopped, he would've asphyxiated.

Am I tough enough to ride a train? I don't know. Sitting around the fire hearing my friends talk, I feel like I don't know anything at all, like I am an impostor, someone who stumbled into this world but doesn't really belong. I want to see the country like my friends have. I want to sleep in the bushes and run from rail cops, and use my wits to puzzle out the mysteries of trainyards. I don't have experience, but I have desire. Maybe that's a good place to start.

A week ago I talked to Jordan on the phone—he told me that he didn't want to go to war, and so he'd gone AWOL from the Marines. Now he was living in Grand Junction again, working as a trash collector for the city, using a fake name so that the military couldn't find him. He was thinking of turning himself in, though. Six months in military prison and his debt would be paid—he wouldn't have to hide anymore. On the phone, he apologized for the way he treated me when we were teenagers. He'd been an addict, he said, and it had changed his personality, but he was clean now. The military had gotten him clean. He said he respected me; he respected the choices I made, how I wasn't afraid to follow my heart. He said he wanted to be as free as I was, one day.

I cried after that phone call, the catharsis of his words unclenching a part of my heart that I hadn't known had been twisted up. I felt serene afterward, full of a calm, intoxicating certainty. Now, sitting on my milk crate next to the fire, I realize that I *am* free. I don't have to be scared. Or rather, I can go after the things that I want, whether I'm afraid or not.

2007

n Greensboro, I live in a redbrick house on a tree-lined street,
in a small room, likely meant to be a storage room, at one end
of the attic. Willow lives in a room just like mine on the other
end of the attic. Our rooms have sloping wooden ceilings and a
single round window that looks out at the yard. In Willow's
room is a futon on the floor and a desk made from a wooden
door on sawhorses. Willow's desk is cluttered with stolen art
supplies, fistfuls of drawing pens organized neatly in yogurt
tubs. Willow sits on a stool in front of this desk late into the
night, drawing forests, mushrooms, flowering plants. The drawings contain hundreds of fine lines, tiny, impossible, intricate
detail. A headlamp is bundled around Willow's wild black hair
and she wears just a sports bra in the stuffy warmth that gathers
in the attic. Magnetic Fields' 69 *Love Songs* plays on repeat
until dawn. The walls in her room are painted bright primary

colors, even the floor. She repaints them in new colors every three weeks.

In my room I've strung up Christmas lights and built a platform bed from scraps of plywood. I've painted the walls fuchsia and pea-soup green. I have a clamshell Mac computer I bought off Craigslist for eighty dollars. I'm working on the great American novel.

Downstairs lives our friend Helena, the painter. Helena's room is full of light. She has lace curtains that move in the air from the yard. Half-finished paintings are propped against the walls—giant, abstract insects, many of them on fire. The floor is obscured with piles of books and clothing.

Willow, Helena, and I dumpster dive much of our food, and we shoplift what we can't dumpster. Mostly, what we eat is bread and foods that are very similar to bread. Rent is paid with our earnings from participating in medical studies in nearby Durham—the studies last days to weeks, and some of them are sketchier than others. During the studies you live in a windowless room with the other test subjects, and medications not yet FDA approved are pumped into your bloodstream in great quantities. No one knows, yet, what the safe limits for these drugs are. That's what you, the guinea pig, are for. The medical studies are terrible, but they keep us from having to get actual jobs, which would get in the way of our art.

The dumpsters in Greensboro, besides being full of bread, often contain birthday cakes. Sheet cakes in all colors and sizes, with misspelled names, botched drawings, crooked edges. We gather these cakes by the dozen, strapping them to the rear racks on our bikes with spent inner tubes. We ride to the trainyard in the empty hours of the night, wait for the trains to come, then throw these cakes at the trains as they pass. The faster the train, the better. The cakes explode on impact. They are vaporized. *Happy Borthday Charile*. Willow has frosting in her hair for days.

Every Sunday, Willow, Helena, and I meet our other friends at a concrete loading dock to play in an anarchist marching band together. Someone has acquired drums; someone else thought up a new beat for us to play in their dreams. A few of us are brilliant with rhythm, and the rest of us, myself included, struggle to stay on the beat. But the effect is transcendent—for an hour time slips away, and the looping rhythm transforms us. We are not individuals. We have always been, and we will always be, parts of a whole. We call ourselves Cakalak Thunder.

At night I lie in bed and look at the way the glitter in the green paint of my room sparkles in the Christmas lights. I pull my sheets up to my chin. They're 1500 thread count, shoplifted from the mall, the softest sheets I've ever owned. I wait for that loosening of reality that comes before sleep, the tug that pulls me under, but it doesn't come. I've been thinking about Barbara again lately; terrible, invasive thoughts, images I can't drive from my brain. Barbara, alone in a room somewhere. Hungry, cold, scared of everything. Barbara in this room day and night, irrespective of what is happening in the rest of the world. In my mind there are floods, famines, earthquakes, and Barbara is still in this room. I'm eating cold fried chicken in a dumpster or sewing a cycling cap from thrifted fabric while outside a rare snow dusts the dogwood trees, and Barbara is still in this room. The planets spin around the sun, and Barbara is still in this room. Barbara is inside this room that is inside me. The room is in my heart.

One morning I open my computer to find an email from Jordan; he's finished his stint in military prison. He's working as a diesel mechanic, and doing well. His letter reminds me of the one he wrote from basic training, when he said he'd talked to

Barbara. He wrote her number in that letter. I jump up from my desk and pull out my stack of journals, flipping through them. The letter falls out, onto the floor. As I unfold the worn notebook paper, my skin prickles and I feel cold. There's the television static, creeping at the corners of my vision. I stumble down the narrow attic steps and lift the receiver of the landline in the front room. I mash the numbers and wait, the pealing of the phone far away, reverberating too loudly into another, parallel world. There are so many ways to die, when you're homeless and schizophrenic in Alaska in winter. You could set your tent on fire in an attempt to drive out Satan, or you could run full speed at the police. You could die of exposure on the street after drinking too much rum and curling up in a doorway wearing just a trench coat as protection from the cold. If Barbara is still alive, it means that she must've gotten help somehow, at least at one point. She must have been given something, even if it was just enough to keep her head above water. Keep her alive for a little while longer.

And if she is alive, shouldn't I be taking care of her? Aren't I the able-bodied daughter, frittering my life away in a brick house filled with sunlight, eating shoplifted goat cheese and writing stories about riding trains? A wave of shame overwhelms me, eclipsing the static at the corners of my vision. *Who am I, anyway?* I should be studying nursing, learning to code, taking welding classes—anything practical that would afford me a good, steady income. I should be saving up so that I can fly to Alaska and rescue her, take her home to a peaceful bit of land I've acquired in the countryside. Hook her up with the very best doctors that can work out the very best medication cocktail so that she can have the very best quality of life possible.

Barbara answers the phone on the third ring.

"This is your daughter," I say.

"Jenni?" she says.

Bile rises in my stomach. I'm sitting on the floor in the front room, the plastic receiver pressed against my cheek. It's warm in the house but I'm shaking with cold.

"Jenni?" she repeats. I realize, then, that I changed my name to Carrot so that I would never have to hear that word again.

"How are you?" I ask, keeping my voice level.

"I'm fine," she says. Her voice is high, nasal, childlike.

"Where are you living?" I ask.

"Oh, Jenni," she says again. "You should've called. You know you can always call me."

I wrap my free arm around my knees, try to stop the shaking.

"Okay," I say.

"Oh, Jenni," she says. "You've got the devil inside of you. Satan, he lives inside of you. I can see all the monkey demons, above your head. Can you see them there? Oh, Jenni, I should've let you die when you were a baby. I should've let you go with Jesus."

The walls in the living room are starting to breathe. They warp softly in and then out again. I'm eight years old, and Barbara is beating me with a wooden kitchen spoon. Her eyes are empty and dark, her mouth in a grimace. Her black hair is coming loose; wisps of it stick to her sweaty forehead. I'm in bed, and she's whaling on me as hard as she can. Because I had begged her for food again.

"You should've died when you were a baby," she repeats.

I'm wandering the playground at recess, looking for something to eat. I find a Doritos bag and there are chip crumbs in the bottom. The other kids are playing four square and tetherball, swinging on the monkey bars. The crushed Doritos don't quiet the burning in my stomach. Every muscle in my body is tensed toward survival. I crawl into the space under the jungle gym and crouch in the wood chips there, surveying the other children like a feral animal. Where is food, and how do I get it?

I hang up the phone. It rings. I pick it up.

"I should've let you die when you were a baby," she repeats again. "I should've let you go with Jesus. . . ."

I hang up again.

The phone rings again.

"DO NOT CALL THIS NUMBER ANYMORE!" I scream into the phone. I smash the landline into its cradle. I grab my bike and push it out of the house, let the screen door slam. Behind me the phone rings, and rings, and rings.

Winter in Greensboro is gentle and mild, like a dream that never comes. Pussy willows grow along the trash-choked creek. The sky is nothing but sun. Florence arrives one day, in a Dodge Neon that trails plumes of burning oil. She's wearing tights and pineapple earrings and she's cut her hair into a mullet with a razor blade. She's running from her red farmhouse banked in new snow and the memory of a man—he'd been handsome but mean and she'd wanted to make a life together, but then everything had ended.

"This town seems like a nice place," she says. "Is that true?"

We're sitting around a fire in the backyard, wearing corsages made of dumpstered roses. I look at Florence and I remember her in Winona, squatting in the fields in her bathing suit, her freckled hands caked with dirt.

Willow is in New York for the holidays and Florence moves into Willow's room, with its glossy red floor and smell of clove cigarettes. In the mornings, I make us eggs and rice and greens and we play cards while we eat and then go dumpstering in Florence's car. We turn the radio way up, and fight over the stations. We steal from the scrapbook aisle at a huge crafts store and then make crafts in Willow's room while eating sugar cookies. Finally, I collapse from the sugar and lie in a heap on the futon, watching Florence make bracelets from old bicycle tubes.

"Where did you come from?" I ask Florence. She crawls into bed and wraps her freckled arms around me and tells me stories about her cats, her bike, her friends and how they like to drink. Her dad was a truck driver and she inherited her grandfather's farm in Minnesota. The winters are too cold in Winona. The summers burn her skin. When she was a teenager, she was into meth; when she was a kid, she huffed propane. Her friends robbed liquor stores. She and her ex-partner had wanted to get goats.

We hold each other on the hard futon, waiting to fall asleep. And then sleep comes and I forget that Florence is there at all.

After talking to my mother on the phone, I'd decided to try to contact my grandmother on my father's side, the one he told me wasn't interested in knowing me. Because what if he was lying? What if she was waiting for my call, sitting in her dusty parlor in San Francisco? Looking out the window at the pigeons in the street, wishing she had a granddaughter. My father had told me that she had been a writer and an editor during her career. I was a writer too. What if I got these genes from her? Maybe my father didn't want her to know me because he was ashamed of how he hadn't paid child support. In the scorched forest of my heart was a small clearing full of lupine and wild paintbrush that was reserved just for her, this grandmother I had never met.

I found her phone number the same way I found my father's address—on the internet. It was listed publicly. One warm afternoon, I called the number and she answered on the second ring.

"My name is Jennifer Quinn," I said. "I think I'm related to you?"

"We're no longer related," she said, her voice clipped. "Never call this number again."

That night I lay in bed and wondered how much rejection was too much to bear. How much rejection could a single person stand? How much pain could a single person stand? When did the pain end and the healing begin? How long did it take to heal? Was one lifetime long enough to even start, much less complete, the process of healing? Or was the certainty of breaking the only thing in life that we could count on for sure? Were we destined to break, and break, and break, until we died?

Florence and I go to a New Year's Eve party. I don't usually drink, but tonight I make an exception, and by midnight I'm moody from wine.

"Kiss me?" I ask Florence, on the deck. I have to shout above the noise. A light rain is falling. Florence pulls the foil from a bottle of champagne and then kisses me. Her eye shadow is the colors of a sunset.

I ask what her plans are.

"I have no plans," she says. "Not right now."

The ghosts have found me by this time, here in Greensboro; they've been drifting like snow in through the open windows, settling into the corners of my living space. Creeping under the blankets at night, sitting on my chest, getting caught behind my eyelids. They're everywhere, on every surface. No one else can see these ghosts; not even I can see them. I can feel them, though. Everything's off about Greensboro now; nothing is right.

I feel spooked, wary, certain that something terrible is about to happen. If I stay here, the ghosts will crush me with their weight. They'll kill me.

I ask Florence if she'll ride trains with me, from Georgia to Alabama to the Mississippi bayou. Hot yards in Texas; New Mexico like the future and the past, like the surface of the moon. Southern Arizona where there is no winter (and there are oranges on the trees!). All the way to California. The Sunset Route, the same train I rode with Sami to escape the Portland rain. Where we went to jail in Sweetwater and I had pinworms in L.A. The train that carries truck trailers of orange juice from Florida to Los Angeles.

Florence says yes.

We start planning our trip together. We have a huge road atlas and we cover it in pencil marks. We're jumping off into the great wide anything; we'll claw our way across the Southwest on the Tropicana train. We collect the gear we need bit by bit, make lists, stress about this and that. Will it be cold? Probably. How many days will it take? How many gallons of water will we need to haul with us?

Florence has never ridden a freight train before. I draw rectangles along the edge of our atlas.

"See? That," I say, "is a stack train."

We talk about the Rockies in Canada, where the train goes through a spiral tunnel built into the mountain itself. How you can ride down the West Coast with winds like ice, and the great middle part of the country with yellow prairies and weather that hits without a cloud in the sky. It's January, and the world feels electric. I feel electric. It feels like movement is the only thing that can soothe me, like I must burn through space and time as though I've been born with more than I can possibly use.

Why not? I figure. There's no place I'd rather be than inside a freight car. We'll eat up the poetry of the passing desert and know that we've got water and a tarp in case it rains. We'll end up west just in time for crocuses and cherry blossoms and the bright wet end of the rainy season, people's hearts exploding like they've just been brought up from the sea floor.

February comes with a clear winter wind and we're off— heavy packs stuffed with woolen things and a cardboard sign that says GEORGIA, hitchhiking thumbs bright red in the cold, going south to find the Juice Train.

That night we're on a dark road in Georgia, tired and wind-burned. We don't know where we are. We lean against a pine tree on the shoulder of the blacktop and watch the silhouette of an old man against the warm yellow windows of his small house. It gets colder and our sweat chills, and ice chunks slosh in the gallons of water that we carry. We walk circles in the fifteen-degree night, kick rocks on the train trestle over I-85.

The next morning, we wake in the frozen dawn and stir, brush the frost from our sleeping bags and knock it from the tarp we'd strung low in the trees. The frustration from last night is gone with our dreams. We stumble, again, under twenty pounds of canned beans, and sleep next to the trainyard in a ditch full of brambles. We find our train, at last, and spend a cold day and black night rumbling toward Louisiana. On the train it's too noisy to talk, so we make faces at each other and stick our filthy fingers into cans of corn, throw liters of bright red piss over the side (we're both on our periods) and laugh, together, until we feel as though we'll throw up. New Orleans is the warm red glow of a city overhead and voices all around us, boots crunching on gravel and the two of us hidden deep in our sleeping bags, hold-ing our breath as the train jumps and startles through the crossings. Finally we are out of it and asleep and in the morning our train is a ship crossing the Mississippi bayou, trees rising out of the still water of a swamp on either side as far as we can see.

Suddenly we're halfway through Texas and the long train slows, then stops. We run our grubby fingers along the atlas and see that we're pretty close to Alpine, although we're not exactly sure what that is. It feels good to stand in the full sun with our backs against the orange freight container, looking at the blue sky and letting the light drive away the stale, dull cold. My mouth tastes like dust. The only sound is the rush of the soundless desert. I pick up a gallon jug and drink for a long time, and Florence shuffles a deck of cards and deals two hands on the floor of the car. So far our train has stopped often and for long periods of time in Texas, pulling off onto stretches of double track in the lonesome desert to wait for other, higher-priority trains to pass. The train will sit silently for hours, with only the *whoosh whoosh* of the winter wind and the *ping* of settling steel. And then, when we've just about forgotten that the train can move at all, when we've accepted it as an immovable thing, a monument to the impermanence of industry, our train will begin to creep—so smoothly at first that we don't notice it until a tree or pole passes above us in the sky.

This morning, we play our card game in the stopped car, and our stomachs growl in the sun-drenched quiet. I reach for my jar of peanut butter but cannot make myself eat one more bite of it. My heavy cold cans of beans aren't appetizing either, nor is the single can of pale green peas, wet and salty and soft, that I packed to break up the monotony of beans.

After eight hours Florence says, "I want to get the fuck out of this metal box." We gather our gallon jugs and blue tarp and throw ourselves over the side, landing squarely on the ballast and walking through brittle sagebrush toward where we imagine the road will be. We turn and look back at our train; it's so long you wouldn't guess that it even had a beginning or an end. I feel a pang of longing looking at it, the train we worked so hard to locate and stow away on, the distance that it took us.

Our legs pump happily on the walk to the road. Blood flows through us; after days of sitting, our metabolisms kick in like flocks of birds.

We find the road and cross, stick out our thumbs toward the west and then put them down again. There is no traffic. Leaning our packs against our legs, we stand upright, our joints loosening like soft butter in the sun. A few cars pass, and then a pickup pulls over for us and we sprint after it, water jugs banging against our sides.

The man driving the pickup has long legs like calipers for squeezing horses and a bright handsome Texas face. His eyes are clear blue glass and he says, "I can take you into Alpine, where you need to go."

"See that train, we just got off that train," we say, to explain why we're standing on the bright empty shoulder, here of all places, our faces smeared in diesel grime, and why we smell like hot dusty sweat gone clammy and then warmed over again.

He drops us at the laundromat and we stuff our filthy things into a washer, scrub our faces with soap in the bathroom, and wipe at ourselves with coarse brown paper towels. In the dumpster behind the grocery store, we find a pecan pie. Fruit and sardines purchased from the store complete our shopping trip, and sometime in the evening the train we left behind rattles through town with a clatter of two tracks joining and a long whistle. We're walking to the catch-out spot; the sun is getting low and the cold is creeping in.

"We'll get the next one," says Florence. "We can find a faster train than that."

There is a wooden shed across a dirt road from the tracks and we poke around in the deep shadow there, use our headlamps to check for hobo loaf (the unburied poops of other train riders) and then set our things in the weeds. Dinner is pecan pie, and then the cold comes in like a flood, so we cover ourselves in our sleeping bags and curl awkwardly on the ground, trying not to fall asleep. Around two A.M. the front of an intermodal train pulls up loudly, headlights sweeping, and then it stops. The train sits quiet while we stuff our sleeping bags away and shake the stiffness from our bodies. We spring down the ballast in the dark, stumbling awkwardly on the sharp, black rocks, until we find a rideable car, just three from the back. Our boots ring out on the metal rungs of the ladder and then we're inside the car, rolling out our bedrolls on the cold steel floor. Stuffing ourselves into our warm bags, we shut our eyes. The train crouches like a cat and then hisses, finally pulling west into the great open desert as the first gray washes the bleary bowl of the sky.

Our train is slower than cold peanut butter, and in the desert, every day, it rains. In El Paso, the highest-security trainyard in the country, we hide beneath our bright blue tarp, and that, along with the spell of our white privilege—we are not the ones the rail cops are looking for here, so close to the Mexican border, so when they do get a good look at us we are presumed innocent, even though we are far from it—keeps us from being pulled off the train. We bail before it pulls into the yard in Yuma, Arizona, and put out our thumbs to hitchhike, but no one will stop but the police. The cops run our IDs while we stand squinting on the pavement in the sun.

"You have a warrant," says one of the cops, to me.

"What?" I say. I close my eyes and think back, finally remembering being pulled off the train here with Sami, when we were headed from Portland to Texas. The kindly rail cop who gave us citations and then told us his shift was almost over, so that we knew what time we could go back to the yard and catch another train. Did I ever pay that ticket?

Oh, fuck.

The back of the cop car is airless and warm. It reminds me of every other time I've been in the back of a cop car. The time I got caught shoplifting in Omaha, Nebraska, when I got off the train to get more water and then decided to hide my pack in the bushes and walk into town and steal a new book to read, because I'd finished *East of Eden* the night before. I smelled bad and I hadn't quite managed to clean all the diesel grime from my hands and face, even though I'd used all the wet wipes I'd had left. The loss prevention agent held me in the back room of the store for hours. He grilled me: *How much meth was I on? Where did I get my meth? Was there any meth in my pockets?* He rifled through the fanny pack I was carrying and instead of drugs he found my small journal, homemade from scrap paper and fabric-covered cardboard and bound with dental floss. I'd had a hard few months, and I'd been writing the most personal things in there—about how much I hated my body. How bad my anxiety and insomnia were. How I cried every day. The pages were literally stained with my tears. The loss prevention agent opened that little book and my stoic, interacting-with-the-cops façade crumbled. I started crying and begged him not to read it. He was angry that I was not, in fact, on meth, and he needed to cover his embarrassment, so he curled his lip and began to read aloud. After a few pages he snorted in disgust, closed the journal, and dropped it onto my lap. The cops came and drove me away and booked me into a holding cell in the Omaha courthouse, a small steel room where I waited twelve hours to see a judge. I curled up on the cold metal bench and closed my eyes, listening to the other minor offenders come and go, the booming of the heavy, solid door. The judge gave me time served, and I was released. It took a long time to figure out what public transportation would take me from downtown Omaha back to that industrial neighborhood on the outskirts of everything, next to the tracks. My pack, miraculously, was still in the weeds where I'd left it.

There was the time I was arrested in Portland during Critical Mass, the monthly event where thousands of people ride their bikes together through the streets, blocking traffic. That month the ride had been to protest the start of the Iraq War. The Portland Police Bureau had announced on the nightly news that they'd be arresting people indiscriminately. There were more beds available in the women's jail, and so they'd mostly arrested women. I was one of them. The cops pulled me off my bike and dragged me across the concrete, zip-tied my wrists, and shoved me into the back of the police cruiser.

I wasn't carrying ID, and I refused to give them my name while I was being booked. I knew I could do this, since my fingerprints weren't yet in the system. It was a way to fuck with them—*I wasn't committing a crime and you arrested me anyway, which is an abuse of power, so I'm going to make things harder for you.* It slowed the machinations of the criminal justice system. Caused problems. Pissed them off. The hope was that it would make the city think twice in the future about arresting people arbitrarily, purely as an intimidation tactic. Legally, I knew, they were allowed to hold me until they found out who I was, but I knew that they wouldn't, because I hadn't actually committed a crime. I was calling their bluff.

My paper bracelet said "Jane Doe" and they held me for four days in the downtown jail. Each cell had two bunks, and each bunk had a window that ran the length of the wall, from which you could look down on the fountains on Third Avenue. The women in the jail were kind to me. They were thrilled by the fact that my bracelet said "Jane Doe" and that I had refused to give my name. My cellmate was in for identity theft. The food was inedible—cold, congealed oatmeal, stale bread. While I was in there, I read *A Separate Peace* and *Slaughterhouse-Five*.

At the police station in Yuma, Arizona, I am given a court date three days from today for the "Failure to Appear" I accrued after neglecting to pay my train ticket. Florence pays my bail— two thousand dollars—with the money she made doing medical studies in North Carolina. It's all the money she has. When the cop picked me up, Florence was left with both our packs, and she had to push them in a shopping cart for four miles in the hot sun to reach the courthouse. She is dehydrated and exhausted, and I am so grateful to her it's physically painful. We fill up our water gallons and stumble through the afternoon to a deep blue canal on the edge of town where we swim until our worries rinse away, then we wash the filth from our clothes and lie down to sleep in the dirt. We're head to head on our blue tarp with the sky turning magenta, then turquoise, then black, and then we're asleep before all the stars are even out.

I make it to my court date this time. The judge serves me with a modest fine. Florence is refunded her bail money and we set out for the more challenging leg of our journey—hitchhiking the length of California, which will bring us the rest of the way to Oregon. We eat and fight and then laugh, we dislike every person who picks us up, the cops are terrible, and we've never felt freer, even though we're trapped in L.A. in the middle of the night with no energy left in our bodies. Florence sits on her pack to roll a cigarette and I say:

"What are we doing now? What are we going to do now?"

We try to take buses out of L.A. but the buses go nowhere. Each neighborhood seems to lead only into itself, and the highway is nowhere to be found. On the northern outskirts of the city, the sun is so hot it burns our faces, our forearms, and the backs of our necks. We walk through labyrinths of concrete courtyards to a rolling, scorched-brown field surrounded by a high chain-link fence. We climb the fence, Florence catching her skirt on the top, and tumble down into the grass on the other side. There's a great oak tree in the center of this field and we run to this tree and allow its shade to swallow us. Florence pulls out her sleeping pad and loses herself in a fitful sleep. We didn't sleep last night, we passed the night wakeful in Union Station after a young man who picked us up at a rest area dropped us in L.A. after all the buses stopped running. Now, in this dry field, Florence is twitching in the dappled light but I've had too much coffee to sleep, so I read a *National Geographic* we got from the free box at the Yuma Public Library, fighting with the wind for control of its pages. I read about Dubai and palm fruit, about orangutans being burned alive in Indonesia.

"Don't you think we should go?" I ask Florence.

"Another hour," she says, red-faced from her bedroll.

I knife open a can of tuna and produce several mayo packets. I dig the corn tortillas from my pack and we laugh at our disgusting lunch and then eat it, wearily lash all our things back together so that we can hoist them into the air, and head toward the freeway, the wall of sound on the other side of all this grass.

It takes about thirty seconds for a cop to kick us off of I-5.

"Fuck," says Florence. We stumble back through a different

part of the field and find ourselves cut off from the neighborhood by another tall fence, this one with barbed wire. Using our hitchhiking sign to cover the wire, we struggle over it, much to the amusement of some guys working on a house across the street. Once we're on the ground, we see a straight, person-sized hole neatly snipped in the fence at ground level. "Fuck," says Florence, again.

Finally, the sunny part of the country is behind us. A snowboarder is taking us all the way up to Portland.

Florence asks him to drop her off in Salem.

"I'm going there for a few days," she says to me, holding my hand between hers. "I'm visiting friends there. You knew that was my plan. I'll meet you in a few days."

I feel a flutter in my chest. The planet we'd created spins wildly out of orbit. The stars fall from the sky.

We leave Florence leaning against the cinderblock wall of a gas station, surrounded by her dirty things. Back in the car, the conversation shrivels up and dies. Buckets of rain pelt the windshield as we near Portland.

That night, safe and sound in the basement guest room at my friend's house, I can almost feel the indentation in the bed next to me where Florence would be. It's an ache so deep that I cry and think, *I didn't know it would be this bad.* I wake at dawn like we had when we were sleeping in the weeds and pull all the things from my pack. Everything smells like corn tortillas and the insides of empty bean cans. I think of walking behind Florence and watching the way her legs bow out as she walks, three pairs of long underwear under a maroon skirt with a crooked hem that swings across her ass with the rhythm of her steps. She'd pull a stick of gum from her pocket for me and tell me not to spit it onto the ground, because a bird will eat it and die. I'd spit out the gum anyway when she wasn't looking and then put my nose against her neck, wrap my arms around her, and inhale the scent of her filthy cashmere sweater, one hundred twenty dollars stolen from the mall and good thing I got her the gray one, because you couldn't even see the dirt.

I fish around for my last clean T-shirt and then put everything back in my pack, pick up the landline, and call her.

"I miss you so bad," says Florence. "I almost cried last night."

But you're still not here, I think. What I don't say is that maybe I am the reason she is not here. That aloneness is the final chapter of every story line of my life. That I'm closed up inside myself like a Russian nesting doll. That she can feel it. I put my heart away for safekeeping so long ago that I don't even remember where it is. Either she'll leave or I'll leave her, there's no other way for this to end.

Florence shows up in Portland the next day, freshly laundered and covered in raindrops. She's brought me dumpstered mango juice and a loaf of olive bread.

"I can't stay for long," she says.

We fall into bed that night and bury ourselves under pounds of blankets in the cold basement room. I wrap my arms around Florence's waist and we both sigh, fitting together like tarnished silver spoons, and I feel the tension drain out of me as I squeeze my eyes shut to keep from crying, to keep from telling her everything I'm thinking, that I want to alter the present and the future and place us side by side in this dark galaxy like twin planets instead of appearing together by chance, each on our way to somewhere else.

Life, I think, is more precious than I can ever remember it being.

And then I am asleep.

The telephone poles are giant candy canes. The streetlights are candy canes. The McDonald's is red and white striped, like a candy cane. I'm in North Pole, Alaska, in the passenger seat of a semi-truck, bouncing as the vehicle jostles along the icy road, my face pressed to the cold window. March, and there's still several feet of snow on the ground. Smoke curls from the stovepipes of the small houses. I'm here to meet Tara, a woman I've only ever talked to on the internet. She lives in a cabin in the snow in the Alaskan interior, without electricity or running water.

A few weeks ago I was in Portland, staying in a small carpeted room in a friend's house. I had a mattress on the floor and my things were in boxes stacked in the corner. The room was lit by a single bare bulb and I hadn't put up any decorations. There was one narrow window that rattled in the constant rain.

I'd just quit my job as a pedicab driver, which I'd only had for two weeks. My shifts started at nine P.M. in downtown Portland, and lasted until four A.M., when the last of the drunks trickled from the bars and found their way home. I paid twenty dollars rent, each night, for my pedicab, which was a bicycle with a narrow bench on the back where two passengers could sit. I parked outside the bars in the cold drizzle, offering people rides. The rides were free—that was the hustle. I pedaled drunks across town, laboriously up hills, at about the same speed they could walk. The people took pity on me, they stared at my ass, and then they tipped.

When the streets were silent and empty, I passed the hours with the other pedicab drivers outside the twenty-four-hour donut shop, spooning cold quinoa from a mason jar, wishing I was at home in bed.

And then I had quit. So then I had no job, and I wasn't sure how I would pay rent the next month. Or how I would buy cabbage and peanut butter and brown rice. On my mattress the night I quit, I was exhausted, but I couldn't sleep. My brain kept going going going, trying to solve this basic puzzle of survival. *I need money to live.* The bare bulb buzzed softly in its fixture. I looked at the stack of cardboard boxes, some of them collapsing, that held everything I owned. How depressing. Running my hands over the bed, I thought, *At least I have nice sheets.*

I opened Craigslist and started scrolling. A listing caught my eye.

Driving to Alaska. Looking for riders.

Now, that's something, I thought. For the past couple of years, I'd gone to Alaska in the summers to work. I'd hitchhiked around the state, brought a tent with me so I could sleep in the trees on the edge of town. Dumpstered corn tortillas and bruised apples. But I'd never thought to go in the winter—I hadn't been in Alaska in the winter since I'd left when I was fourteen years old. How would I get around? Where would I sleep? In the summer there were boatloads of seasonal jobs. What could I do in the winter? I needed money. And I needed to get out of Portland. Out of this sad room where I couldn't sleep or imagine a future for myself.

A year ago I'd found a blog online called hobostripper.com, written by a woman named Tara Burns. Tara lived in a van and traveled around North America, stripping, sleeping on forest service roads, gathering plants for medicine, and snaring rabbits. Tara was queer, the same age as me, and she was also from Alaska—she'd grown up in a remote part of the state, in a cabin with a dirt floor and walls made of spruce poles. When she was a kid, her family ate moose, caribou, fish, and beaver, burned wood for their heat, and made their own parkas out of caribou skins. What little cash they needed came from selling the furs of the animals her father trapped. They had a dog team to run their traplines, and the nearest village was several days' boat ride away. Even that tiny village wasn't on any road system—you had to fly out of there to get to a town that could be considered civilization.

I'd emailed Tara and we'd become friends, writing long letters back and forth about our families, our longings, our hopes and dreams and fears.

Becoming friends with Tara online was a balm for my tired heart. I felt a great kinship to her, and the more we emailed, the more I wanted to meet her.

Recently Tara had bought a piece of land on a large river just south of the Arctic Circle. The land was five acres of flat forest with a one-room cabin. No electricity, no plumbing, no running water. You walked across the wide frozen river to get to the property, or you took a boat there in the summer. Tara had just moved onto the land and was writing and making poplar salve and selling kinky hypnosis videos on the internet. In my bedroom at one in the morning, under the bare bulb on my nice sheets, I penned another email to Tara. If I found a ride to Alaska, could she help me get a job?

You should come stay on my land with me, she wrote back within minutes. *And we can totally find you a job.*

The next morning, I called the number listed in the Craigslist ad for the man driving north. His name was Asaf and his speech was loud and gruff, but not unkind. He was Israeli American, he said. What kind of vehicle was he driving? I asked. It was over three thousand miles from Portland to Alaska, so if his car was a gas guzzler and we were splitting gas, then it might be cheaper for me to fly.

"I don't want any money for gas," he said. "I just want the company."

I listened for hints of an ulterior motive, but there were none. There would be two other riders, he said, also from Craigslist. This put me at ease. A person looking to victimize three people would be a pretty ambitious serial killer, I told myself.

Asaf said that he was moving to Anchorage and leaving March 1. It would take us four days to reach Alaska.

On a Sunday, in the gray hour before dawn, a sleek SUV pulled up and idled on the curb in front of my house. I pushed my way through the wet roses, dragging a brown leather suitcase from the Goodwill, a tall pack on my back. Everything else I owned I'd wrapped in garbage bags, as protection against the damp, and stored in a friend's basement. Now the birds were up, but I felt like I was still asleep—it had been too warm in the house last night and I'd lain awake for many hours. I'd eaten only a banana for breakfast.

There was a storage trailer hitched to the rear of the SUV.

"Everything I own is in there," said Asaf. He was standing in the rain, moving luggage around in the rear of the car. He was middle-aged, with a thick Israeli accent. He had a big smile and slightly bloodshot eyes. The license plate on the SUV read SHOW BIZ. "I work in the entertainment industry," he said, speaking loudly, almost shouting. "But I'm moving to Anchorage to be Sarah Palin's advisor."

"Do you know Sarah Palin?" I asked, handing him my suitcase.

"No, but I'm going to find her."

"All right," I said.

In the backseat was a young couple who introduced themselves as Meadow and Barry. Meadow wore a torn dress, knit leg warmers, and an oversized hoodie. Her blond hair was loose around her face. Barry had a push-broom mustache and cloudy brown eyes. He clutched a thermos of steaming coffee. Meadow was hand-rolling a cigarette. She tucked the cigarette behind her ear and extended her small, warm hand for me to shake.

"Barry and I met in San Francisco a few months ago," said Meadow, as Asaf pulled onto the wet, empty freeway and steered the SUV north, toward Canada. "I was sleeping in the park, and I heard him playing his guitar." She laughed hoarsely. "Now we're headed back to Alaska, where I'm from."

The sun came up as we crossed into Washington, and the gray day softened. Asaf told us about his passion for Sarah Palin's political career. "She needs an advisor like me," he said, in his loud, almost-shouting voice. He told us that he was a millionaire.

"Keanu Reeves calls me on my birthday." Asaf passed back a Ziploc baggie of sesame cookies. "You want some? My mother made these for the trip."

Meadow told us about growing up in Cantwell, a little nowhere village in the Alaskan interior. She had lived with her father in an unfinished one-room cabin. Her mother died when she was small. Her father taught her how to fish, hunt, and gather berries.

"He was a drunk," said Meadow, "but a happy drunk."

"What's Barry's story?" I asked. Barry had fallen asleep, his head resting against the window, the large thermos still clutched tightly in his hands.

"He comes from a rich family," said Meadow. "He ran away."

Around midday we reached Canadian customs at the U.S.-Canada border. I was eating a recycled yogurt tub of leftovers—sweet potatoes and ground beef—and Meadow had produced two bruised apples from her fringed leather bag. Asaf had a turkey sandwich from the gas station as his lunch.

"Shit," said Asaf, as we pulled into the line of waiting cars. "We don't have a story. We're supposed to have a story. Otherwise they won't let us in! Okay okay okay. Here's what we say. We've all known each other. For a long time. Ten years!"

"We're all in a band together!" said Meadow. "And we're on tour!"

I laughed. Barry woke and rubbed his hands over his face.

"Can I play the accordion?" I asked.

"Shhh!" Asaf hushed us, as the customs agent approached the SUV. Asaf handed over our passports and the customs agent peered inside. Had we ever been arrested? No. How long had we known each other? Ten years. We were a band. On tour. I held my breath. Of course I had been arrested, but I knew better than to say so. They'd have no way of knowing unless they ran a background check on me, and they wouldn't do that as long as our story was solid, right?

The customs agent handed our passports back to Asaf. We were free.

In British Columbia the rain turned to snow. Piles and piles of snow, mounded up along the roadsides, heaped on the roofs of the houses. Snow falling from the heavy clouds; fat, slow flakes pinwheeling down to the pillowed earth. The thermometer on the car's dashboard was dropping. While I knew that it was still winter in Alaska, I had not taken into consideration that it would be winter *on the way* to Alaska as well.

Neither had Meadow.

"Where are you planning to sleep tonight?" she asked me quietly.

I laughed. "I don't know. I thought I could sleep outside. But this . . . I guess I don't have any idea. I don't have money for hotel rooms."

"Same," she said, drawing her ill-fitting hoodie more tightly around her.

Asaf fished a camera from the console between the two front seats and held it against the glass of the windshield. He focused on the little screen, attempting to frame the shot. The car began to creep into the oncoming lane.

"Asaf!" I shouted, gripping my seat. He swerved back into our lane and snapped the picture. The roads were coated in ice, and snow was still falling. He accelerated around a curve— I looked at the speedometer and saw that we were going seventy miles an hour—and lifted the camera to frame another shot. The car again swerved into the oncoming lane.

"Asaf!" Meadow and I shouted, in unison. He ignored us.

The car swerved back and forth, from one lane to the other, as he stared at the tiny camera screen. We hadn't seen anyone else in a while, on this frozen highway in the middle of nowhere. But what if there was an oncoming car suddenly? We'd be dead.

The highway uncurled itself and Asaf accelerated to eighty.

"Dude!" yelled Meadow. "You need to slow down!" Barry had fallen asleep again and his mouth was slack, his breath fogging the passenger window. Asaf acted as though we hadn't said anything at all. "What the fuck do we do?" Meadow whispered to me. *Click, click, click.* Asaf's camera captured more shots of the snowy countryside.

We stopped for gas at a little roadhouse in the middle of a great expanse of undulating white, and Meadow anxiously smoked a cigarette while I ate a bag of potato chips. Smoke curled from the stovepipe on the roof of the roadhouse, and firewood was stacked neatly against the side of the wooden building. Nearby, an ax rested on a wooden chopping block. Bright shavings littered the clean snow.

"I'll sit in the front passenger seat," I said. "Maybe I can get him to slow down."

It was no use, though. I cajoled, I whined, I even shouted a little, matching the volume of his own speech. Asaf ignored me. He held the camera against the windshield and looked at the little screen—*click. Click. Click.* "I want to photograph everything," he said. Each bend in the road, each distant line of mountains. He swerved slowly, gently, into the oncoming lane and back. Always staying between sixty and eighty miles per hour, on this highway slick with ice, as it wound around the mountain, just a guardrail between us and the abyss.

"Why don't you let me drive for a while?" I asked. "Or Meadow? You must be getting tired."

"No," he said. "Then I could not say that I drove all the way to Alaska. I want to be able to say that I drove all the way to Alaska."

Asaf had reserved a hotel room in Prince George for the night, and we pulled in around eight. Asaf, in an act of strange, incredible generosity, had called ahead to all his reservations and upgraded the rooms so that there was enough space to sleep all four of us. Because where else would we sleep? It was sixteen degrees outside and snowing. He didn't want any money from us, he reiterated. It was his treat.

Asaf flopped on one of the beds in our room and turned on the television. Barry sat on the other bed, playing his guitar. I opened a can of chili for dinner.

"You need to shower," said Asaf, suddenly, to Meadow.

"I don't want to shower," said Meadow.

"It's important to shower," said Asaf.

"Sure, fine, whatever," said Meadow. She heaved her backpack onto the bed Barry was sitting on and headed for the bathroom. I pulled the sleeping bag from my pack and spread it in the narrow space between that bed and the wall. The heater ticked, radiating an intense, dry heat. My skin felt parched and tight, as though it might crack. Outside, the snow fell silently, piling up in the village and in the quiet forest that stretched beyond it, into forever.

Around noon the next day, we stopped at another small roadhouse, a ramshackle building with two ancient gas pumps. The cold had deepened as we'd hurtled farther north, and the air bit at my face. Inside the small building one could order a slice of pie or drink a cup of coffee. I spun a rack of old postcards and thumbed through a shelf of worn romance novels. *Take a book, leave a book,* said a handwritten sign.

"What do we do?" said Meadow, next to me. All morning we'd been taking turns sitting in the front seat, next to Asaf, and shouting at him. All morning he had acted as though he couldn't hear us. He'd kept the speedometer between sixty and eighty, all while taking constant photographs, *click click click,* and swerving across the icy highway, toward one snowbank and then the other. There was little other traffic but now and then a truck would blast by, spitting gravel. Asaf would not slow down. Now, Meadow and I ran through a list of ways to physically stop him:

1. Hide his camera
2. Throw the camera out the window
3. Steal his keys

We couldn't do any of those things to him, though. He'd been so nice. So generous. He was driving all three of us all the way to Alaska for no money, and he'd upgraded all his hotel rooms so that we would have a place to sleep! There was no way we could be that rude.

On the third day, Meadow and I gave up. We were in the Yukon Territory, a few hours east of Whitehorse. The world was a blur of white, the flat boreal forest with its drunken spruce trees stretching on to the horizon in all directions. The temperature gauge on the car's dash said fifteen below zero. I was in the middle row of seats, eating a can of black beans. Meadow and Barry were in the back row of seats, stretched out together, napping.

Asaf was taking a photo of a frozen lake when he lost control of the vehicle and we slid toward the snowbank on our right. He yanked the wheel as hard as he could and we spun across the icy road, the car and trailer turning, pointing south. We hit the snowbank on the other side of the road, and the SUV flipped onto its hood. The can of beans I was eating flew out of my hands as we rolled, staining my face, clothes, and the roof of the SUV with purple juice. The trailer caught like an anchor in the snowbank, and the SUV righted itself. The world was suddenly very, very still.

Asaf shoved open the driver's-side door and lurched out into the deep snow. He appeared to be unhurt. I was unhurt. Were Meadow and Barry okay? They hadn't been wearing seatbelts. They were sitting up now, alarmed. A little trickle of blood was running from Barry's nose. "I'm fine," he said, wiping it with the sleeve of his sweater.

The front end of the SUV was smashed in. The right-side windows were all shattered.

"My stuff!" Asaf was screaming, his voice cracking, standing on the frozen highway, waving his arms in the air. "My things! My life is ruined!" The trailer we were towing had busted open in the wreck, and all of Asaf's furniture—a shitty-looking desk, an office chair, lamps—was strewn about in the snow.

"You almost killed us!" I shrieked at him. I was shaking. It was fifteen degrees below zero, and I didn't have gloves on, or a coat, or a hat. I couldn't feel the cold, though. "You asshole! You're a horrible driver and you almost killed us!" Asaf ignored me. He had a cellphone but there was no cell reception here, no way of calling anyone. The last village we passed had been an hour ago.

"What do we do now?" said Meadow, dreamily.

A snowplow rumbled along the highway at that very moment, heading back in the direction of the last village that we passed.

Asaf stood in the highway, waving his hands in the air, and the plow grumbled to a stop.

"What are you doing?" I shouted at him.

"I've totaled this car," he said. He pulled the keys from the SUV's ignition and pocketed them. "I'll get a new one. Put my things in the backseat." He heaved himself up into the cab of the snowplow and was gone.

"What the fuck!" I screamed after the receding snowplow. I turned to Meadow and Barry, who were standing, befuddled, next to the wreckage, Meadow in all her ill-fitting layers and Barry in just his heavy wool fisherman's sweater and jeans. "He took the keys. It's fifteen below. What the fuck are we even supposed to do?"

Meadow shrugged. "I guess we'll wait for him, and ride with him when he gets a new car?" she said quietly.

"Fuck that!" I was still screaming. I couldn't seem to calm myself. "I'm not riding any farther with that asshole. What a fucking asshole. He almost killed us!" A car crept along the icy road headed west and I stuck out my thumb but the car passed without slowing. I realized that I didn't even have my things, and that there was still purple bean juice all over my face. I gathered my backpack and my heavy leather suitcase. I washed my face with snow, and dug out my warm coat, hat, and woolen gloves, and put them on. If I'd known that I would be hitching, I wouldn't have brought so much stuff. Definitely not this dumb heavy suitcase. And I only had these thin wool gloves.

"All right," said Meadow, watching me. "I guess we'll come with you." She collected her and Barry's things—a canvas backpack, a fringed leather purse, and a guitar.

A tow truck pulled up with Asaf just as a dirty, snow-caked

sedan stopped for us. Asaf climbed down from the tow truck and stared at us while we loaded our things into the sedan.

"You're leaving me?" he said. He was standing in the frozen road, the tow truck rumbling beside him. He appeared to be crestfallen.

"Yeah," I said. "Of course we are. You almost killed us. Remember?"

"But . . . you're leaving me?" the pain in his face was deep and real.

"Yes, Asaf!" I shouted at him. "We are leaving you!"

I was shaking from the shock of the accident as I folded myself into the backseat of the sedan. The car was completely full of the driver's belongings—more full than any hitchhiking ride that had ever stopped for me. The driver was a young man, maybe twenty, with bloodshot eyes and only a Hawaiian shirt on for warmth against the cold. He was driving to the North Slope of Alaska, he said, where he had work in the oil industry. In the sedan was everything he owned, stacked from the floorboards to the roof. I sat next to a tall stack of boxes, and clothing spilled onto my lap. Clutching my pack and suitcase in my arms, I smashed myself against the door as best I could. In the front passenger seat, Meadow sat on Barry's lap and held their belongings against her chest. Our driver tore off the cap on a 5-Hour Energy shot with his teeth and poured it down his throat. The smell of sucrose and B vitamins filled the cab.

"I haven't slept since Seattle," he said. He hit the gas and peeled out onto the icy highway, tires screaming, and accelerated to ninety miles an hour. *Oh my God.* I stared at the speedometer, willing it down.

The young man caught my eye in the rearview mirror.

"Does that scare you?" he said. "DOES THAT SCARE YOU?" He tapped the brakes, and the rear tires fishtailed a little on the ice.

"So," said Meadow calmly, her face a mask of tranquility, "you're from Seattle?"

By the time we reached Whitehorse a few hours later, the last of the daylight was gone, and we'd convinced the young man to stop and rest for the night.

"We'll pay for the hotel room," we said. "Don't worry."

Whitehorse was a small, artsy little town, asleep under the heavy cloak of winter, and we found a room for a hundred dollars, which was nearly the last of all of our money. Meadow, Barry, and our new friend dropped their things in the room and wandered off to find a bar, while I brewed tea in the motel coffee maker and sat on the bed, eating an orange, still shaking. I unstuffed my sleeping bag and lay down in my spot between the bed and the wall but couldn't sleep—my nerves felt full of electricity. At an indeterminate hour the three returned, drunk and covered in shiny green Saint Patrick's Day confetti. Meadow and Barry were arguing. The young man took off his shirt, flexed his six-pack in the mirror a few times, and then collapsed on top of the covers, starfish position, instantly asleep. I pretended to be asleep as well, and eventually I was.

I said goodbye to my fellow travelers in the morning. I didn't want to ride one more day with another reckless driver. One accident on this trip, I figured, was enough for me. And I needed a day to rest. Walking slowly down the sidewalks of Whitehorse, my boots crunching on the snow, I looked at the murals and the bulletin boards at the food co-op—"Intern needed on organic farm, four hours per day, as many fresh vegetables as you want." The notice was soggy from weathering the seasons. I reached the hostel. Up a set of stairs was a sunlit kitchen where a Japanese hipster sat at the table, making paper cranes. There was a teakettle and a shelf cluttered with boxes of tea. In another room someone was playing the flute. I sank into an overstuffed couch. It was so peaceful I almost started to cry.

I peeled twenty-five dollars off my small roll of money for a bunk, and that night I slept as though I had died. In the morning I fried a few eggs and the Japanese man gave me a paper crane.

"For good luck," he said. "No more car accidents."

I hoisted my pack and suitcase, cursing myself again for bringing too much luggage, and set out to hitchhike the rest of the way to Alaska.

Midday, I was picked up by a First Nations woman and her three young nieces. The girls stared at me as we drove west through the bright wintertime—at my wind-burned face, my red fingers, the snot running from my nose. They were coming from a grocery store resupply trip in town, and the SUV was piled with cases of food. They offered to take me home with them, to Kluane Lake, and put me up for the night. I said yes—a place to stay on this frozen journey was a godsend.

The family lived in a warm, split-level home on the banks of the lake, which was a flat, white expanse that danced with wind-blown drifts. We ate moose meat stew for dinner and then I tucked myself in on the living room couch, lay looking up at all the family photographs on the walls as the house rustled, and then finally fell still.

In the morning they fed me frosted cornflakes and the children watched as I ate.

"We know a great place to drop you off," said the woman. "A really good hitching spot."

The spot was a gas station about ten miles out of town, at a lonely highway intersection. I realized, too late, that the gas station was closed. The doors were boarded up, snowdrifts piled against the pump. LONG LIVE, said the letters on a signboard outside the entrance. I raised my thumb and then dropped it again. There was no traffic. Curtains of dust-fine snow swirled across the empty highway. The world was white and devoid of life—white forest, white road, white sky. It felt like it was ten degrees below zero, or colder. I jumped up and down in the squeaky snow to stop my shivering. All I had, still, were thin wool gloves, and I stuffed my numb hands into my pockets. *Fuck.*

Twenty minutes later a car approached. I waved my hands in the air, like the kid in *Hatchet* when he sees a plane and wants to be rescued. The driver slowed down and smiled at me, standing there on the desolate roadside bundled up with my scarf over my face and desperation in my eyes, and then he blew past, blasting me with bits of ice and snow. The cold wind pummeled me. *Fuck! Fuck fuck.* My toes were going numb one by one, and I could no longer make a fist with my hand. Across the highway, set back into the trees a bit, was a cabin. I stomped through the deep snow to reach it. The front door and windows were boarded up, but the sheet of plywood on one of the windows was loose, and I pried at it—if I could only get inside, I could start a fire in the woodstove and get warm. My hands wouldn't work well enough to grip the wood, though, and I started to cry. Tears froze to my eyelashes, sticking them together. *Fuck!*

A small hatchback approached, headed in the direction from which I'd come. I stuck out my thumb and the car rolled to a stop.

I squeezed into the backseat, pushing aside trash to make a space for my luggage. A small, bug-eyed dog cowered on the floorboards. The driver and his passenger each had an open beer and the car stank of stale cigarette smoke. My eyes itched from the heater. I pulled off the wool gloves and tried, unsuccessfully, to uncurl my pinky finger. I petted the dog with my numb, cold hands.

"Thanks for stopping," I said. The men lifted their beers in cheers and then continued their conversation, ignoring me.

There was an open gas station in Destruction Bay, a big gleaming log structure that was also a diner and a motel. It shone like a mirage in the middle of the great, frozen world. I piled my things at one of the tables and ordered a chili cheeseburger. In the bathroom I ran my hands under warm water until they felt normal again.

I hitched from the inside of the gas station, this time, approaching people and asking if they were driving to Alaska and if they had space for me. Eventually a fleece-wearing couple headed to Alaska said yeah, they could take me along, and I hoisted myself into the warm leather world of their shiny new pickup, aglow with gratitude. We pulled out, headed west with the heater all the way up (and heated seats!) just as the bright winter sun broke through the haze, setting the mountains on fire. In the valley below us I could see a herd of caribou. A red fox darted across the road. An audiobook droned softly in the car, a low-voiced person pontificating on the hero's journey. According to the book, there were three different ways the hero character could manifest: as a person who died and was born again, as a person who defeated some great evil, and as a person who was a vehicle for the energy of life itself. We stopped to take pictures at an overlook and startled a flock of ravens who were eating the eyes from a caribou head.

My kind drivers were headed to Anchorage, not Fairbanks, where I would meet Tara, so at Tok Junction, where the highway split, they bought me a room in a low, dark wooden motel. I was more grateful than I knew how to express, as they had spared me a night in the freezing snowbanks, one that I couldn't have survived. I ate a can of black beans and washed my shirts in the sink, plunging them up and down in the warm gray water.

The truck driver drops me in the empty parking lot of a mall in North Pole, Alaska, and rumbles away. He's headed to the North Slope on the Dalton Highway—he was kind enough to pick me up this morning in Tok Junction. The mall is flanked by closed-up strip malls, and once inside I see that many of the stores here are closed as well—a locked crafts store, a framing shop gone dark. There is only a JCPenney and the soft jazz music that wafts from the sound system. Tara and I agreed to meet here—North Pole is just outside of Fairbanks, and Tara's land is two hours from there. I sit on a bench in the empty mall with my pack between my legs, waiting. Then there's the swoosh of insulated Carhartt coveralls and Tara appears at the end of the long corridor.

It is so strange to see her here in the physical realm. A real live person in a heavy winter coat and plastic bunny boots, the military kind that inflate against the cold. She is tall, and her face is round and pale. We hug, and space and time ripple all around me, illusions and realities whispering against each other, worlds swirling together and apart, like braids in a river. Her hair is curly and fine, and her eyes are shining dark stones in the round flesh of her face. She smells of smoked fish.

"Shall we go to the cabin?" she says. Her voice is delicate and high.

The walls inside Tara's cabin are a white that's aged to pale yellow from wood smoke. There's a window that looks out at the slough, which is a flat current of water that cuts through the snowy forest. Yesterday, after Tara picked me up, we walked across the frozen, wind-blasted river, which is a quarter of a mile wide. We parked Tara's van on one side, at a pullout in the trees, after driving two hours from Fairbanks. And then we walked across the river. The snow squelched beneath our feet; the sky was an empty blue. We dragged plastic sleds by ropes that were strung around our hips. In the sleds were four cabbages, several pounds of carrots, dried pinto beans, red lentils, brown rice, cans of coconut milk, cumin powder, cooking oil, bacon, a huge sack of apples, and my luggage. We'd picked up the supplies in Fairbanks. Once across the river, we pulled the sleds a quarter mile through a forest of birch trees to the cabin, struggling in the deep snow.

Tara's cabin is a small rectangle, one room, the outside sided in honey-colored spruce. The window trim is a cheery green. There is no running water, just a plastic bucket that Tara uses to haul snow from the yard to the huge pot on top of the woodstove, where it is melted and becomes drinking water, dishwater, water for the dog, a border collie who lies on the bed, chewing huge moose bones he's dragged from the woods. There is no plumbing, just a little outhouse that smells of plywood and has a view of the forest. A small iron gadget called a thermopile sits on top of the woodstove and creates just enough electricity to charge a cellphone. At night there are candles and oil lamps for light.

This morning, my first morning waking up in the cabin, we

used the sleds to haul rounds of wood from the forest, which Tara had cut from downed trees with a borrowed chain saw. The wood was a half mile away and we tromped back and forth, the sleds tied to our hips as though we were ponies. We split the rounds with the maul on the stump in front of the house and stacked the chunks next to the woodstove to last through the next few nights. March is bright sun and clear days, but the world is still mostly frozen here, and the daily low is fifteen below zero.

Next to the cabin is a shed where whitefish, pulled from the river in warmer seasons, are stacked on a table like kindling, frozen solid. There are also chunks of roadkill moose wrapped in butcher paper. Now, Tara takes an ax and hacks a fish from the pile and brings it inside, adding it to the pot on the woodstove, which holds remnants of last night's stew. To the whitefish she adds potatoes, carrots, onions, and green curry paste. The floor of the cabin is littered with broken eggshells and sacks of fish eggs, pulled from the bellies of whitefish and dropped there for the dog to eat. Tara has been fermenting teff flour with water in a glass bowl next to the woodstove, and we'll fry up some of this for an approximation of injera and dip it into the stew. We are famished from hauling and chopping wood in the cold.

Tara has a thermos of tea to which she adds new herbs whenever the flavor gets faint, mugwort and lavender fading into raspberry leaf and comfrey, all of it steeped in melted snow water. I drink this tea from a mason jar, watching the birch seeds swirl in the water, tiny kites that have been tossed on the wind. It tastes like wintertime, cold and milky and distilled.

After dinner we wash our dishes in a chipped enamel bowl on a white table beneath the window that lets in the best light. A little water, a little sopping with the dishrag—the dishes are never really clean. Having to work so hard to get water—a full bucket of snow takes forever to melt, and makes just a few inches of liquid—leaves Tara much less inclined to do an extraneous wiping down. There is a broom, and I use it to sweep the cabin floor, shooing the broken eggshells and dog hair out the door, where they mar the pure white snow.

When darkness comes, we light the candles and oil lamps and I sit in the rocking chair next to the woodstove while Tara lies on the bed, one arm around the dog. She has been reading *Pilgrim at Tinker Creek* too—we've been emailing back and forth about the book for months—and we take turns reading aloud from the battered paperback copy that Finch gave me years ago. The cabin creaks and pops as the cold settles in, and I get up every now and then to feed more logs into the glowing woodstove. I lose track of time and look up, and Tara is asleep. I close the draw on the woodstove and crawl into the top bunk, pulling a stained quilt over myself. The bed smells like a limp feather pillow that's never been washed. The smell is deeply comforting to me.

In the morning the window that faces the slough is sparkling with frost. I step outside in the biting air to pee in the snow, and then walk a few paces farther to fill the snow bucket. The snow is a flat plane of light from which birch trees spring, blond striped pillars that cut the light into bars, make a sort of grid to measure space. The birch trees make sheets of paper that I peel off with my bare hands, which are red and wet from scooping snow.

I like being here, with Tara, in this land outside of time. The forest and the snow and the frozen river are made new every day, and the heavy questions of existence that dogged me in Portland seem irrelevant now. Tara feels like family, even though I only just met her. I wonder if the ghosts can even find me here, in this wild land. Maybe they can't. And maybe, one of these nights, talking with Tara in the yellow light from the oil lamp, we'll stumble upon answers; answers to the riddles that are stuck like thorns into the darkest parts of our hearts.

In the afternoon, once we've finished hauling and chopping wood again, Tara tells me stories from her own childhood in a one-room cabin made of spruce poles on the banks of the Coleen River. In the dark mornings, her father would depart with the dog team to check his traplines. Her mother sewed winter parkas for Tara and her baby sister from caribou hides that she had tanned herself. Her father sold the pelts of the animals he trapped for money to buy flour, salt, and gas for their boat. As Tara relates these tales of connectedness with the land, of learning to dog mush when she was small and the darkness of those early winters, she also weaves in anecdotes of her father's sadistic abuse. He is a violent man, and throughout her childhood she was his primary victim. So these stories, which contain so much wonder and beauty, are also suffused with deep grief.

Tara's two rifles lean, at the ready, next to the cabin door. She takes me outside and we stand in the snow in the bright, cold afternoon and she teaches me how to shoot. She has a plywood nativity scene that she found in the shed when she first bought this land. We prop one of the Wise Men up in the snow. "We don't want your frankincense," we tell him. *Bang.* "We don't want your myrrh."

In the clearing behind the house, we build an altar to Durga, the Indian goddess of vengeance. We say that in a different time, in a different world, we would be assassins. We would live short, violent lives avenging the wrongs that had been committed by child abusers. We would chop their dicks off and set the men on fire, drag them through the main street of the village while tossing money to the poor.

When she was a kid, everyone said Tara's father was a brilliant pianist. In the summer, when the river was high and before
the salmon ran, they'd go to town and he'd play piano in the bar.
The other drunk musicians who had come to Alaska in converted
school buses with their bohemian dreams spoke worshipfully of
him. All the men played music together and everyone was on
acid and no one took care of the babies. The sun never set, freeing them from the constructs of time. Their babies cried from
hunger and shit themselves and sometimes fell into the river and
drowned.

One day men on snow machines appear at our cabin, having
crossed the river from the nearest village, and they offer us oily
strips of dried salmon. We stand in the snow eating the sweet red
fish, chewing it like candy, as they eye us up and down and take
in the cabin, the chopping block, the Wise Man full of bullet
holes.

"Do you have guns?" they ask Tara.

"Yes," she says. They ask her if she needs more guns. Guns to
shoot bears, rapists, ghosts. We don't worry about the bears—
there are only black bears on this part of the river, no grizzlies.
Tara says that every springtime, a mother black bear wanders
through with her cubs and gnaws the door latch of the shed
where the frozen fish are kept. Tara wants to shoot a black bear
to get a bucket of bear fat, which would last a long time.

Tara tried to run away a few times when she was thirteen
years old and they were spending the summer in Fairbanks. She
kept a backpack with her birth certificate, important photos, and
a change of clothes and she would slip out of the house when her
dad was sleeping and run to the road and stick out her thumb.
Her father would find her and convince her to come home,
promise her that things would be different. They never were,

though, and she would run away again. She lived on the streets and was in and out of foster care for a few years. She did sex work and found that her clients were more helpful and caring than social workers. Finally, at sixteen, she escaped Alaska, going first to Texas and then moving every few months, running from various fucked-up situations until she paid cash for a double-wide in Pennsylvania and enrolled in college with the money she'd made sucking dick.

Tara graduated with a degree in psychology and bought a Chevy Astro minivan, which she converted into a camper. She pulled the seats out, added a cot from the military surplus store and a sleeping bag so fluffy she could sleep in it anywhere, even in the wintertime. Under the bed went crates to store her belongings—canning jars, cooking oil, weathered books, four-inch Lucite heels. She drove to North Dakota, where there were scores of lonely men working in the oil fields. The men had nothing to do on the weekends but drink in the bars, and she danced until money rained from the sky and she could gather it up and save it for her future. She drove all over the country, washed herself in gas station bathrooms and danced in dive-bar strip clubs. She brushed her long hair and dabbed coconut oil on her eyelashes. She'd dance in any one place for a week at a time, and sleep a dreamless sleep each night safe in her sleeping bag, the stars winking companionably above her. In the bright daylight before work, she'd snare rabbits and walk through fields of dry grass, gathering medicinal plants, which she stuffed into mason jars full of grain alcohol, distilling them into tinctures. She sold the little blue tincture bottles online—medicine for menstrual cramps, for sleeplessness, for winter colds.

Tara was happy. She read books by headlamp—Audre Lorde, Phoolan Devi. She roasted the rabbits she snared over a crackling fire in the dark and listened to the earth humming all around her. After several years she saved up enough money to buy this piece of land.

Her father still lives in Alaska. He still plays piano in the bars with the drunk people who adore him. He's found a new woman to beat and he beats his sled dogs and has a violent assault conviction and multiple restraining orders on his public record, but everyone ignores this because he's such a good musician, and a man.

One day I go out walking on the frozen river alone. The ice is still solid, it seems, although I am no expert in this arena. The wind stings and burns and I wrap my face in gray herringbone wool and put on every layer that I have. Tara's life is beautiful, and the stories about her father fill me with rage—a rage that warms my core, a rage as familiar as my own skin. A rage that has nowhere to go. I want to loose this rage onto something bigger than myself, so I go to the frozen river. The snow on the ice has been sculpted into drifts by the wind, and these drifts have a hard crust just thick enough to hold me. In some spots my boots punch through but there is only more snow underneath, and I imagine the river to be a clear brittle mass, frozen all the way to the bottom, fish trapped in place, suspended mid-swim. I'm looking for a cabin upriver that an old man in the village told me about. He drew me a map with a ballpoint pen when I was doing sudoku at the community center, waiting for Tara to finish filling out some paperwork. The old man wore suspenders and offered me soda and pretzels from a big plastic barrel. When I declined the pretzels, he told me about the cabin, drawing his map on a scrap of newspaper—one line for the river, one line for the creek, a box for the wee house. Now I want to find it, but the sucking gray wind is discouraging me. The wind wants to dry up my lungs, freeze their moisture into food for its cruel, hungry heart. The whole earth, it seems to me, has a cruel, hungry heart. How sad is a single life, though, if this is true? I don't want this to be true, but the facts that I've collected along my way seem to say that it is. I scramble up the steep riverbank, floundering around in the deep loose stuff, prick my mittened fingers on the bare wild rosebushes. When I get back to the cabin, Tara tells me that it can be dangerous to go walking on the river in March just for fun. Where we cross to get to the road to the village is solid, but in other places there are warm springs that run from the creek, with fast-moving water that never freezes. She says that soon the whole river will melt, nearly all at once, and it will crack and scream and flood, and for a week or two the world will be a mosh pit of ice floes and you're stuck on either this side of the river or that one. When the ice is gone, Tara has a little metal motorboat we can use to cross; the engine is old and dies mid-stroke but she only has to set the spark plugs on fire and it works again.

"In the meantime, just be careful," she says. "If it seems sketchy one day but you really need to cross, cut a long pole and carry the pole horizontally like you're walking a tightrope. That way, if you fall through the ice, the pole will catch you. And if you fall in, you'll need to throw yourself up onto the bank. You can't really pull yourself up. Just think of a seal, and throw yourself up onto the ice."

I lie on the bed in the smoky cabin interior and ask Tara if she thinks that the earth has a cruel, hungry heart. And if it does, what's the point of being alive?

"I don't know," says Tara. "Things can be beautiful sometimes. I'm trying to figure that one out."

We drive a few hours in to Fairbanks to buy more supplies.

Produce is wilted and expensive and we place it in the cart carefully, as though it is gold. On the drive back to the cabin, Tara tells me about eating the crispy fat of beaver tails when she was a kid, about her mother washing diapers in snow she had melted and boiled. In the evenings they dipped Strike Anywhere matches in candlewax by the light of a kerosene lantern to waterproof them. They had film canisters of these matches in everything, said Tara—their coat pockets, the dogsled, the bag they took trapping. In case they fell through the ice and needed to make a fire after climbing out, soaked and cold.

"You should always have one in your pocket," she says. "So you can build a fire no matter what."

I've been staying with Tara for two weeks when my money runs out completely. I have no more dollars for cabbage, or pinto beans, or cooking oil. Tara's mother, Sandra, who left her father years ago, is remarried and now lives in a tiny village in the boreal forest about fifty miles to the south. She works as the special education teacher in the small K–12 school there.

Tara uses Sandra's washer and dryer for laundry and Sandra watches Tara's dog when she's traveling, sometimes for months at a time. "We never talk about my father."

Sandra needs an aide, but so far the school hasn't been able to find one for her—the village, called Andrews, is too remote to attract many residents; it consists of a few dozen plywood-sided houses in a tilted bit of forest far from any river or mountain, a dark, frozen land that becomes a wet mosquito bog in the summer. Andrews was built to serve a nearby military base, which is locked and gated and whose secretive operations have spawned numerous conspiracy theories over the years: Laser guns? A huge mind-control satellite dish? The people who live in An-drews either work at the military base, and are poor, or moved there when the State of Alaska was giving away land parcels in the town in an attempt to keep the population large enough to warrant funding for the school, which needs thirty students to stay open. There was one caveat for the folks, also poor, who came for the free land: they had to stay for at least two years, or the land went back to the state. Some of these families stayed, mostly the ones like Tara's, with paranoid, addict fathers who thought they were messiahs and wanted to raise their children on fear and the Bible alone. Their daughters wear only dresses and their sons wear only camo. They eat Top Ramen, mostly, and moose and salmon in their seasons.

It is the first week of April. Sandra interviews me on the phone and decides that I'll do just fine as her aide until the school year is up, in June. Sandra has an empty room in her house; I can stay there. Her husband lives in another village, and works as an engineer in the uranium mine there—I won't be seeing much of him. On weekends I can come back to Tara's land. My pay will be fifteen dollars an hour, and I start in a week.

I have a job until the end of May now. It's not full-time but it's enough to get me thinking about things I can do with the money when I have it—buy a car off Craigslist, an old Subaru with a red body and a blue hood, maybe, or something I can live in, al-though where I want to live is here, in this cabin with Tara, with the woodstove and the dog and the paperback books, and our long evenings talking in circles trying to puzzle out the tangles of existence. I'm tired of leaving. I'm tired of anxiety creeping up every three months like an alarm in my brain I can't turn off. I feel like I've been playing the same level in a video game over and over, and at the end I keep dying. Maybe this time, if I stay, my character won't die. Maybe I'll beat the final boss, the dark mass of tar around my own heart.

We add more ingredients to the stew pot for dinner. Bits of the roadkill moose that I will be too scared to eat—esophagus, spinal cord, a femur full of marrow. Turnips and purple cabbage and soft, dirty carrots from the galvanized tub on the floor of the shed. There's one last whitefish in the shed, lying frozen on the plywood table in the dusty light from the window. We've got to eat it all up, says Tara, before the world thaws. I can't wait for the snow to recede so I can see all the junk that's lying behind the cabin, the old wooden boxes and metal tubs and cracked plastic buckets. I can't wait to see the forest floor, the leaves on the birch trees. I can't wait to see summer come hot and fast like a woodstove fire of dry spruce wood with the damper and the flue wide open.

I love my job. Sandra's classroom is filled with books, educational materials, sunshine, and toys. There are a couple of short tables with child-sized chairs. The children, who are between the ages of six and ten, trickle in throughout the day and we do activities with them; we look at books, answer questions on worksheets, build things with blocks. The children have ADHD, or fetal alcohol syndrome, or brain damage from being shaken as babies. We have lunch in the cafeteria and play basketball in the gym. At recess, the kids fling themselves from the tops of the playground equipment, push each other into the snow, pump their legs recklessly on the swings. I've never done any work like this. It is deeply gratifying.

After my workday ends, I walk back to Sandra's place, past the unfinished houses of the villagers, sided in Tyvek, mostly, smoke pumping from the stovepipes, ATVs parked askew in the snow. There are plenty of abandoned houses too. These are the people who came for the free land but didn't stay. They built their humble houses and stacked their cordwood but they didn't stay. Now the doors are open to the elements, the window glass shattered, plaster moldering in the spring warmth. I go inside some of these houses, walk their empty rooms. There are old children's toys, shirts still hang in the closet. Hidden among the trees are derelict converted school buses. I climb into one bus, stepping over the shattered glass. I touch the rusted bedsteads, pull open the dresser drawers, and imagine the hippies arriving here in the seventies, the same time my parents came to Anchorage. How many children lived in this bus? I picture their tattered layers of clothing, the babies crying.

Most nights Sandra works late and I am alone in the house. I eat ice cream and watch cable TV and consider my loneliness. Sandra has a parrot that waddles back and forth on top of its tall cage in the corner of the room, periodically letting out loud shrieks. The sun stays up late too, and I can hear the neighborhood kids outside, screaming as they tool around on their ATVs. When I'm finally tired, I sleep, pulling a dark shirt over my eyes to block the sun, which is still bright at ten P.M.

On Saturday after my first week at Sandra's, I'm back at Tara's cabin, lying in bed reading *Pilgrim at Tinker Creek* aloud while she washes the dinner dishes with a rag and an amber glass of snow water. It's an old copy of the book that Tara got on interlibrary loan, and on the inside of the dust jacket is a picture of young Annie Dillard, with all the wisdom of her twenty-five years, lips parted, looking out at the world like a vessel shot through with light, a conduit to God, which she defines, in the book, as Nature.

We read *Pilgrim* until the light is gone completely in the four-paned window, although the snow is still glowing outside when I squat to pee, and I can make out the shapes of the shed and the chopping block. It's nearly eleven o'clock! There is an abundance of daylight now. A cornucopia of sunshine. I feel like the richest person on earth.

I do not mind that it's April and the world has not yet thawed. The icicles glint like crystals in the doorway, and sounds are incredibly clear, like the air, and fresh, like the water in the creek. The snow is bluish with light and the shadows, bright shadows, are more bluish still. The sky is endless from six A.M. until ten and it bleeds into the night a little more each day. And you can start to smell the earth, where it softens beneath the snow. I can't believe it will eventually be summer here, hot good dry summer, with a pounding sun and an empty sky, and dust. The rivers will unstick themselves and flow, and salmon will swim up from the sea to spawn. People in the villages have built fish wheels, and the current of the river turns the wheel, and the baskets scoop the fish, and the people cut the fish and hang them to dry on wooden racks, with the smoke of green poplar to keep the flies from laying maggots.

I like so much about this quiet life, in this cabin with Tara. I like the herbs hanging to dry in the dusty corners, and the white-painted table where we wash the dishes. I like the way Tara subsists on potatoes and fish, and then finally, with a sigh, grows weary of them. I like how she tucks her .45 into the back of her pants when we walk to the village, the careful way she crosses the frozen river, the way she brushes her hair with rosemary oil, and the way the smell of rosemary lingers for the rest of the day.

. . .

One weekend we drive south to visit a friend of Tara's, in Anchorage. It's icy in the city and the skies are leaden and the air smells of the sea. I sit on the broken curb in front of Tara's friend's house and listen to the *ai ai ai* of the seagulls. The Pacific Ocean is close, I know, dark and full of secrets, crashing itself against the mudflats. I shut my eyes and can smell spring, growth waiting beneath the snow. I think of the time, six years ago, when I hitchhiked up here to find my father. I haven't seen him since. I wanted a relationship, but you can't wish a father into existence. My ideas of him had been pure fantasy, and when, even after meeting him, I still had no father, I was heartbroken. Now he is no one to me, and I am no one to him. He is a stranger again. I think of my mother. She's here in Anchorage, somewhere, as well. But where? The memories come back and I shut my eyes. I'm a kid again, I'm hungry, I'm wandering the streets in desperation. Everything is closed off to me, no magic tickets to open doors, no hot soup to eat. I'm gazing in the windows of restaurants and wondering how anyone anywhere is rich enough to eat in restaurants, to pay that many dollars for a little meal and to sit in the warmth, with the condiments in their orderly metal stands, the sugars and Sweet'N Lows so tidy, everything so calm around them. How is anyone in the world rich enough for that?

I haven't seen my mother in twelve years. I remember when I last talked to her on the phone a few years ago, when I was in Greensboro, North Carolina. She was living indoors then. But where? A halfway house? Where do schizophrenic homeless people live in Anchorage, when they're not on the streets? She told me I should've died when I was a baby. A few phrases of lucid conversation—she acted as though I was still a child, but at least her words made sense—and then she was gone. *I should've died when I was a baby. I had the devil inside me, and she should've let me die.*

I open my eyes and look at the broken concrete of the driveway. My mouth tastes like metal, and I've started to shake, so I focus on the smell of the sea, imagining the mud beach, the flat gray water. The ridgelines of volcanoes in the distance. Being in Anchorage always makes me feel this way. Darkness, creeping in at the edges. Threatening to subsume me.

I have never tried to find my mother. Seeing her, I think, would crumble this fragile scaffolding I've managed to build, this perception of reality on which I've hung my version of a life. I'm balancing on thin wood, telling myself I'm okay, I'm not in danger, everything is going to be okay. Seeing Barbara would destroy everything. I would fall, reeling, into the dark hole in which she dwells, like a gremlin. My first world. What still feels, in my bones, like the truest world.

But the shaking doesn't stop, so I think about the volcanoes across the water. When I was seven years old, one of the volcanoes, Mount Redoubt, erupted. The skies turned dark and for days ash fell like fine, dirty snow. A man on a bicycle saw me collecting the ash in a pickle jar and he handed me his paper dust mask.

A little kid rides by on a pink bicycle. She's riding in the gutter, rowing the ground with her feet. I remember when I was her age and I lived just down the road, in a neighborhood like this, with potholed asphalt and trash in the street. I'd walk the silty sidewalks with my paper bag of cheeseburgers from Burger King, and at the traffic light I'd hit the metal button, *pong pong*, and stand, head down against the wind, bare hands cold around the paper sack, waiting for the light to change. Sometimes it's

raining, in my memory, and the rain is all the loneliness and iso-
lation that exists in the whole world, and this rain hits the dirty
snowbanks, whose gravelly crusts are sprinkled with straw wrappers, crushed drink cups, and Cheetos bags. I walked for miles
on those sidewalks. This walking is what I always remember first.
Head down, hungry, lonely, nothing in my pockets. Not wanting
to go home. Looking for a dumpster of chalky old candy bars or
a dollar for a cheeseburger, or a warm place to get out of the
cold.

And yet, it's amazing, sitting here on Tara's friend's front
stoop, what I also remember. The good. I remember the hope I
would feel in the springtime, when the world was opening up. I
had a fierce belief, even then, in the godlike power of springtime. The seasons were each a god, I was sure, the passage of
time, a god, the sea was a god, the trampoline of moss in the
forest was a god. I was in awe of all of it, and it would make me
drunk, and I would fall down into it, the idea that this could be,
in the end, the truest core of everything. Beneath the sadness
and disappointment and grief. You fall and you fall and this is
what finally catches you—this loamy forest floor, this soft light
that's filtered through the spruce boughs. What was flaking paint,
despair, secondhand smoke? What was hunger? It was nothing
in the face of the forests and the tide, the flowers in the springtime, the howling of wolves in the high mountains, the glittering
white snowbanks in the dark of winter.

Tara and I spend the night curled together on the narrow bed
in her van. We forgot to bring warm blankets, which is hilarious,
and we laugh about it. To pass the cold hours, we read aloud
from *Pilgrim at Tinker Creek*. In the morning we eat sausage
and hash browns from the grocery store deli and split an organic
cucumber and then drive around town, running errands. It's late

afternoon when we pull onto the highway headed back north, toward Tara's cabin, and dark when we see the antlers silhouetted in the headlights, on the side of the highway outside Denali National Park.

We pull off the road and walk toward the fallen creature, put our hands in its wind-blown fur. The caribou is still warm. It lies on the concrete shoulder in a dark pool of its own blood. Tara tells me that it's against the law to take home roadkill in Alaska. You're supposed to call a hotline, and someone in a nearby village will pick up the dead animal and take it to a family in need. What if we took this caribou, though? We could eat it. We would put it to good use. But how? How does one process an animal this large?

"My mom will know what to do," says Tara.

It's four A.M. when we reach Sandra's house in Andrews. It took us a long time to get the caribou into the van—it was far too large for us to lift on our own, so we waited in the dark until we saw headlights on the lonely highway, and flagged down a pickup truck. The driver helped us hoist the caribou into the back of the van, where it rested on the floor next to the bed, and then he drove away without asking any questions. I think he understood.

Sandra is awake, waiting for us in the empty garage, a blue tarpaulin spread across the floor. In her fists are several rusty kitchen knives. White plastic buckets are arranged at the end of the tarp. We've woken her before she would normally get up for work, but she doesn't complain. She helps us pull the caribou out of the van and across the ground, onto the tarp.

"These knives are dull," Sandra tells us as we arrange the caribou belly-up on the floor. "Dull knives are best for skinning. That way you're less likely to cut into the skin, or the membrane between the skin and the muscles."

Tara opens the animal down the belly slowly, so as not to damage any of the organs. The three of us grasp the edges of the skin and work the dull knives underneath it, pulling it back inch by inch. There are circles of white, here and there, on the underside of the skin, which I recognize from the Farley Mowat books I've read—Farley Mowat was a Canadian biologist who spent decades in the Arctic in the first half of the twentieth century, working with caribou, among other creatures. Botflies. These are botflies. I cut open one of these white lumps and my fears are confirmed—there's a fat larva in there, the size of a walnut, wriggling back and forth. I drop my knife and take a few steps back, feeling like I might throw up.

The botflies are, interestingly, the only part of this process that overwhelms me, which makes me feel proud. Since I eat meat, I want to be able to face the truth of a dead animal. After the skin with its terrible wriggling larvae is off, the rest of the work is not so bad. The inside of the caribou is steaming—this is why, says Sandra, you've got to gut an animal right away after it dies; otherwise, the hot organs will cause the carcass to ferment. It's beautiful, inside the caribou, a whole galaxy of complex organs, and nutrient-rich blood that was so recently pumping around. I think about the full life this caribou lived, out in the wild. Eating lichen and migrating over the land, watching storms. Weathering winter, exalting in the brief flush of summer. The tundra is made of lichen—the caribou have found a way to metabolize the lichen, and everything else eats the caribou. Caribou are the creatures that tether so much other life to this huge, wild land.

Once Sandra feels confident that we know what we're doing, she ducks out to catch a few hours of sleep before the school day begins. I'll join her, at noon, for the second half of the day. Until then I'll be here, in this garage, covered in warm blood. No sleep for me.

The sun rises and we grow bleary with exhaustion as we do the slow, steady work of dismantling this giant beast. As Tara and I wearily work side by side, our clothes and arms covered in blood and our hair matted, our exhaustion turns to something else, a sort of strange, transcendental deliriousness.

"Don't tell anyone about the caribou," says Tara. Her voice is hoarse with fatigue. She's cutting meat off one of the leg bones and dropping it into the stew pot. Her face is smeared with blood. "Taking roadkill home is illegal. My mom could get in trouble."

"By who?" I snap, as I maneuver a hindquarter in the sink, trying to rinse off the last of the hair. "The roadkill police? Literally who would care?" Her fear irks me. In this strange worn-out hour Tara's fear feels, in my body, like my mother's fear, a tide against which I struggled for years.

"Just don't tell anyone about it, okay?" says Tara.

"You're being paranoid," I say. "No one cares."

Tara looks at me, and I see the dark parts of her eyes close up, and suddenly she's far away.

We don't speak for the rest of the morning as we continue processing the caribou. At noon I shower, put on a clean shirt, and walk the two blocks to the small village school, feeling shaky and strange. When I am off at four, I return to the house and take over for Tara, who leaves to drive back to her cabin, where she will sleep at last. By evening I am pulling the jars of stew from their steaming water bath and lining them up on dish towels to cool. Jerky is drying in the dehydrator, and steaks are frozen in Ziploc bags in Sandra's chest freezer. We have mopped up all the blood. We're finished.

On Friday, when I email Tara to ask if I can come to the cabin for the weekend, she doesn't respond. Something has shifted between us, something has flipped. I don't know if it's her, or me, or both of us. I stay in Andrews for the weekend, spend my time wandering the forests there, discovering what lies beneath the melting snow—ancient moose skeletons, hunks of rusted metal, antique liquor bottles.

Weeks pass and one day winter is gone completely, and it's summer, and the school year has ended. The sun hangs stubbornly in the sky, and hordes of mosquitoes rise up from the bogs. I have just enough money—twelve hundred dollars—to buy an old van in which I can live. I feel heavy with loneliness. I email Tara again, and again she doesn't respond. I have a nagging feeling that I've done something wrong, but I don't know what it is. Or has Tara done something wrong? Or is it my clumsy attempts at relationships that have always been, and will always be, wrong? Either way I need to find another job, so I drive to Fairbanks. Fairbanks is where the people are.

In Fairbanks I find Meadow, my companion from my Craigslist ride north. She's living in an abandoned cabin in the woods, on a rough jeep road beyond the edge of town. The windows of the cabin have no glass, and the insulation of one wall has been eaten out by squirrels. There's a loft with a stained futon and a single, tattered blanket. The woodstove doesn't draw, and the cabin is thick with smoke. Dark mildew flowers on the plaster. A small low table is cluttered with empty wine bottles. Meadow and Barry have arranged knickknacks on the windowsill. A wall calendar hanging next to the door reads June 1996.

"How did you find this cabin?" I ask.

"Just wandering around in the woods, I guess," Meadow says. She's wearing a stained satin slip and smoking a Marlboro, sitting on the decomposing porch, looking out at the dark forest. She doesn't seem to notice the mosquitoes at all. "After we moved in, a woman came by. She said her son built this place, but that he'd died more than ten years ago, before he had a chance to finish it. She said we could stay, as long as we swept up the broken glass."

Meadow lends me an old mountain bike that she bought on the street for twenty-five dollars. Sandra's husband has a mechanic shop in town that he rarely uses, and he lets me park my van in the fenced-in lot out back. The lot is full of fireweed, and willows grow from the rusted carcasses of old vehicles. I pull one of the captain's chairs from my van and set it on a wooden flatbed trailer where it can catch the light. Now I have a living room. In the endless evenings I sit in this captain's chair and read books set in the Far North. I have a case of caribou stew in a cardboard box under my bed, and a small cooler in which I keep carrots and other sturdy vegetables. I eat my dinner while the sun sinks into peachy-orange milk in the dusty sky, feeling the mosquitoes land on the tops of my feet.

I find a job as a gardener for a sprawling estate twenty minutes outside of town. The estate hosts weddings, and the grounds are dotted with hundreds of flower beds: pansies and marigolds and petunias. The estate sits on a hillside far above Fairbanks, and from the grounds I can see the Tanana Valley, wide and green and glittering with lakes, stretching all the way to the Alaska Range. The flowers are dewy and fragrant in the warm, still afternoons, and I haul the hose or the watering can from flower bed to flower bed, no sound but the twittering of the birds. My boss is a drunk; she tools around the property on her ATV, gripping a tumbler of booze. She yells at me, tells me I'm fucking up, then disappears for the rest of the day. Bumblebees dip in and out of the flowers. I throw dog food to the koi in the koi pond, I clean the algae from the filters. My heart feels empty.

At the library in town, I email Tara. *How are you?* I say. *How is the dog?* She doesn't respond.

I find a lake, ringed in gravel, that sits on the outskirts of town. After work I park my van next to the lake and roll down all the windows. The water smells of soaked leaves and phosphorus, and above it the sky is empty and blue. The light comes in the open doors of the van, a big rectangle of sun, and warms the beige carpet, the bed, the wooden cabinet that holds my dry goods. On top of the cabinet is a cast-iron skillet I found at the dump. I use it to poach my eggs in canned soup on my little two-burner propane stove.

I lie in the rectangle of sun, feeling my muscles creak and pop. My work is hard, and at the end of the day I'm tired. It's full-fledged summer now, and the sun doesn't set. I haven't been sleeping much.

I pull myself up and walk through the trees to the edge of the lake, take off all my clothes, and wade into the cool, broth-colored water. Leafy underwater plants brush my legs. I drop all the way in, rise up, and wave my arms and legs around. When I lie back in the water, I am weightless. The lake smell is on my face. The water is all around me, holding me up with its million tiny hands. The weariness has left me. There are barn swallows flying over. I can see their soft white underbellies. On the elastic surface of the water there are spiders, small beetles, the parasols of dandelion seeds.

Climbing out of the water, I feel my heaviness return. But I am cooler now, cleansed by the lake. The tannins of decomposing leaves. Duck shit. Fish. Now that I'm heavy again, the small shore rocks hurt the soles of my feet. It is hard being a land mammal. A tired land mammal. I feel old. Ancient. Close to death.

The sun is lower now and the shadows are long, the way they'll stay for the rest of the night. I climb into the front passenger seat and put my feet up on the dash, check my cellphone. It's a flip phone, prepaid, ten cents a minute. No one has called me. I could go to the library, I think, and check my email. I could read magazines there. Bits of plant matter float in my open window, carried on the air.

Meadow tells me about a show at the Sea Otter Saloon—Girl Haggard, an all-woman Merle Haggard cover band. There's a wedding on the grounds at work tonight, and I have to set up the big canvas tents, lug a hundred plastic chairs across the grass, hand out mushrooms stuffed with breadcrumbs and tiny glass flutes of champagne. The bride is beautiful. At the end of the night I carry the demolished cake into the kitchen and set it on the stainless steel counter. Only the rich chocolate edges are left, the buttercream fluting. The heel of a slice. Each crumb glistens. I eat a few handfuls. It tastes incredible. The cake-stained paper doilies go in the trash; the crystal champagne glasses get soaped clean. There is a muslin bag of jelly beans, knotted with a ribbon that says HAPPILY FOREVER. I put these in my pocket for later.

Outside, the sunlight is long and filled with dust from the road. My van edges between the parked cars of the guests, with my HAPPILY FOREVER jelly beans sitting on the dash. It feels good to reach the open road that leads back to town. There are three country music stations on the radio, and I switch between them as I drive. The good wind comes in through the rolled-down window and stirs the dust that coats everything.

Cake is the only thing in my stomach, so I buy a package of sushi from the deli at the grocery store and park next to the Sea Otter Saloon, in the huge lot for a sporting goods store, to eat it. The show has already started and there are folks milling around outside, smoking cigarettes. There's a man selling hot dogs from a metal cart. The crowd is mostly young men with beards and they watch me, in my van. I've never been to this bar before. I don't like to drink, but I am trying to make some friends tonight. Why are the men pointing at me, though? I ignore them and focus on my sushi. I squeeze out too much wasabi. Tamari is everywhere.

There is a loud clang, and my van shakes. I put down my sushi, confused. Then my van lurches backward.

I open the door and jump out. There is a tow truck behind the van, the kind with the big flatbed that lowers to make a ramp. My van is being winched, slowly, onto the ramp.

"Hey!" I shout, above the rumbling of the truck. "Hey!"

The man standing next to the truck looks at me. He motions with his arm, and the winching motion stops. But there is a winching feeling in my gut.

"I was in there!" I shout. "I had just parked!" My laughter is loud and ridiculous.

"You're on private property," the man shouts back. He's my age, wearing a crass T-shirt with the sleeves cut off. His upper arms are soft, and covered in tattoos. The side of the truck says FAIRBANKS I TOW. "You want your van back, it's a hundred dollars."

"I just parked!" I say. "There aren't any signs! I hadn't even gone into the bar!" I think of my flip phone, inside the van. I think of my paycheck, all of my worldly belongings.

The man shrugs, blank faced, and points to a concrete barrier, two feet high, that sits at the end of the row of parking spaces. In stencil spray paint it says: LOT CLOSED 10 P.M. TO 6 A.M. UNAUTHORIZED VEHICLES WILL BE TOWED AT OWNER'S EXPENSE.

My watch says it's 10:30 P.M. The men outside the bar are laughing loudly, slapping their pant legs. Raising their glasses of beer in the air. Shouting. They're laughing at the tow truck driver. They're laughing at me.

"I don't have a hundred dollars!" I shout. "Why can't you put my van back down?"

"Hundred dollars," says the man. His partner steps down from the cab and stands next to him. The truck rumbles. "More if we have to wait."

There is no strength left inside me. I do not understand why everyone is laughing at me.

"You're not taking my van! What is this, some sort of scam?" Against my will, water comes out of my eyeballs and fucks up my vision, ruins my voice. Now I can hardly speak.

"A hundred dollars or we take the van." The tow truck drivers look at each other. "You want us to call the trooper?"

"Yes! Call the fucking trooper!" I am shameless now, screaming through my snot, pacing along the concrete. The second man gets on his cellphone. He is bearded and wearing dirty Carhartts. They could be brothers. I imagine them in their house in the woods. It is cluttered and has no siding, only Tyvek.

A few minutes later the trooper appears. He greets the tow truck drivers by name and nods at each of them in turn. My cheeks are flushed, and I can't stop crying.

"I had just parked and was eating sushi in my van and had only been here four minutes—"

"ID," he says.

I hand him my ID. He looks it over and hands it back.

"This is private property," he says. "You got an issue, you take it up with the sporting goods store."

He tips his hat at the drivers, gets in his car, and leaves. The men stand sideways, watching him go. They do not look at me.

"It's a hundred fifty now, for the wait," they say.

The thing winches tighter in my gut. It is a taut rope, pulling my insides too close together. I walk away, and then I turn and screech at them, through my snot:

"Is this fun for you? Is this what you do? Wait for the lot to close at ten, then circle around, looking for people still parked here, who have no idea they can't park here? I have never even been to this bar before!"

They say nothing. They are being strong. It is good money for them, predatory towing. This sporting goods store allows it. Some businesses will not allow it.

"You can pick up your van from the impound lot tomorrow," says the one with the crass T-shirt. He looks down at the black pavement. "It'll cost three-fifty. You want a receipt?"

"No!" I shriek. My voice warbles. I am frantic, inconsolable. I want to kill them. I want to take out a knife and gouge their eyes out. I want to steal their tow truck. The chain clinks, the truck rumbles, and my van begins to move onto the bed again. I do not have my cellphone. I do not have my money, hidden under the cutting board in the cabinet in my van. I do not have a blanket. I do not have a place to stay or a way to get to work tomorrow.

"Okay! I'll pay you the hundred and fifty dollars!" The van

stops moving. I jump onto the truck bed and climb inside, find
the money, a small stack of twenties. It is my first paycheck. So
my car insurance payment will be late again this month.

The man hands me a receipt on yellow paper. He still cannot
look at me. Hostility wafts off him like cologne. Things are
spelled wrong on the receipt. My van comes back down slowly
on the chain.

"You're a fucking douchebag," I say as he lowers my van.

He looks straight ahead. "I don't care what you think of me,"
he says. "I don't care what you think of me." I want to shoot him
with a paintball gun. I want to chase him through the woods. It
doesn't do any good. He is already unhappy, I can tell. The whole
world is unhappy. Nothing does any good.

Shaking, I get in my van, circle the lot, and, laughing hysteri-
cally, park on the opposite side. The drivers look at me and jump
into their truck, which comes rumbling to life and peels out
across the lot, toward me. I scream and pull into traffic. I am
insane. I am insane.

I drive east out of town. The sun is low, the sky and dust glow
golden, like fire. This week I am house-sitting for my boss's next-
door neighbor. They are leaving on a fishing trip in the morning.
"Park in our driveway tonight," they had said. "We'll be gone
when you get up in the morning. You can let the dogs out then."
I am headed to their house, driving fast. It is a nice two-story
place in the woods. They have a big garden, a greenhouse. Three
dogs.

The sun is in my rearview mirror, the clear blue of the sky. I
grip my steering wheel and scream as loudly as I possibly can.
My body shudders. I have no tears left. I open my mouth and
scream again. It is a perfect summer night. I scream again, and
the noise terrorizes the empty space around me, bounces off the

wind from my open window. I keep screaming, all the way to the house. There's a spot for me in the trees next to their driveway. It is around midnight. I step out and pee in the grass. Outside, the air has gone gray. A gentle dusk has settled.

Pulling the van's mini blinds down against the light, I crawl carefully under the mosquito netting and curl up on the bed in back. I lie on my side, my knees tight against my chest, making myself as small as possible. Instead of breathing, I shake. The screen of my flip phone glows gently. I count forward. In Oregon it is three A.M. There is no one I can call. My body shudders. I am hyperventilating now. There is an ache inside me. It eats my bone marrow. The entire world hates me. And the hate is attacking me. There is no one who wants me to live, and so I am dying. Hyperventilating. My bones are hollow gourds, my stomach is bottomless, my lungs are echo chambers. There is no one in the world to talk to, so I am dying. My only friends are the petunias and the bumblebees, so I am dying. My boss is a grumpy drunk and I have spoken aloud to no one but her and the bank teller in the last two weeks, so I am dying. It makes perfect sense. I have ceased to exist. I am dying.

I die until five A.M. At five A.M. I turn on my phone and dial 1-800-SUICIDE. I do not know if it's a real phone number, but "suicide" has seven letters, which seems serendipitous.

"I need to talk to someone and I don't have anyone to talk to," I say to the man who answers the phone. His voice is quiet and flat, like the voice of someone watching television. "Uh-huh," he says.

"I live in my van and I don't have any money," I say. "I am small," I say. "I am helpless. I am barely alive."

Uh-huh.

I tell him everything that happened and everything I am

afraid of, my voice squeaking higher and higher like a cartoon mouse. When I am finished talking, I don't know what to say, so I thank him and hang up the phone. The man doesn't offer any solutions. There aren't any solutions. There was only the pressure of my own existence, cracking my heart in two. Now this man has it. He has grown special pockets to carry it. He carries pieces of many people, in his special pockets. The pieces are heavy, but he carries them just so, and maybe they won't hurt him.

In the morning when I wake, the world is empty. It has evaporated and left me with its house, and three dogs. A small terrier and two springer spaniels. A big house, with big, empty rooms. Antique couches, sad lamps. Still walls. Little light. There is a wraparound deck with wooden chairs. I sit on the deck after work and watch the light move across the grass. In the kitchen, I open all the cupboards and rifle through the snacks. Fat-free potato chips, boxes of Jell-O. Fat-free mayonnaise. There are lots of prescription medications. I take them out and line them up on the counter, one by one. For the heart, for the blood pressure, for the joints, for things I do not know and cannot imagine. I open the fridge and eat slices of fat-free American cheese.

On the deck I read a book. The book cannot hold me. The potted flowers need watering. There is a wilting sun and a bucket of Miracle-Gro. The afternoon is silent. The terrier is on a long tie-out and he bites at the grass where I peed next to the steps; he bites and tears and rips at it, swallowing the grass.

I unleash the dogs and herd them into the woods. We go running down the leafy path, sticks and plants swiping at our ankles. The sun comes through in bars and patches, the air rushes past us. The little terrier carries a stick larger than his own body, joyously, like an ant. The springer spaniels bound stupidly, afraid of nothing. We run down a hill, through the woods. I trip and stumble over fallen logs. The mud of decomposition smears my calves. We run fast to keep ahead of the mosquitoes, which hide on the backsides of leaves, in pockets of shade. We have to run fast to escape the coming evening.

At the bottom of the hill is a meadow. A mud path, a clutter of raspberry canes. The ground is sponge and blueberry bushes. Moose tracks are everywhere. We keep running, through the meadow, through the grass, into the woods again. I cannot see it, but below us is the valley. There is the river, the horizon to infinity, the silence of the huge blue sky. I urge the dogs on. The sun or rain falls down on us. It doesn't matter.

2019

A t six A.M. I wake in darkness. For a moment I can't remember where I am, and then it comes back to me—I'm in my van, in the desert west of Phoenix, Arizona. I parked here last night under the nearly full moon. In a few days I'll reach Death Valley, where I'll hike 135 miles from Badwater Basin, the hottest place on earth, to the summit of Tumanguya, aka Mount Whitney, the highest point in the Lower 48.

I pull the magnetic covers from the windows of my van, letting in the predawn light, and rub the sleep from my face. The morning smells of creosote and warm earth. I light my camp stove, heat water for instant coffee. Sleep eluded me last night. I long to go somewhere cold, where I can burrow into the bed in my van and just sleep and sleep. Maybe Lone Pine, today's destination, will be that place. Six years ago I discovered long-distance hiking, wherein one walks great distances with only what can fit in a backpack, and I've hiked ten thousand miles since, including from Mexico to Canada three times. Walking through nature until I become rangy, wild, and interwoven with the very fabric of the mountains is now one of my favorite things in the world.

A week ago my grandmother passed away in Colorado. I visited just a few times after moving out at age seventeen, and those visits were awkward and strange. My blood family exists for me mostly as snapshots. Memories that live forever in the past tense. But two weeks ago an aunt I rarely hear from texted me—Grandma was dying, she said, and I should try to call her.

I've longed for my grandmother's love since I was a teenager, although I don't like to admit it to myself. My grandmother wasn't capable of giving love, though. She had a cold heart. It was what allowed her to survive her life.

My grandfather answered when I dialed their number, his voice gruff. Grandma was no longer speaking, he told me. She had a few days left at most. No, I couldn't try to talk to her.

"Are those dogs barking?" asked my grandpa.

"Yeah," I said. "I have two dogs." Grandpa was silent on the line. He didn't ask me where I was living, or what my life was like. The gulf between us was so large it had become a sea, and it was hard to remember that this water had ever been narrow enough to leap across.

They had been married for more than sixty years. All that time my grandma had cooked his meals for him, laundered his Wranglers and his plaid shirts that had gone thin and soft with age, hung them on the line with wooden clothespins to dry in the sun. She had scrubbed their house until it shone, slept next to him in their bed, woken in the night to his snoring. She'd tended watermelons and tomatoes in their garden, sliced homegrown cucumbers into bowls of vinegar to eat with their sandwiches, bought packs of new tube socks for him when his boots wore holes in the old ones. How many packages of tube socks marked the passage of that much time?

"Take care of yourself, Jenni," said Grandpa on the phone.

"My name is Carrot," I said. "My name has been Carrot for eighteen years."

"What kind of a name is that?" he snorted.

As I drive across the desert, I press my hand to my chest, searching for my feelings about my grandmother passing. They're deep under the bones of my rib cage, in a spot I can't quite reach. I have always wanted to know my grandmother's inner world. To understand her. And now she's dead, and I never will. I wish my grandmother loved me, but I can't be sure that she did. And now she's gone.

Last summer I began to try to find my mother. I hadn't seen her since I left Alaska as a teenager. I wasn't totally sure she was still alive, but if she was, she'd be sixty-two years old, having somehow survived twenty-one winters homeless in Anchorage. The fact of her age was what pushed me to finally begin my search—I imagined she was okay in the summertime, in the warm dappled forests, but the winters were likely growing more difficult to endure. When it came to my mother, my heart was a bruised plum, but I didn't want her to die alone in a snowbank, so I gritted my teeth and bought a plane ticket to Anchorage in August. I would look for her for a single week, I told myself. If she could endure winters as a homeless person, then I could endure seven days grappling with the reality of her existence.

On my first day in Anchorage, I found a man who knew her. I was at a drop-in center for homeless folks that was three blocks from the apartment where I was staying, in the spare bedroom of a stranger I'd met online. At the drop-in center I sat in a torn vinyl chair in front of a chipped desk, behind which sat a large man, the director of the center.

"I know Barbara," he said. "I used to see her often. Tiny, frail lady, always had her little suitcase with her. A bit of a loner." He smiled, as though at a fond memory. "I haven't seen her in, oh . . . five years."

That was the final dead end of all my leads for the day. I'd followed various ribbons as they unfurled until this bonanza, a man who knew her—and he hadn't seen her in a very long time.

"Try to get support while you're doing this," he said, his eyes kind. "Talk to someone who knows about grief. Don't white-knuckle your way through this." I started crying, and he handed me a box of tissues. I felt like he could see right through me.

The desert, warm and open, passes by outside the bug-splattered windshield of my van. In the evening I reach San Bernardino and pick up Laurie and Plants, two other long-distance hikers, who are joining me on this hike. We're meeting another hiker, Pilar, in Lone Pine tomorrow. I am looking forward to being around people in the wilderness, even people I've only just met. Sharing the rushing quiet of nature with a handful of other human beings is the purest form of companionship I have found.

The highway to Lone Pine is dark and lonely, and it's hard to stay awake. At last Plants, Laurie, and I reach the Alabama Hills, those piles of smooth, sand-colored boulders at the base of the Sierras, where there is camping. The road here is sandy and the huge rocks are pale in the moonlight. Rising in the west are the mountains of the High Sierra, the peaks jagged and aglow. There's Tumanguya, where we'll finish our hike.

There are RVs parked in seemingly every dark pullout in the Alabama Hills, and we drive farther and farther into the rocks. Then we dip down into a wash and my van can't get up the other side. The sand is too deep! We roll back and forth, wheels spinning.

"Maybe we should try turning around?" says Plants. This is tricky, because it means leaving the road for the even deeper sand of the wash. Maybe we can do it?

We can't. The back tires of my van are wedged deeply in the sand. It's a nice, level spot, though. I guess we're camping here.

Laurie and I fit on the bed and Plants curls into a fetal position on the small square of floor.

"I'm the husky," he says. Plants has the driest sense of humor of anyone I've ever met in my life. It's nine-thirty P.M., hiker midnight, and we're all exhausted. I turn off the lights and the night comes in, cold and vast. I pull the sleeping bag over my head and I'm gone.

My second day in Anchorage, I parked at Loussac Library, the big library where, as a kid, I would hide from the cold or, alternately, from my home life, which was messier and scarier than the weather. In the library, as a kid, I sat in antique leather chairs under walls of beautiful old books, reading magazines by the light of a stained-glass lamp. The air was quiet. Predictable. Sometimes my mother was there with me, muttering to herself in a chair in the corner. Sometimes she was hiding too.

Anchorage is full of forests, undeveloped chunks of land tucked between wide, car-choked boulevards, and these forests, besides having grizzly bears, wolves, and streams that run with salmon, also hold many homeless camps. These forests are wild, they harken to another time; they exist outside of society. And if you come here to hide, you can exist outside of society too. Was my mother in one of these camps? I wasn't sure.

"Barbara, yeah," said a woman in the homeless camp in the woods behind Loussac. We were standing among the birch trees. The air was warm, and I could feel the loamy ground beneath my feet. *It's nice here,* I thought. I imagined my mother in this forest, in her tent—did she own a tent? If not, how did she stay dry in the rain? What did she do in winter?

"She used to come into McDonald's when I worked there," the woman was saying. "I would give her free food. Talks to herself a lot. I last saw her two days ago, in Walmart. She goes in there to wash up, I think."

The woman's pit bull whined inside his wire kennel. The light dissolved in the boughs of the trees and then re-formed, pooling on the mossy ground. Here was someone who'd seen my mother recently, which meant that she was definitely still alive. That sudden truth was like this forest light: gentle, golden, all around me. Nearby was a folding table with blue jugs of water. Boxes of food and piles of blankets were stacked next to it. An older white man and an Inupiat elder sat in folding chairs at the entrance of the camp, where the mowed park ended and the path into the forest began.

"We do security here," said the white man. "We take shifts."

It's nice here, I thought again.

I stopped by the apartment complex where we had lived for four years, the longest we'd spent in any single spot. It was unchanged—packs of loose children, circling on bikes like feral dogs. Peeling paint, broken window blinds. The air smelled of baby formula and Top Ramen. Here was the ground-floor window my brother would climb out of when he ran away. Here was the hole in the fence through which we'd sneak over to the mall and pull broken electronics and expired candy bars from their dumpster. Everything seemed smaller now, almost depressingly so. Was this really the hill we sledded down? Where I collected dandelions in the summertime? Were these the trees I loved? I walked behind what had been our apartment, as close to the back door as I dared. Was my name still carved into the wood of the patio? I wandered the complex, looking at the drab buildings, the windows open to let in the good summer air. Children swarmed around me and then past, like schools of salmon. Dirty children, clutching Popsicle sticks, their hair uncombed. Were these children loved? What worlds did they disappear into, behind the closed doors of their apartments? What did these children imagine the future to be? Did they dream of running away, and wonder what would happen if they did? I wished I could tell them that I had been here too, and that I had been just as scared. I hadn't known what else the world held, besides this basic, essential darkness. But I had gotten away. I had learned that you couldn't escape the darkness entirely, but you could learn to live above it. Grief was an ocean but you could reach the surface and bob there, where the light was.

The corridor leading to the front door of our apartment was dark and somehow still smelled like Smarties candies, a scent so familiar I felt it in my body like an old friend. *Home.* This smell was one of my homes. How many homes do we acquire during the long unspooling of a human life?

I wake at six A.M. in my van in the Alabama Hills after sleeping eight whole hours. I feel so good, like I could punch through a wall. Plants and Laurie are still asleep, motionless in their sleeping bags. Outside is the palest shade of dawn, and I squat to pee in the sand. It's too cold to be awake! I shiver back into my bag and drift off, to anxiety dreams. At eight I'm awake again, feeling groggy and strange. The sun is up now and the others are awake and blinking. I set up the folding table and chairs outside in the bright desert and heat water for coffee.

"Looks like you're stuck in the wash," says a man, from above us on the ridge. He's got a dog with him.

"We sure are," I say. "You know how to get vans unstuck?"

The man lights up at this call of duty. He circles the van, inspecting the tires. "You got a shovel?" he asks.

"Nah. Got a piece of cardboard maybe."

"Here's what you do," he says. "You take air out of the tires for more traction." He depresses a tire valve, and it begins to hiss. "You dig out the sand in front of the tires with your hands, to make a flat spot for the tire to roll. You put the cardboard under the tire that's most stuck. You straighten the wheels. You rock back and forth. You make your friends push."

I kneel down and dig the sand from in front of the tires. I am so grateful.

"You want me to drive it out while you all push?" he asks.

"Yeah, thanks," I say, relieved. The man starts the van, three of us lean on the rear end, the tires spin, and suddenly the van is free. The man revs it to the top of the hill.

"I feel like we all just had a dad for a minute," I say to the others, laughing.

We meet Pilar in Lone Pine. She drove down from Northern California, where she's been living in a cabin in the woods. We take a table in the crowded Alabama Cafe and order giant plates of food. There's a parade today, and older white men are dressed as cowboys. The fantasy of colonization is strong in the rural

West. I think about my great-grandparents, homesteading in what is now a suburb of Denver. For white people of North America, colonization is our only remembered connection to the earth. How fucked-up and sad is that, I think, as I pour hazelnut creamer into my second cup of coffee and touch my face, which feels hot. I'm sunburned already, somehow. Plants, who is vegan, tears into a plate of sautéed zucchini. Restaurants have hilarious ideas of what a vegan meal is. He's not complaining, though.

At the store we buy ten gallons of water to cache in the desert, some canned goods for our resupply box at Panamint Springs, the campground we'll reach a few days into our hike, and several bags of candy corn. We pack all these things into the trunk of Pilar's car. My van will stay in Lone Pine, parked behind the small grocery store.

Death Valley is a dry place, even drier than the Sonoran Desert, where I live, and as we drop down into it on the winding road my nostrils sting and my throat goes hoarse. The mountains are raw and bare, the valleys scoured featureless by the wind. The air is thick. My mouth feels wrong. I drink water, but it doesn't help.

At Badwater Basin the sun is setting, the sky lavender and orange above the white salt flats. A crowd of people swirls on the salt, taking selfies from every angle. It's not very hot right now— the air is a warm bath. I take a deep breath, looking out across the salt flats. We're 282 feet below sea level. Across the expanse of white is Telescope Ridge, ten thousand feet above sea level. Tonight, we cross the flat. Tomorrow, we climb ten thousand feet up to that ridge and then descend seven thousand feet down the other side. The next day, we cross a long, exposed, hot valley before finally reaching our first stop—Panamint Springs Resort, with its showers and burgers.

Am I strong enough for this hike? Or will this hike break me, crumbling me into a thousand small pieces that will blow away on the wind? There's only one way to find out.

I buckle my hip belt. I feel good right now. My pack is light, filled with minimal layers: my one-person tarp, four liters of water, no stove, and only three days of food. I think that I can do this.

After stopping by my old apartment building that second day in Anchorage, I bought a pre-roll at the weed store and met Tara at her friend's house, where she was staying for a few days, sleeping on the couch. Tara hadn't spoken to me for years after I'd snapped at her that night we were processing the roadkill caribou. Tara and I are both too sensitive, but in different ways. The summer of the caribou we'd understood each other intensely, until we hadn't anymore. After three years of silence, she responded to one of my emails, saying that she was passing through Oregon. She stayed with me in the trailer in the woods where I was living. I made pot roast in the Dutch oven and we talked about our feelings and listened to the rain. I knew that she would never see exactly what I saw, and I would never see exactly what she saw, but we could learn to dance around each other's sensitivities, to show up without getting so close that we got burned. Maybe that's all human relationships are—accepting the fact that we'll never be truly seen but sticking around anyway, for the pure animal comfort of knowing someone over the span of a life.

Now Tara was in Anchorage for a social justice conference. Next week she'd head north again, back to her cabin on the river. I lit the pre-roll and we smoked it on the back deck with the mosquitoes and the wild roses and she told me about her day, about standing in fluorescent-lit rooms for hours speaking about the criminalization of sex work. I'm not much of a weed smoker but I wanted to numb out, wanted Tara to talk and talk forever so I could just listen and I wouldn't have to hear my own thoughts, wouldn't have to feel the rough waves of grief crashing against my shores, threatening to pull me out to sea. I got as high as I could and Tara watched TV with me until it got so late I was able to sleep. Tara got it. She didn't ask me why I was sad. She got it more than anyone I knew. Tara was the person I texted late at night, racked with insomnia on a full moon, having just decided that I was unlovable trash, that I was a terrible person, and that death was the only thing that would ever bring relief.

"I understand," she'd say. And I knew that she did.

The sun is setting over the salt flats of Badwater Basin in Death Valley. The salt flats are amorphous. They contain multitudes. They are free from the constructs of inherent form. They are alternatingly smooth and spiky, brittle and soft. Our minds and feet work to make sense of these textures as we wander across the expanse of white. The lavender and orange of the sky intensifies, until it feels as though we are suspended within it. I stop and bend over, plucking a piece of salt, putting it in my mouth. It tastes like metal and the earth.

Tonight is the full moon in Aries. This bloated moon spills over the crest of the pink mountains behind us, casting long moon shadows just as the last of the daylight fades in the west. We don't need headlamps. The night is dark and also bright. *Cronch, cronch, cronch* go our footsteps as they break through the crusts of salt. The *cronch*ing echoes in the thick air, which swallows all other sound.

The first water source on this route is Hanaupah Canyon, fifteen miles from the start. We'd considered walking there tonight. But after six miles we leave the salt flats and start climbing on a dirt road, eating pieces of the elevation gain that will eventually bring us to the cold piñon forest of Telescope Ridge. It's night, the adrenaline has left us. We're beat. Who walks this late?

"This reminds me of when I worked overnight as a baker," says Pilar.

I sweep my arms. "All of this is bread," I say.

We throw our bedrolls in the dirt. This is as good a place to sleep as any.

I eat my cold-soaked instant refried beans with tortilla chips. The texture and flavor of the beans are pretty bad. Pilar passes around a bag of candy corn. The candy smells like, and has the texture of, vanilla-scented taper candles. I eat a whole handful, biting each piece into three, according to the color demarcations. Dinner finished, I tend to my butt chafing with baby wipes and Vagisil, then inflate my sleeping pad under the moon.

I have not "cowboy camped" in a long time. When you cowboy camp, you do not set up a tent. Your roof is the stars, and you are cradled by the wind. Insects crawl over you in the night. They pause on the bridge of your nose. They check their watches. They are running late. They hurry down your cheeks, muttering to themselves. They don't think of you, of your heavy human worries. They have their own lives.

The moon shines on our faces like a flashlight. The air dries the sweat from my clothes. Is it too bright to sleep? Eventually the answer is no.

.   .   .

My third day in Anchorage, I walked to a homeless café and discovered that half the staff knew Barbara.

"Little old white lady?" said a big man in a fluorescent safety
vest. "Sometimes uses a walker? Keeps to herself? She's in here
all the time. Was just in here this morning."

"What?" I said, feeling my skin start to tingle. I looked at the
clock. It was noon. I sat at one of the long tables, next to the
people eating lunch. Sloppy joes and boiled carrots on a plastic
tray. I looked around the huge room, checking all the faces but
moving my eyes quickly. If any of these folks were paranoid like
Barbara, they wouldn't want me looking directly at them. I tried
to imagine my mother now, aged twenty-two years since the last
time I saw her. In 1997, at forty, her hair was already silver. Her
face was haunted. The flesh of her body hung from her bones.
Her illness had accelerated time, rocketed her into the future,
toward death.

"What are you looking at me for?" shouted the woman sitting
next to me at the table.

"I'm looking for my mother," I said.

"Your mother robbed a bank," mumbled the woman. "She
went to Cancún. She went to the moon."

I left the café and walked in the bright afternoon light to the
women's shelter.

"We can't confirm or deny that Barbara is here, or has ever
stayed here," said the woman at the front desk. All of the shelters
had given me some version of this answer. It was meant to protect Barbara, to allow her confidentiality. "You can leave a note,"
said the woman. "And if Barbara is here I will pass it along."

"We used to stay here sometimes when I was a kid," I said.
"Memories, you know?" The woman smiled. I pushed the note
across the desk. "She can't read," I said.

In Death Valley, the alarm on my phone goes off at five A.M. and wakes me into a world that is suspiciously like yesterday. It's dark. Dry. Moony. I slept maybe five hours? Oh well. I select "Eye of the Tiger" from the music on my phone and turn the volume all the way up. The others laugh themselves awake. We need to start hiking at this terrible hour because it's going to take us an absurd amount of time to get to the top of this mountain. We knocked out one thousand feet of climbing last night. Just nine thousand more to go today! I mix protein powder with water in the screw-top container that still tastes like yesterday's beans. I'm determined to be a good sport about these early wake-ups for as long as I can. Coffee will help. I shake a packet of instant coffee into my water bottle and swish it around. It tastes terrible, but it works.

The moon is setting behind Telescope Ridge as we work our way up Hanaupah Canyon on a jeep road. The road is distinct at first, then less so, then there is only the dry wash and picking one's way through piles of rock, stretches of sand, brush.

I've been thinking a lot about the wave-particle duality of light, the concept in quantum mechanics wherein light can act either as a particle or as a wave. The funny thing here is that this doesn't make any sense—according to our understanding of physics, objects are either particles or waves, but never both. And yet, light can be both. We've been studying the wave-particle duality of light for hundreds of years, and we still don't understand how it's possible. The short answer is that it's not possible. And yet, it is.

The sun rises over the salt flats that are below us already, somehow. We hear the happy burbling waters of Hanaupah

Spring and then we see them, bursting from the earth into a tangle of bushes and reeds. The water is clear and cold, and it runs over a bed of clean gravel. Bright yellow flowers hang over it. We crouch in the shade and shove chips into our mouths. I'm soaked in sweat and the cortisol of the morning is wearing off. I'm tired. Eight thousand feet of climbing left until we reach the top of the ridge. *Fuck!*

On my sixth day in Anchorage, I walked to the Catholic church downtown where Barbara would take me when I was small. Where she would speak in tongues in the little room off the main worship hall, the one with the metal rack of novena candles in red glass, and I would wander the empty pews, fingering the curled songbooks. That day, there was a mass in Spanish going on and I stood in the foyer with the women bouncing their babies, quieting them. Did Barbara still come to this church? Did they know her here? Everywhere, in this city, were people who knew her. Somehow she had made herself a life here. Somehow she'd stayed alive. Through the grace of God. Through the small righteous fire that burned inside her.

Next door was the gift shop where, as a kid, I would lust after turquoise rosaries in pleather snap pouches that we could never afford. I was an adult now, impossibly tall and stronger than the sun, and I could buy whatever rosary I wanted. I selected a rose-colored glass one that sparkled and fought back tears as I paid six dollars at the register. Had the rosaries here always been this cheap? Had six dollars really been so much? Any amount was too much, I remembered, when you had no money at all.

My mother is a paranoid schizophrenic who does not want to be found. The information I had acquired on her whereabouts

was from someone at a shelter or homeless café who was breaking the rules—the most recent one was a volunteer offering that
he'd been seeing her around for a year, that she'd gone off her
meds and had been extra cantankerous but now she was back on
them. He told me to return at six P.M., but when I knocked on
the door of the shelter that evening another worker told me,
with a serene face, that she couldn't give me any information
due to confidentiality laws, nor would she be able to give me
information at any time in the future. I knew why these rules
existed, and I respected them. I respected my mother's auton-
omy. Would she even know me if she saw me? So much time had
passed. I had changed my name. Our worlds had diverged. We
each existed for the other as mythologies, memories that bore
little resemblance to what lived today. Her delusions, I knew,
often centered around being chased—by demons, by other people. How would it make her feel to know that someone was trying to find her now, even if my intentions were good? I didn't
need to have a relationship with my mother, if she didn't want
that. I didn't want to cause her more stress. And yet, I wanted
her to be safe. I wanted a warm room for her, where she could
live out the rest of her days.

I pocketed my rosary and walked quickly down the street as
the city buses rumbled past. At six A.M. the next day, before the
homeless café opened for breakfast, I would fly back to the
Lower 48. I now knew that Barbara went there most mornings,
but I wouldn't get another chance to cross paths with her. Once
back at the apartment where I was staying, I packed my things,
my head so heavy it felt as though I would fall, and if I did, I
would most likely break. I'd already decided that I would come
back to Anchorage in the winter, to look for her again. Maybe

there was a way. Maybe she didn't have to freeze to death, alone in the woods. Maybe that didn't have to be the ending to her story. Barbara couldn't give me anything, but maybe I could give her this one thing. I'd spent so long running from her, from the pain that threatened to overtake me. It was time to stop. To stand still, to ever so slowly turn and face the tsunami behind me. Barbara would be there, looking at me. Holding my heart in her hands, the hot meat of it, as it pumped blood onto the floor.

Our morning break at the clear waters of Hanaupah Canyon is over. I roll up the Ziploc bag of smashed tortilla chips I was eating and stash it away. I clip my pack back onto my body. It is time to climb the mountain. The mountain in question is a sharply angled slope, pebbled with scree and loose rock, and the climb is going to be brutal. Partly because of how steep it is, and partly because we're carrying eight liters of water each. I begin the slow, steady work. I am panting, stopping every few feet to rest. Picking my way around obstacles. Pausing to laugh at the absurdity of it all.

Do you ever exercise until you are exhausted, sit down in the fragrant piñon duff knowing that you cannot possibly go on, and then stand up with great effort, swaying under the weight of your pack, and continue climbing? Today I do this about eleven times. The hours turn liquid and slip by. Time is marked in snack breaks, shaky breaths, the twinges in my knees, tablets of fizzy electrolytes dropped into my water bottle, and the increasing tension in my Achilles tendons, which feel as though they're going to snap like old rubber bands. I cannot possibly go on. But I do. We all do.

I think about how subjective reality is, how even looking directly at a thing, saying it out loud, will alter it. This is what physicists found while studying the wave-particle duality of light—that the intention of their experiments, whether they were looking to show that light was a particle or that light was a wave, would influence the results. Basically, whichever they tested for, the universe said *yes*. Is light a particle? *Yes*. But is it a wave? *Yes*. Einstein, who was frustrated by this, said:

> It seems as though we must use sometimes the one theory and sometimes the other, while at times we may use either. We are faced with a new kind of difficulty. We have two contradictory pictures of reality; separately neither of them fully explains the phenomena of light, but together they do.

The air grows thinner and now we're more out of breath. Seven thousand feet. Eight thousand feet. Nine thousand feet. The world is bright and then we're in the shade of the piñon forest; the air is warm, then cool. The sun is at our backs, then directly above us, then shining into my left eye, then at our fronts. Step. Step. Step. Pause.

The last two thousand feet of climbing happens in a single mile. This is just as fucked-up as it sounds. The scree is too steep. The brush is too steep. We fall back a half step with each step forward that we take. We push our way through thorns. I have been beyond exhausted for hours. I have been exhausted since the day I was born. I want to cry in frustration. Life is suffering. I go on.

When I reach the top of the mountain, I feel nothing, just a shaking, hollow fatigue. Nine thousand feet of climbing today in ten miles, and for what? There's a biting cold wind and the sun is setting. We have to get off this ridge and as far down the other side as we can before dark. These last five miles of climbing took us eight hours to complete.

I pull on all my layers, feeling the sharp pains of the thorns embedded in my fingers, the burn of the hotspots on the pads of my feet. It's so cold and I can't get warm—I seem to have used up every last bit of heat in my body to get to the top of this climb.

My grandma's funeral service is tomorrow, in Grand Junction, Colorado. I won't be there. I'll be here instead, in Death Valley, crossing a playa under the full moon. What happens to our inner mysteries after we die? I imagine another life, in the future or happening simultaneously, whichever way reincarnation plays out. I am there, and so is my grandma, and my mother. Except this time, we're three aspen trees in a grove, or three birds in a flight of swallows. Or I am their mother, and I do a better job. Or the same job, because we're all doing the best that we can. We're all just holding on, waiting for the waves to stop shaking us, staying alive if only because we know that if we died, we'd just wake up somewhere worse.

We live in a universe in which multiple things are true at once. Sitting at the Formica table with my grandma, cutting the earwigs from a bushel of peaches. My grandpa pulling off my nose but it was his thumb all along, then laughing at his own joke. In the rocking chair with Barbara, in that gray time before memory begins. *You are my sunshine, my only sunshine.*

Tara's father, playing the piano in a windowless bar in Fairbanks, Alaska. Tara's father, whose mother survived a concentration camp in Poland. The sound coming from the piano is so beautiful that Tara's father ceases to exist—he is no longer an old man who beats his sled dogs. He is a network of nerve endings leading to piano keys. He is music.

My brother in Afghanistan, where he works as a diesel mechanic for the U.S. military. Standing on a concrete balcony watching the sun set over the desert, the light marigold and rose.

And me, on this mountain. I am new. I am as clean and empty as the wind.

Acknowledgments

This book has been many years in the making, and I am deeply indebted to all the wonderful people who supported me and offered me encouragement along the way: my agent, Rebecca Friedman, whose warmth and generosity of spirit buoyed me countless times; my editor, Annie Chagnot, whose feedback was crucial and brilliant and who was kind, even when she didn't have to be; everyone at The Dial Press; all of the punk houses that sheltered me in my twenties, when I was a young oogle who refused to work very much because I was "focusing on my writing" and so was always broke and mooching off my friends—the Wych Elm house, Mississippi Co-op, the Sassy Shack, the Ramshackle, Mimosa Street house, and the Mendenhall house, as well as others I am forgetting; Tara, whose friendship has served as a container for so many of my complicated feelings about the nature of embodiment and whose influence has shaped the way

I write memoir; and all of the other friends who took a chance on me in the years contained in this story, who helped teach me how to be a person in the world and who are now characters in this book. You are important to me, I am thinking fondly of you, and if we haven't talked in a while, I miss you.

About the Author

CARROT QUINN is the author of the book *Thru-Hiking Will Break Your Heart*. She lives in the open spaces of the western United States with her two Chihuahuas.

About the Type

This book was set in Caledonia, a typeface designed in 1939 by W. A. Dwiggins (1880–1956) for the Mergenthaler Linotype Company. Its name is the ancient Roman term for Scotland, because the face was intended to have a Scottish-Roman flavor. Caledonia is considered to be a well-proportioned, businesslike face with little contrast between its thick and thin lines.